Experiment Central

Understanding Scientific Principles
Through Projects

Experiment Central

Understanding Scientific Principles
Through Projects
Second Edition

VOLUME 4: L-PH

M. Rae Nelson
Kristine Krapp, editor

U·X·L
A part of Gale, Cengage Learning

LINDENHURST MEMORIAL LIBRARY
One Lee Avenue
Lindenhurst, New York 11757

Detroit • New York • San Francisco • New Haven, Conn • Waterville, Maine • London

GALE
CENGAGE Learning

Experiment Central
Understanding Scientific
Principles Through Projects
Second Edition
M. Rae Nelson

Project Editor: Kristine Krapp

Managing Editor: Debra Kirby

Rights Acquisition and Management:
  Margaret Abendroth, Robyn Young

Composition: Evi Abou-El-Seoud, Mary
  Beth Trimper

Manufacturing: Wendy Blurton

Product Manager: Julia Furtaw

Product Design: Jennifer Wahi

© 2010 Gale, Cengage Learning

For product information and technology assistance, contact us at
Gale Customer Support, 1-800-877-4253.
For permission to use material from this text or product, submit all requests online at **www.cengage.com/permissions.**
Further permissions questions can be e-mailed to
permissionrequest@cengage.com

Cover photographs: Images courtesy of Dreamstime, Photos.com, and iStockPhoto.

Library of Congress Cataloging-in-Publication Data

Experiment central : understanding scientific principles through projects. -- 2nd ed. / M. Rae Nelson, Kristine Krapp, editors.   p. cm. --
  Includes bibliographical references and index.
    ISBN 978-1-4144-7613-1 (set) -- ISBN 978-1-4144-7614-8 (vol. 1) --
ISBN 978-1-4144-7615-5 (vol. 2) -- ISBN 978-1-4144-7616-2 (vol. 3) --
ISBN 978-1-4144-7617-9 (vol. 4) -- ISBN 978-1-4144-7618-6 (vol. 5) --
ISBN 978-1-4144-7619-3 (vol. 6)
    1. Science--Experiments--Juvenile literature. I. Nelson, M. Rae. II. Krapp, Kristine M.

Q164.E96 2010
507.8--dc22   2009050304

Gale
27500 Drake Rd.
Farmington Hills, MI, 48331-3535

978-1-4144-7613-1 (set)	1-4144-7613-2 (set)
978-1-4144-7614-8 (vol. 1)	1-4144-7614-0 (vol. 1)
978-1-4144-7615-5 (vol. 2)	1-4144-7615-9 (vol. 2)
978-1-4144-7616-2 (vol. 3)	1-4144-7616-7 (vol. 3)
978-1-4144-7617-9 (vol. 4)	1-4144-7617-5 (vol. 4)
978-1-4144-7618-6 (vol. 5)	1-4144-7618-3 (vol. 5)
978-1-4144-7619-3 (vol. 6)	1-4144-7619-1 (vol. 6)

This title is also available as an e-book.
ISBN-13: 978-1-4144-7620-9 (set)
ISBN-10: 1-4144-7620-5 (set)
Contact your Gale sales representative for ordering information.

Printed by China Translation & Printing Services Limited, Guangdong Province, China. 1st printing. 05/2010
1 2 3 4 5 6 7 14 13 12 11 10

Table of Contents

Experiment Central, 2nd edition

Experiment Central, 2nd edition

Experiment Central, 2nd edition

Experiment Central, 2nd edition

Experiment Central, 2nd edition

Reader's Guide

Experiment Central: Understanding Scientific Principles Through Projects provides in one resource a wide variety of science experiments covering nine key science curriculum fields—astronomy, biology, botany, chemistry, ecology, food science, geology, meteorology, and physics—spanning the earth sciences, life sciences, and physical sciences.

Experiment Central, 2nd edition combines, expands, and updates the original four-volume and two-volume UXL sets. This new edition includes 20 new chapters, 60 new experiments, and more than 35 enhanced experiments. Each chapter explores a scientific subject and offers experiments or projects that utilize or reinforce the topic studied. Chapters are alphabetically arranged according to scientific concept, including: Air and Water Pollution, Color, Eclipses, Forensic Science, Genetics, Magnetism, Mountains, Periodic Table, Renewable Energy, Storms and Water Cycle. Two to three experiments or projects are included in each chapter.

Entry format

Chapters are presented in a standard, easy-to-follow format. All chapters open with an explanatory overview section designed to introduce students to the scientific concept and provide the background behind a concept s discovery or important figures who helped advance the study of the field.

Each experiment is divided into eight standard sections to help students follow the experimental process clearly from beginning to end. Sections are:

- Purpose/Hypothesis
- Level of Difficulty

- Materials Needed
- Approximate Budget
- Timetable
- Step-by-Step Instructions
- Summary of Results
- Change the Variables

Chapters also include a "Design Your Own Experiment" section that allows students to apply what they have learned about a particular concept and to create their own experiments. This section is divided into:

- How to Select a Topic Relating to this Concept
- Steps in the Scientific Method
- Recording Data and Summarizing the Results
- Related Projects

Special Features

A "Words to Know" sidebar provides definitions of terms used in each chapter. A cumulative glossary collected from all the "Words to Know" sections is included in the beginning of each volume.

The "Experiments by Scientific Field" section categorizes experiments by scientific curriculum area. This section cumulates all experiments across the six-volume series.

The Parent's and Teacher's Guide recommends that a responsible adult always oversee a student's experiment and provides several safety guidelines for all students to follow.

Standard sidebars accompany experiments and projects.

- "What Are the Variables?" explains the factors that may have an impact on the outcome of a particular experiment.
- "How to Experiment Safely" clearly explains any risks involved with the experiment and how to avoid them.
- "Troubleshooter's Guide" presents problems that a student might encounter with an experiment, possible causes of the problem, and ways to remedy the problem.

Over 450 photos enhance the text; approximately 450 custom illustrations show the steps in the experiments.

Four indexes cumulate information from all the experiments in this six-volume set, including:

- Budget Index categorizes the experiments by approximate cost.
- Level of Difficulty Index lists experiments according to "easy," "moderate," or "difficult," or a combination thereof.
- Timetable Index categorizes each experiment by the amount of time needed to complete it, including setup and follow-through time.
- General Subject Index provides access to all major terms, people, places, and topics covered in the set.

Acknowledgments

The author wishes to acknowledge and thank Laurie Curtis, teacher/researcher; Cindy O'Neill, science educator; and Joyce Nelson, chemist, for their contributions to this edition as consultants.

Comments and Suggestions

We welcome your comments on *Experiment Central*. Please write: Editors, *Experiment Central*, U*X*L, 27500 Drake Rd. Farmington Hills, MI 48331-3535; call toll-free: 1-800-347-4253; or visit us at www.gale.cengage.com.

Parent's and Teacher's Guide

The experiments and projects in *Experiment Central* have been carefully constructed with issues of safety in mind, but your guidance and supervision are still required. Following the safety guidelines that accompany each experiment and project (found in the "How to Experiment Safely" sidebar box), as well as putting to work the safe practices listed below, will help your child or student avoid accidents. Oversee your child or student during experiments, and make sure he or she follows these safety guidelines:

- Always wear safety goggle is there is any possiblity of sharp objects, small particles, splashes of liquid, or gas fumes getting in someone's eyes.

- Always wear protective gloves when handling materials that could irritate the skin.

- Never leave an open flame, such as a lit candle, unattended. Never wear loose clothing around an open flame.

- Follow instructions carefully when using electrical equipment, including batteries, to avoid getting shocked.

- Be cautious when handling sharp objects or glass equipment that might break. Point scissors away from you and use them carefully.

- Always ask for help in cleaning up spills, broken glass, or other hazardous materials.

- Always use protective gloves when handling hot objects. Set them down only on a protected surface that will not be damaged by heat.

- Always wash your hands thoroughly after handling material that might contain harmful microorganisms, such as soil and pond water.

- Do not substitute materials in an experiment without asking a knowledgeable adult about possible reactions.

- Do not use or mix unidentified liquids or powders. The result might be an explosion or poisonous fumes.

- Never taste or eat any substances being used in an experiment.

- Always wear old clothing or a protective apron to avoid staining your clothes.

Experiments by Scientific Field

Chapter name in brackets, followed by experiment name. The numeral before the colon indicates volume; numbers after the colon indicate page number.

CHEMISTRY

ECOLOGY

FOOD SCIENCE

GEOLOGY

Words to Know

A

Abdomen: The third segment of an insect body.

Abscission: Barrier of special cells created at the base of leaves in autumn.

Absolute dating: The age of an object correlated to a specific fixed time, as established by some precise dating method.

Acceleration: The rate at which the velocity and/or direction of an object is changing with respect to time.

Acid: Substance that when dissolved in water is capable of reacting with a base to form salts and release hydrogen ions.

Acid rain: A form of precipitation that is significantly more acidic than neutral water, often produced as the result of industrial processes and pollution.

Acoustics: The science concerned with the production, properties, and propagation of sound waves.

Acronym: A word or phrase formed from the first letter of other words.

Active solar energy system: A solar energy system that uses pumps or fans to circulate heat captured from the Sun.

Additive: A chemical compound that is added to foods to give them some desirable quality, such as preventing them from spoiling.

Adhesion: Attraction between two different substances.

Adhesive: A substance that bonds or adheres two substances together.

Aeration: Mixing a gas, like oxygen, with a liquid, like water.

Aerobic: A process that requires oxygen.

Aerodynamics: The study of the motion of gases (particularly air) and the motion and control of objects in the air.

Agar: A nutrient rich, gelatinous substance that is used to grow bacteria.

Air: Gaseous mixture that covers Earth, composed mainly of nitrogen (about 78%) and oxygen (about 21%) with lesser amounts of argon, carbon dioxide, and other gases.

Air density: The ratio of the mass of a substance to the volume it occupies.

Air mass: A large body of air that has similar characteristics.

Air pressure: The force exerted by the weight of the atmosphere above a point on or above Earth's surface.

Alga/Algae: Single-celled or multicellular plants or plant-like organisms that contain chlorophyll, thus making their own food by photosynthesis. Algae grow mainly in water.

Alignment: Adjustment in a certain direction or orientation.

Alkali metals: The first group of elements in the periodic table, these metals have a single electron in the outermost shell.

Alkaline: Having a pH of more than 7.

Alleles: One version of the same gene.

Alloy: A mixture of two or more metals with properties different from those metals of which it is made.

Amine: An organic compound derived from ammonia.

Amino acid: One of a group of organic compounds that make up proteins.

Amnesia: Partial or total memory loss.

Amperage: A measurement of current. The common unit of measure is the ampere or amp.

Amphibians: Animals that live on land and breathe air but return to the water to reproduce.

Amplitude: The maximum displacement (difference between an original position and a later position) of the material that is vibrating. Amplitude can be thought of visually as the highest and lowest point of a wave.

Anaerobic: A process that does not require oxygen.

Anal fin: Fin on the belly of a fish, used for balance.

Anatomy: The study of the structure of living things.

Anemometer: A device that measures wind speed.

Angiosperm: A flowering plant that has its seeds produced within an ovary.

Animalcules: Life forms that Anton van Leeuwenhoek named when he first saw them under his microscope; they later became known as protozoa and bacteria.

Anther: The male reproductive organs of the plant, located on the tip of a flower's stamen.

Anthocyanin: Red pigment found in leaves, petals, stems, and other parts of a plant.

Antibiotic: A substance produced by or derived from certain fungi and other organisms, that can destroy or inhibit the growth of other microorganisms.

Antibiotic resistance: The ability of microorganisms to change so that they are not killed by antibiotics.

Antibody: A protein produced by certain cells of the body as an immune (disease-fighting) response to a specific foreign antigen.

Antigen: A substance that causes the production of an antibody when injected directly into the body.

Antioxidants: Used as a food additive, these substances can prevent food spoilage by reducing the food's exposure to air.

Aquifer: Underground layer of sand, gravel, or spongy rock that collects water.

Arch: A curved structure that spans an opening and supports a weight above the opening.

Artesian well: A well in which water is forced out under pressure.

Asexual reproduction: A reproductive process that does not involve the union of two individuals in the exchange of genetic material.

Astronomers: Scientists who study the positions, motions, and composition of stars and other objects in the sky.

Astronomy: The study of the physical properties of objects and matter outside Earth's atmosphere.

Atmosphere: Layers of air that surround Earth.

Atmospheric pressure: The pressure exerted by the atmosphere at Earth's surface due to the weight of the air.

Atom: The smallest unit of an element, made up of protons and neutrons in a central nucleus surrounded by moving electrons.

Atomic mass: Also known as atomic weight, the average mass of the atoms in an element; the number that appears under the element symbol in the periodic table.

Atomic number: The number of protons (or electrons) in an atom; the number that appears over the element symbol in the periodic table.

Atomic symbol: The one- or two-letter abbreviation for a chemical element.

Autotroph: An organism that can build all the food and produce all the energy it needs with its own resources.

Auxins: A group of plant hormones responsible for patterns of plant growth.

Axis: An imaginary straight line around which an object, like a planet, spins or turns. Earth's axis is a line that goes through the North and South Poles.

B

Bacteria: Single-celled microorganisms that live in soil, water, plants, and animals that play a key role in the decay of organic matter and the cycling of nutrients. Some are agents of disease.

Bacteriology: The scientific study of bacteria, their characteristics, and their activities as related to medicine, industry, and agriculture.

Barometer: An instrument for measuring atmospheric pressure, used especially in weather forecasting.

Base: Substance that when dissolved in water is capable of reacting with an acid to form salts and release hydrogen ions; has a pH of more than 7.

Base pairs: In DNA, the pairing of two nucleotides with each other: adenine (A) with thymine (T), and guanine (G) with cytosine (C).

Beam: A straight, horizontal structure that spans an opening and supports a weight above the opening.

Bedrock: Solid layer of rock lying beneath the soil and other loose material.

Beriberi: A disease caused by a deficiency of thiamine and characterized by nerve and gastrointestinal disorders.

Biochemical oxygen demand (BOD5): The amount of oxygen microorganisms use over a five-day period in 68°F (20°C) water to decay organic matter.

Biodegradable: Capable of being decomposed by biological agents.

Biological variables: Living factors such as bacteria, fungi, and animals that can affect the processes that occur in nature and in an experiment.

Bioluminescence: The chemical phenomenon in which an organism can produce its own light.

Biomass: Organic materials that are used to produce usable energy.

Biomes: Large geographical areas with specific climates and soils, as well as distinct plant and animal communities that are interdependent.

Biomimetics: The development of materials that are found in nature.

Biopesticide: Pesticide produced from substances found in nature.

Bivalve: Bivalves are characterized by shells that are divided into two parts or valves that completely enclose the mollusk like the clam or scallop.

Blanching: A cooking technique in which the food, usually vegetables and fruits, are briefly cooked in boiling water and then plunged into cold water.

Blood pattern analysis: The study of the shape, location, and pattern of blood in order to understand how it got there.

Blueshift: The shortening of the frequency of light waves toward the blue end of the visible light spectrum as they travel towards an observer; most commonly used to describe movement of stars towards Earth.

Boiling point: The temperature at which a substance changes from a liquid to a gas or vapor.

Bond: The force that holds two atoms together.

Bone joint: A place in the body where two or more bones are connected.

Bone marrow: The spongy center of many bones in which blood cells are manufactured.

Bone tissue: A group of similar cells in the bone with a common function.

Bony fish: The largest group of fish, whose skeleton is made of bone.

Boreal: Northern.

Botany: The branch of biology involving the scientific study of plant life.

Braided rivers: Wide, shallow rivers with multiple channels and pebbly islands in the middle.

Buoyancy: The tendency of a liquid to exert a lifting effect on a body immersed in it.

By-product: A secondary substance produced as the result of a physical or chemical process, in addition to the main product.

C

Calcium carbonate: A substance that is secreted by a mollusk to create the shell it lives in.

Calibration: To standardize or adjust a measuring instrument so its measurements are correct.

Cambium: The tissue below the bark that produces new cells, which become wood and bark.

Camouflage: Markings or coloring that help hide an animal by making it blend into the surrounding environment.

Cancellous bone: Also called spongy bone, the inner layer of a bone that has cells with large spaces in between them filled with marrow.

Canning: A method of preserving food using airtight, vacuum-sealed containers and heat processing.

Capillary action: The tendency of water to rise through a narrow tube by the force of adhesion between the water and the walls of the tube.

Caramelization: The process of heating sugars to the point at which they break down and lead to the formation of new compounds.

Carbohydrate: A compound consisting of carbon, hydrogen, and oxygen found in plants and used as a food by humans and other animals.

Carbonic acid: A weak acid that forms from the mixture of water and carbon dioxide.

Carnivore: A meat-eating organism.

Carotene: Yellow-orange pigment in plants.

Cartilage: The connective tissue that covers and protects the bones.

Cartilaginous fish: The second largest group of fish whose skeleton is made of cartilage

Cast: In paleontology, the fossil formed when a mold is later filled in by mud or mineral matter.

Catalase: An enzyme found in animal liver tissue that breaks down hydrogen peroxide into oxygen and water.

Catalyst: A compound that starts or speeds up the rate of a chemical reaction without undergoing any change in its own composition.

Caudal fin: Tail fin of a fish used for fast swimming.

Cave: Also called cavern, a hollow or natural passage under or into the ground large enough for a person to enter.

Celestial bodies: Describing planets or other objects in space.

Cell membrane: The layer that surrounds the cell, but is inside the cell wall, allowing some molecules to enter and keeping others out of the cell.

Cell theory: All living things have one or more similar cells that carry out the same functions for the living process.

Cell wall: A tough outer covering over the cell membrane of bacteria and plant cells.

Cells: The basic unit for living organisms; cells are structured to perform highly specialized functions.

Centrifugal force: The apparent force pushing a rotating body away from the center of rotation.

Centrifuge: A device that rapidly spins a solution so that the heavier components will separate from the lighter ones.

Centripetal force: Rotating force that moves towards the center or axis.

Cerebral cortex: The outer layer of the brain.

Channel: A shallow trench carved into the ground by the pressure and movement of a river.

Chemical change: The change of one or more substances into other substances.

Chemical energy: Energy stored in chemical bonds.

Chemical property: A characteristic of a substance that allows it to undergo a chemical change. Chemical properties include flammability and sensitivity to light.

Chemical reaction: Any chemical change in which at least one new substance is formed.

Chemosense: A sense stimulated by specific chemicals that cause the sensory cell to transmit a signal to the brain.

Chitin: Substance that makes up the exoskeleton of crustaceans.

Chlorophyll: A green pigment found in plants that absorbs sunlight, providing the energy used in photosynthesis, or the conversion of carbon dioxide and water to complex carbohydrates.

Chloroplasts: Small structures in plant cells that contain chlorophyll and in which the process of photosynthesis takes place.

Chromatography: A method for identifying the components of a substance based on their characteristic colors.

Chromosome: A structure of DNA found in the cell nucleus.

Cilia: Hairlike structures on olfactory receptor cells that sense odor molecules.

Circuit: The complete path of an electric current including the source of electric energy.

Circumference: The distance around a circle.

Clay: Type of soil comprising the smallest soil particles.

Cleavage: The tendency of a mineral to split along certain planes.

Climate: The average weather that a region experiences over a long period.

Coagulation: The clumping together of particles in a mixture, often because the repelling force separating them is disrupted.

Cohesion: Attraction between like substances.

Cold blooded: When an animals body temperature rises or falls to match the environment.

Collagen: A protein in bone that gives the bone elasticity.

Colloid: A mixture containing particles suspended in, but not dissolved in, a dispersing medium.

Colony: A mass of microorganisms that have been bred in a medium.

Colorfast: The ability of a material to keep its dye and not fade or change color.

Coma: Glowing cloud of gas surrounding the nucleus of a comet.

Combustion: Any chemical reaction in which heat, and usually light, is produced. It is commonly the burning of organic substances during which oxygen from the air is used to form carbon dioxide and water vapor.

Comet: An icy body orbiting in the solar system, which partially vaporizes when it nears the Sun and develops a diffuse envelope of dust and gas as well as one or more tails.

Comet head: The nucleus and the coma of a comet.

Comet nucleus: The core or center of a comet. (Plural: Comet nuclei.)

Comet tail: The most distinctive feature of comets; comets can display two basic types of tails: one gaseous and the other largely composed of dust.

Compact bone: The outer, hard layer of the bone.

Complete metamorphosis: Metamorphosis in which a larva becomes a pupa before changing into an adult form.

Composting: The process in which organic compounds break down and become dark, fertile soil called humus.

Compression: A type of force on an object where the object is pushed or squeezed from each end.

Concave: Hollowed or rounded inward, like the inside of a bowl.

Concave lens: A lens that is thinner in the middle than at the edges.

Concentration: The amount of a substance present in a given volume, such as the number of molecules in a liter.

Condensation: The process by which a gas changes into a liquid.

Conduction: The flow of heat through a solid.

Conductivity: The ability of a material to carry an electrical current.

Conductor: A substance able to carry an electrical current.

Cones: Cells in the retina that can perceive color.

Confined aquifer: An aquifer with a layer of impermeable rock above it where the water is held under pressure.

Coniferous: Refers to trees, such as pines and firs, that bear cones and have needle-like leaves that are not shed all at once.

Conservation of energy: The law of physics that states that energy can be transformed from one form to another, but can be neither created nor destroyed.

Constellations: Patterns of stars in the night sky. There are eighty-eight known constellations.

Continental drift: The theory that continents move apart slowly at a predictable rate.

Contract: To shorten, pull together.

Control experiment: A set-up that is identical to the experiment but is not affected by the variable that will be changed during the experiment.

Convection: The circulatory motion that occurs in a gas or liquid at a nonuniform temperature owing to the variation of its density and the action of gravity.

Convection current: A circular movement of a fluid in response to alternating heating and cooling.

Convex: Curved or rounded outward, like the outside of a ball.

Convex lens: A lens that is thicker in the middle than at the edges.

Coprolites: The fossilized droppings of animals.

Coriolis force: A force that makes a moving object appear to travel in a curved path over the surface of a spinning body.

Corona: The outermost atmospheric layer of the Sun.

Corrosion: An oxidation-reduction reaction in which a metal is oxidized (reacted with oxygen) and oxygen is reduced, usually in the presence of moisture.

Cotyledon: Seed leaves, which contain the stored source of food for the embryo.

Crater: An indentation caused by an object hitting the surface of a planet or moon.

Crest: The highest point reached by a wave.

Cross-pollination: The process by which pollen from one plant pollinates another plant of the same species.

Crust: The hard outer shell of Earth that floats upon the softer, denser mantle.

Experiment Central, 2nd edition

Crustacean: A type of arthropod characterized by hard and thick skin, and having shells that are jointed. This group includes the lobster, crab, and crayfish.

Crystal: Naturally occurring solid composed of atoms or molecules arranged in an orderly pattern that repeats at regular intervals.

Crystal faces: The flat, smooth surfaces of a crystal.

Crystal lattice: The regular and repeating pattern of the atoms in a crystal.

Cultures: Microorganisms growing in prepared nutrients.

Cumulonimbus cloud: The parent cloud of a thunderstorm; a tall, vertically developed cloud capable of producing heavy rain, high winds, and lightning.

Current: The flow of electrical charge from one point to another.

Currents: The horizontal and vertical circulation of ocean waters.

Cyanobacteria: Oxygen-producing, aquatic bacteria capable of manufacturing its own food; resembles algae.

Cycles: Occurrence of events that take place on a regular, repeating basis.

Cytology: The branch of biology concerned with the study of cells.

Cytoplasm: The semifluid substance inside a cell that surrounds the nucleus and other membrane-enclosed organelles.

D

Decanting: The process of separating a suspension by waiting for its heavier components to settle out and then pouring off the lighter ones.

Decibel (dB): A unit of measurement for the amplitude of sound.

Deciduous: Plants that lose their leaves during some season of the year, and then grow them back during another season.

Decompose: To break down into two or more simpler substances.

Decomposition: The breakdown of complex molecules of dead organisms into simple nutrients that can be reutilized by living organisms.

Decomposition reaction: A chemical reaction in which one substance is broken down into two or more substances.

Deficiency disease: A disease marked by a lack of an essential nutrient in the diet.

Degrade: Break down.

Dehydration: The removal of water from a material.

Denaturization: Altering an enzyme so it no longer works.

Density: The mass of a substance divided by its volume.

Density ball: A ball with the fixed standard of 1.0 gram per milliliter, which is the exact density of pure water.

Deoxyribonucleic acid (DNA): Large, complex molecules found in the nuclei of cells that carry genetic information for an organism's development; double helix. (Pronounced DEE-ox-see-rye-bo-noo-klay-ick acid)

Dependent variable: The variable in an experiment whose value depends on the value of another variable in the experiment.

Deposition: Dropping of sediments that occurs when a river loses its energy of motion.

Desert: A biome with a hot-to-cool climate and dry weather.

Desertification: Transformation of arid or semiarid productive land into desert.

Dewpoint: The point at which water vapor begins to condense.

Dicot: Plants with a pair of embryonic seeds that appear at germination.

Diffraction: The bending of light or another form of electromagnetic radiation as it passes through a tiny hole or around a sharp edge.

Diffraction grating: A device consisting of a surface into which are etched very fine, closely spaced grooves that cause different wavelengths of light to reflect or refract (bend) by different amounts.

Diffusion: Random movement of molecules that leads to a net movement of molecules from a region of high concentration to a region of low concentration.

Disinfection: Using chemicals to kill harmful organisms.

Dissolved oxygen: Oxygen molecules that have dissolved in water.

Distillation: The process of separating liquids from solids or from other liquids with different boiling points by a method of evaporation and condensation, so that each component in a mixture can be collected separately in its pure form.

DNA fingerprinting: A technique that uses DNA fragments to identify the unique DNA sequences of an individual.

DNA replication: The process by which one DNA strand unwinds and duplicates all its information, creating two new DNA strands that are identical to each other and to the original strand.

DNA (deoxyribonucleic acid): Large, complex molecules found in nuclei of cells that carry genetic information for an organism's development.

Domain: Small regions in iron that possess their own magnetic charges.

Dominant gene: A gene that passes on a certain characteristic, even when there is only one copy (allele) of the gene.

Doppler effect: The change in wavelength and frequency (number of vibrations per second) of either light or sound as the source is moving either towards or away from the observer.

Dormant: A state of inactivity in an organism.

Dorsal fin: The fin located on the back of a fish, used for balance.

Double helix: The shape taken by DNA (deoxyribonucleic acid) molecules in a nucleus.

Drought: A prolonged period of dry weather that damages crops or prevents their growth.

Dry cell: A source of electricity that uses a non-liquid electrolyte.

Dust tail: One of two types of tails a comet may have, it is composed mainly of dust and it points away from the Sun.

Dye: A colored substance that is used to give color to a material.

Dynamic equilibrium: A situation in which substances are moving into and out of cell walls at an equal rate.

E

Earthquake: An unpredictable event in which masses of rock suddenly shift or rupture below Earth's surface, releasing enormous amounts of energy and sending out shockwaves that sometimes cause the ground to shake dramatically.

Eclipse: A phenomenon in which the light from a celestial body is temporarily cut off by the presence of another.

Ecologists: Scientists who study the interrelationship of organisms and their environments.

Ecosystem: An ecological community, including plants, animals and microorganisms, considered together with their environment.

Efficiency: The amount of power output divided by the amount of power input. It is a measure of how well a device converts one form of power into another.

Effort: The force applied to move a load using a simple machine.

Elastomers: Any of various polymers having rubbery properties.

Electric charge repulsion: Repulsion of particles caused by a layer of negative ions surrounding each particle. The repulsion prevents coagulation and promotes the even dispersion of such particles through a mixtures.

Electrical energy: Kinetic energy resulting from the motion of electrons within any object that conducts electricity.

Electricity: A form of energy caused by the presence of electrical charges in matter.

Electrode: A material that will conduct an electrical current, usually a metal; used to carry electrons into or out of a battery.

Electrolyte: Any substance that, when dissolved in water, conducts an electric current.

Electromagnetic spectrum: The complete array of electromagnetic radiation, including radio waves (at the longest-wavelength end), microwaves, infrared radiation, visible light, ultraviolet radiation, X rays, and gamma rays (at the shortest-wavelength end).

Electromagnetism: A form of magnetic energy produced by the flow of an electric current through a metal core. Also, the study of electric and magnetic fields and their interaction with charges and currents.

Electron: A subatomic particle with a single negative electrical change that orbits the nucleus of an atom.

Electroplating: The process of coating one metal with another metal by means of an electrical current.

Electroscope: A device that determines whether an object is electrically charged.

Element: A pure substance composed of just one type of atom that cannot be broken down into anything simpler by ordinary chemical means.

Elevation: Height above sea level.

Elliptical: An orbital path which is egg-shaped or resembles an elongated circle.

Elongation: The percentage increase in length that occurs before a material breaks under tension.

Embryo: The seed of a plant, which through germination can develop into a new plant.

Embryonic: The earliest stages of development.

Endothermic reaction: A chemical reaction that absorbs heat or light energy, such as photosynthesis, the production of food by plant cells.

Energy: The ability to cause an action or to perform work.

Entomology: The study of insects.

Environmental variables: Nonliving factors such as air temperature, water, pollution, and pH that can affect processes that occur in nature and in an experiment.

Enzyme: Any of numerous complex proteins produced by living cells that act as catalysts, speeding up the rate of chemical reactions in living organisms.

Enzymology: The science of studying enzymes.

Ephemerals: Plants that lie dormant in dry soil for years until major rainstorms occur.

Epicenter: The location where the seismic waves of an earthquake first appear on the surface, usually almost directly above the focus.

Equilibrium: A balancing or canceling out of opposing forces, so that an object will remain at rest.

Erosion: The process by which topsoil is carried away by water, wind, or ice action.

Ethnobotany: The study of how cultures use plants in everyday life.

Eukaryotic: Multicellular organism whose cells contain distinct nuclei, which contain the genetic material. (Pronounced yoo-KAR-ee-ah-tic)

Euphotic zone: The upper part of the ocean where sunlight penetrates, supporting plant life, such as phytoplankton.

Eutrophication: The process by which high nutrient concentrations in a body of water eventually cause the natural wildlife to die.

Evaporation: The process by which liquid changes into a gas.

Exoskeleton: A hard outer covering on animals, which provide protection and structure.

Exothermic reaction: A chemical reaction that releases heat or light energy, such as the burning of fuel.

Experiment: A controlled observation.

Extremophiles: Bacteria that thrive in environments too harsh to support most life forms.

F

False memory: A memory of an event that never happened or an altered memory from what happened.

Family: A group of elements in the same column of the periodic table or in closely related columns of the table. A family of chemical compounds share similar structures and properties.

Fat: A type of lipid, or chemical compound used as a source of energy, to provide insulation and to protect organs in an animal body.

Fat-soluble vitamins: Vitamins such as A, D, E, and K that can be dissolved in the fat of plants and animals.

Fault: A crack running through rock as the result of tectonic forces.

Fault blocks: Pieces of rock from Earth's crust that press against each other and cause earthquakes when they suddenly shift or rupture from the pressure.

Fault mountain: A mountain that is formed when Earth's plates come together and cause rocks to break and move upwards.

Fermentation: A chemical reaction in which enzymes break down complex organic compounds (for example, carbohydrates and sugars) into simpler ones (for example, ethyl alcohol).

Filament: In a flower, stalk of the stamen that bears the anther.

Filtration: The mechanical separation of a liquid from the undissolved particles floating in it.

Fireball: Meteors that create an intense, bright light and, sometimes, an explosion.

First law of motion (Newton's): An object at rest or moving in a certain direction and speed will remain at rest or moving in the same motion and speed unless acted upon by a force.

Fish: Animals that live in water who have gills, fins, and are cold blooded.

Fixative: A substance that mixes with the dye to hold it to the material.

Flagella: Whiplike structures used by some organisms for movement. (Singular: flagellum.)

Flammability: The ability of a material to ignite and burn.

Flower: The reproductive part of a flowering plant.

Fluid: A substance that flows; a liquid or gas.

Fluorescence: The emission of visible light from an object when the object is bombarded with electromagnetic radiation, such as ultraviolet rays. The emission of visible light stops after the radiation source has been removed.

Focal length: The distance from the lens to the point where the light rays come together to a focus.

Focal point: The point at which rays of light converge or from which they diverge.

Focus: The point within Earth where a sudden shift or rupture occurs.

Fold mountain: A mountain that is formed when Earth's plates come together and push rocks up into folds.

Food webs: Interconnected sets of food chains, which are a sequence of organisms directly dependent on one another for food.

Force: A physical interaction (pushing or pulling) tending to change the state of motion (velocity) of an object.

Forensic science: The application of science to the law and justice system.

Fortified: The addition of nutrients, such as vitamins or minerals, to food.

Fossil: The remains, trace, or impressions of a living organism that inhabited Earth more than ten thousand years ago.

Fossil fuel: A fuel such as coal, oil, or natural gas that is formed over millions of years from the remains of plants and animals.

Fossil record: The documentation of fossils placed in relationship to one another; a key source to understand the evolution of life on Earth.

Fracture: A mineral's tendency to break into curved, rough, or jagged surfaces.

Frequency: The rate at which vibrations take place (number of times per second the motion is repeated), given in cycles per second or in hertz (Hz). Also, the number of waves that pass a given point in a given period of time.

Friction: A force that resists the motion of an object, resulting when two objects rub against one another.

Front: The area between air masses of different temperatures or densities.

Fuel cell: A device that uses hydrogen as the fuel to produce electricity and heat with water as a byproduct.

Fulcrum: The point at which a lever arm pivots.

Fungi: Kingdom of various single-celled or multicellular organisms, including mushrooms, molds, yeasts, and mildews, that do not contain chlorophyll.

Funnel cloud: A fully developed tornado vortex before it has touched the ground.

Fusion: Combining of nuclei of two or more lighter elements into one nucleus of a heavier element; the process stars use to produce energy to produce light and support themselves against their own gravity.

G

Galaxy: A large collection of stars and clusters of stars containing anywhere from a few million to a few trillion stars.

Gastropod: The largest group of mollusks; characterized by a single shell that is often coiled in a spiral. Snails are gastropods.

Gene: A segment of a DNA (deoxyribonucleic acid) molecule contained in the nucleus of a cell that acts as a kind of code for the production of some specific protein. Genes carry instructions for the formation, functioning, and transmission of specific traits from one generation to another.

Generator: A device that converts mechanical energy into electrical energy,

Genetic engineering: A technique that modifies the DNA of living cells in order to make them change its characteristics. Also called genetic modification.

Genetic material: Material that transfers characteristics from a parent to its offspring.

Geology: The study of the origin, history and structure of Earth.

Geothermal energy: Energy from deep within Earth.

Geotropism: The tendency of roots to bend toward Earth.

Germ theory of disease: The theory that disease is caused by micro-organisms or germs, and not by spontaneous generation.

Germination: First stage in development of a plant seed.

Gibbous moon: A phase of the Moon when more than half of its surface is lighted.

Gills: Special organ located behind the head of a fish that takes in oxygen from the water.

Glacier: A large mass of ice formed from snow that has packed together and which moves slowly down a slope under its own weight.

Global warming: Warming of Earth's atmosphere as a result of an increase in the concentration of gases that store heat, such as carbon dioxide.

Glucose: A simple sugar broken down in cells to produce energy.

Gnomon: The perpendicular piece of the sundial that casts the shadow.

Golgi body: An organelles that sorts, modifies, and packages molecules.

Gravity: Force of attraction between objects, the strength of which depends on the mass of each object and the distance between them.

Greenhouse effect: The warming of Earth's atmosphere due to water vapor, carbon dioxide, and other gases in the atmosphere that trap heat radiated from Earth's surface.

Greenhouse gases: Gases that absorb infrared radiation and warm the air before the heat energy escapes into space.

Greenwich Mean Time (GMT): The time at an imaginary line that runs north and south through Greenwich, England, used as the standard for time throughout the world.

Groundwater: Water that soaks into the ground and is stored in the small spaces between the rocks and soil.

Group: A vertical column of the periodic table that contains elements possessing similar chemical characteristics.

H

Hardwood: Wood from angiosperm, mostly deciduous, trees.

Heartwood: The inner layers of wood that provide structure and have no living cells.

Heat: A form of energy produced by the motion of molecules that make up a substance.

Heat capacity: The measure of how well a substance stores heat.

Heat energy: The energy produced when two substances that have different temperatures are combined.

Heliotropism: The tendency of plants to turn towards the Sun throughout the day.

Herbivore: A plant-eating organism.

Hertz (Hz): The unit of measurement of frequency; a measure of the number of waves that pass a given point per second of time.

Heterogeneous: Different throughout.

Heterotrophs: Organisms that cannot make their own food and that must, therefore, obtain their food from other organisms.

High air pressure: An area where the air is cooler and more dense, and the air pressure is higher than normal.

Hippocampus: A part of the brain associated with learning and memory.

Homogenous: The same throughout.

Hormones: Chemicals produced in the cells of plants and animals that control bodily functions.

Hue: The color or shade.

Humidity: The amount of water vapor (moisture) contained in the air.

Humus: Fragrant, spongy, nutrient-rich decayed plant or animal matter.

Hydrologic cycle: Continual movement of water from the atmosphere to Earth's surface through precipitation and back to the atmosphere through evaporation and transpiration.

Hydrologists: Scientists who study water and its cycle.

Hydrology: The study of water and its cycle.

Hydrometer: An instrument that determines the specific gravity of a liquid.

Hydrophilic: A substance that is attracted to and readily mixes with water.

Hydrophobic: A substance that is repelled by and does not mix with water.

Hydropower: Energy produced from capturing moving water.

Hydrotropism: The tendency of roots to grow toward a water source.

Hypertonic solution: A solution with a higher concentration of materials than a cell immersed in the solution.

Hypha: Slender, cottony filaments making up the body of multicellular fungi. (Plural: hyphae)

Hypothesis: An idea in the form of a statement that can be tested by observation and/or experiment.

Hypotonic solution: A solution with a lower concentration of materials than a cell immersed in the solution.

I

Igneous rock: Rock formed from the cooling and hardening of magma.

Immiscible: Incapable of being mixed.

Imperfect flower: Flowers that have only the male reproductive organ (stamen) or the female reproductive organs (pistil).

Impermeable: Not allowing substances to pass through.

Impurities: Chemicals or other pollutants in water.

Inclined plane: A simple machine with no moving parts; a slanted surface.

Incomplete metamorphosis: Metamorphosis in which a nymph form gradually becomes an adult through molting.

Independent variable: The variable in an experiment that determines the final result of the experiment.

Indicator: Pigments that change color when they come into contact with acidic or basic solutions.

Inertia: The tendency of an object to continue in its state of motion.

Infrared radiation: Electromagnetic radiation of a wavelength shorter than radio waves but longer than visible light that takes the form of heat.

Inner core: Very dense, solid center of Earth.

Inorganic: Not containing carbon; not derived from a living organism.

Insect: A six-legged invertebrate whose body has three segments.

Insoluble: A substance that cannot be dissolved in some other substance.

Insulated wire: Electrical wire coated with a non-conducting material such as plastic.

Insulation: A material that is a poor conductor of heat or electricity.

Insulator: A material through which little or no electrical current or heat energy will flow.

Interference fringes: Bands of color that fan out around an object.

Internal skeleton: An animal that has a backbone.

Invertebrate: An animal that lacks a backbone or internal skeleton.

Ion: An atom or groups of atoms that carry an electrical charge—either positive or negative—as a result of losing or gaining one or more electrons.

Ion tail: One of two types of tails a comet may have, it is composed mainly of charged particles and it points away from the Sun.

Ionic conduction: The flow of an electrical current by the movement of charged particles, or ions.

Isobars: Continuous lines that connect areas with the same air pressure.

Isotonic solutions: Two solutions that have the same concentration of solute particles and therefore the same osmotic pressure.

J

Jawless fish: The smallest group of fishes, who lacks a jaw.

K

Kinetic energy: The energy of an object or system due to its motion.

Kingdom: One of the five classifications in the widely accepted classification system that designates all living organisms into animals, plants, fungi, protists, and monerans.

L

Labyrinth: A lung-like organ located above the gills that allows the fish to breathe in oxygen from the air.

Lactobacilli: A strain of bacteria.

Landfill: A method of disposing of waste materials by placing them in a depression in the ground or piling them in a mound. In a sanitary landfill, the daily deposits of waste materials are covered with a layer of soil.

Larva: Immature form (wormlike in insects; fishlike in amphibians) of an organism capable of surviving on its own. A larva does not resemble the parent and must go through metamorphosis, or change, to reach its adult stage.

Lava: Molten rock that occurs at the surface of Earth, usually through volcanic eruptions.

Lava cave: A cave formed from the flow of lava streaming over solid matter.

Leach: The movement of dissolved minerals or chemicals with water as it percolates, or oozes, downward through the soil.

Leaching: The movement of dissolved chemicals with water that is percolating, or oozing, downward through the soil.

Leavening agent: A substance used to make foods like dough and batter to rise.

Leeward: The side away from the wind or flow direction.

Lens: A piece of transparent material with two curved surfaces that bend rays of light passing through it.

Lichen: An organism composed of a fungus and a photosynthetic organism in a symbiotic relationship.

Lift: Upward force on the wings of an aircraft created by differences in air pressure on top of and underneath the wings.

Ligaments: Tough, fibrous tissue connecting bones.

Light: A form of energy that travels in waves.

Light-year: Distance light travels in one year in the vacuum of space, roughly 5.9 trillion miles (9.5 trillion kilometers).

The Local Group: A cluster of thirty galaxies, including the Milky Way, pulled together by gravity.

Long-term memory: The last category of memory in which memories are stored away and can last for years.

Low air pressure: An area where the air is warmer and less dense, and the air pressure is lower than normal.

Luminescent: Producing light through a chemical process.

Luminol: A compound used to detect blood.

Lunar eclipse: An eclipse that occurs when Earth passes between the Sun and the Moon, casting a shadow on the Moon.

Luster: A glow of reflected light; a sheen.

M

Machine: Any device that makes work easier by providing a mechanical advantage.

Macrominerals: Minerals needed in relatively large quantities.

Macroorganisms: Visible organisms that aid in breaking down organic matter.

Magma: Molten rock deep within Earth that consists of liquids, gases, and particles of rocks and crystals. Magma underlies areas of volcanic activity and at Earth's surface is called lava.

Magma chambers: Pools of bubbling liquid rock that are the source of energy causing volcanoes to be active.

Magma surge: A swell or rising wave of magma caused by the movement and friction of tectonic plates, which heats and melts rock, adding to the magma and its force.

Magnet: A material that attracts other like materials, especially metals.

Magnetic circuit: A series of magnetic domains aligned in the same direction.

Magnetic field: The space around an electric current or a magnet in which a magnetic force can be observed.

Magnetism: A fundamental force in nature caused by the motion of electrons in an atom.

Maillard reaction: A reaction caused by heat and sugars and resulting in foods browning and flavors.

Mammals: Animals that have a backbone, are warm blooded, have mammary glands to feed their young and have or are born with hair.

Mantle: Thick dense layer of rock that underlies Earth's crust and overlies the core; also soft tissue that is located between the shell and an animal's inner organs. The mantle produces the calcium carbonate substance that create the shell of the animal.

Manure: The waste matter of animals.

Mass: Measure of the total amount of matter in an object. Also, an object's quantity of matter as shown by its gravitational pull on another object.

Matter: Anything that has mass and takes up space.

Meandering river: A lowland river that twists and turns along its route to the sea.

Medium: A material that contains the nutrients required for a particular microorganism to grow.

Melting point: The temperature at which a substance changes from a solid to a liquid.

Memory: The process of retaining and recalling past events and experiences.

Meniscus: The curved surface of a column of liquid.

Metabolism: The process by which living organisms convert food into energy and waste products.

Metamorphic rock: Rock formed by transformation of pre-existing rock through changes in temperature and pressure.

Metamorphosis: Transformation of an immature animal into an adult.

Meteor: An object from space that becomes glowing hot when it passes into Earth's atmosphere; also called shooting star.

Meteor shower: A group of meteors that occurs when Earth's orbit intersects the orbit of a meteor stream.

Meteorites: A meteor that is large enough to survive its passage through the atmosphere and hit the ground.

Meteoroid: A piece of debris that is traveling in space.

Meteorologist: Scientist who studies the weather and the atmosphere.

Microbiology: Branch of biology dealing with microscopic forms of life.

Microclimate: A unique climate that exists only in a small, localized area.

Microorganisms: Living organisms so small that they can be seen only with the aid of a microscope.

Micropyle: Seed opening that enables water to enter easily.

Microvilli: The extension of each taste cell that pokes through the taste pore and first senses the chemicals.

Milky Way: The galaxy in which our solar system is located.

Mimicry: A characteristic in which an animal is protected against predators by resembling another, more distasteful animal.

Mineral: An inorganic substance found in nature with a definite chemical composition and structure. As a nutrient, it helps build bones and soft tissues and regulates body functions.

Mixture: A combination of two or more substances that are not chemically combined with each other and that can exist in any proportion.

Mnemonics: Techniques to improve memory.

Mold: In paleontology, the fossil formed when acidic water dissolves a shell or bone around which sand or mud has already hardened.

Molecule: The smallest particle of a substance that retains all the properties of the substance and is composed of one or more atoms.

Mollusk: An invertebrate animal usually enclosed in a shell, the largest group of shelled animals.

Molting: A process by which an animal sheds its skin or shell.

Monocot: Plants with a single embryonic leaf at germination.

Monomer: A small molecule that can be combined with itself many times over to make a large molecule, the polymer.

Moraine: Mass of boulders, stones, and other rock debris carried along and deposited by a glacier.

Mordant: A substance that fixes the dye to the material.

Mountain: A landform that stands well above its surroundings; higher than a hill.

Mucus: A thick, slippery substance that serves as a protective lubricant coating in passages of the body that communicate with the air.

Multicellular: Living things with many cells joined together.

Muscle fibers: Stacks of long, thin cells that make up muscle; there are three types of muscle fiber: skeletal, cardiac, and smooth.

Mycelium: In fungi, the mass of threadlike, branching hyphae.

N

Nanobots: A nanoscale robot.

Nanometer: A unit of length; this measurement is equal to one-billionth of a meter.

Nanotechnology: Technology that involves working and developing technologies on the nanometer (atomic and molecular) scale.

Nansen bottles: Self-closing containers with thermometers that draw in water at different depths.

Nebula: Bright or dark cloud, often composed of gases and dust, hovering in the space between the stars.

Nectar: A sweet liquid, found inside a flower, that attracts pollinators.

Neutralization: A chemical reaction in which the mixing of an acidic solution with a basic (alkaline) solution results in a solution that has the properties of neither an acid nor a base.

Neutron: A subatomic particle with a mass of about one atomic mass unit and no electrical charge that is found in the nucleus of an atom.

Newtonian fluid: A fluid that follows certain properties, such as the viscosity remains constant at a given temperature.

Niche: The specific location and place in the food chain that an organism occupies in its environment.

Noble gases: Also known as inert or rare gases; the elements argon, helium, krypton, neon, radon, and xenon, which are nonreactive gases and form few compounds with other elements.

Non-Newtonian fluid: A fluid whose property do not follow Newtonian properties, such as viscosity can vary based on the stress.

Nonpoint source: An unidentified source of pollution, which may actually be a number of sources.

Nucleation: The process by which crystals start growing.

Nucleotide: The basic unit of a nucleic acid. It consists of a simple sugar, a phosphate group, and a nitrogen-containing base. (Pronounced noo-KLEE-uh-tide.)

Nucleus: The central part of the cell that contains the DNA; the central core of an atom, consisting of protons and (usually) neutrons.

Nutrient: A substance needed by an organism in order for it to survive, grow, and develop.

Nutrition: The study of the food nutrients an organism needs in order to maintain well-being.

Nymph: An immature form in the life cycle of insects that go through an incomplete metamorphosis.

O

Objective lens: In a refracting telescope, the lens farthest away from the eye that collects the light.

Oceanographer: A person who studies the chemistry of the oceans, as well as their currents, marine life, and the ocean floor.

Oceanography: The study of the chemistry of the oceans, as well as their currents, marine life, and the ocean bed.

Olfactory: Relating to the sense of smell.

Olfactory bulb: The part of the brain that processes olfactory (smell) information.

Olfactory epithelium: The patch of mucous membrane at the top of the nasal cavity that contains the olfactory (smell) nerve cells.

Olfactory receptor cells: Nerve cells in the olfactory epithelium that detect odors and transmit the information to the brain.

Oort cloud: Region of space beyond our solar system that theoretically contains about one trillion inactive comets.

Optics: The study of the nature of light and its properties.

Orbit: The path followed by a body (such as a planet) in its travel around another body (such as the Sun).

Organelle: A membrane-enclosed structure that performs a specific function within a cell.

Organic: Containing carbon; also referring to materials that are derived from living organisms.

Oscillation: A repeated back-and-forth movement.

Osmosis: The movement of fluids and substances dissolved in liquids across a semipermeable membrane from an area of its greater concentration to an area of its lesser concentration until all substances involved reach a balance.

Outer core: A liquid core that surrounds Earth's solid inner core; made mostly of iron.

Ovary: In a plant, the base part of the pistil that bears ovules and develops into a fruit.

Ovule: Structure within the ovary that develops into a seed after fertilization.

Oxidation: A chemical reaction in which oxygen reacts with some other substance and in which ions, atoms, or molecules lose electrons.

Oxidation state: The sum of an atom's positive and negative charges.

Oxidation-reduction reaction: A chemical reaction in which one substance loses one or more electrons and the other substance gains one or more electrons.

Oxidizing agent: A chemical substance that gives up oxygen or takes on electrons from another substance.

P

Paleontologist: Scientist who studies the life of past geological periods as known from fossil remains.

Papain: An enzyme obtained from the fruit of the papaya used as a meat tenderizer, as a drug to clean cuts and wounds, and as a digestive aid for stomach disorders.

Papillae: The raised bumps on the tongue that contain the taste buds.

Parent material: The underlying rock from which soil forms.

Partial solar/lunar eclipse: An eclipse in which our view of the Sun/Moon is only partially blocked.

Particulate matter: Solid matter in the form of tiny particles in the atmosphere. (Pronounced par-TIK-you-let.)

Passive solar energy system: A solar energy system in which the heat of the Sun is captured, used, and stored by means of the design of a building and the materials from which it is made.

Pasteurization: The process of slow heating that kills bacteria and other microorganisms.

Peaks: The points at which the energy in a wave is maximum.

Pectin: A natural carbohydrate found in fruits and vegetables.

Pectoral fin: Pair of fins located on the side of a fish, used for steering.

Pedigree: A diagram that illustrates the pattern of inheritance of a genetic trait in a family.

Pelvic fin: Pair of fins located toward the belly of a fish, used for stability.

Pendulum: A free-swinging weight, usually consisting of a heavy object attached to the end of a long rod or string, suspended from a fixed point.

Penicillin: A mold from the fungi group of microorganisms; used as an antibiotic.

Pepsin: Digestive enzyme that breaks down protein.

Percolate: To pass through a permeable substance.

Perfect flower: Flowers that have both male and female reproductive organs.

Period: A horizontal row in the periodic table.

Periodic table: A chart organizing elements by atomic number and chemical properties into groups and periods.

Permeable: Having pores that permit a liquid or a gas to pass through.

Permineralization: A form of preservation in which mineral matter has filled in the inner and outer spaces of the cell.

Pest: Any living thing that is unwanted by humans or causes injury and disease to crops and other growth.

Pesticide: Substance used to reduce the abundance of pests.

Petal: Leafy structure of a flower just inside the sepals; they are often brightly colored and have many different shapes.

Petrifaction: Process of turning organic material into rock by the replacement of that material with minerals.

pH: A measure of the acidity or alkalinity of a solution referring to the concentration of hydrogen ions present in a liter of a given fluid. The pH scale ranges from 0 (greatest concentration of hydrogen ions and therefore most acidic) to 14 (least concentration of hydrogen ions and therefore most alkaline), with 7 representing a neutral solution, such as pure water.

Pharmacology: The science dealing with the properties, reactions, and therapeutic values of drugs.

Phases: Changes in the portion of the Moon's surface that is illuminated by light from the Sun as the Moon revolves around Earth.

Phloem: The plant tissue that carries dissolved nutrients through the plant.

Phosphorescence: The emission of visible light from an object when the object is bombarded with electromagnetic radiation, such as ultraviolet rays. The object stores part of the radiation energy and the emission of visible light continues for a period ranging from a fraction of a second to several days after the radiation source has been removed.

Photoelectric effect: The phenomenon in which light falling upon certain metals stimulates the emission of electrons and changes light into electricity.

Photosynthesis: Chemical process by which plants containing chlorophyll use sunlight to manufacture their own food by converting carbon dioxide and water to carbohydrates, releasing oxygen as a by-product.

Phototropism: The tendency of a plant to grow toward a source of light.

Photovoltaic cells: A device made of silicon that converts sunlight into electricity.

Physical change: A change in which the substance keeps its molecular identity, such as a piece of chalk that has been ground up.

Physical property: A characteristic that you can detect with your senses, such as color and shape.

Physiologist: A scientist who studies the functions and processes of living organisms.

Phytoplankton: Microscopic aquatic plants that live suspended in the water.

Pigment: A substance that displays a color because of the wavelengths of light that it reflects.

Pili: Short projections that assist bacteria in attaching to tissues.

Pistil: Female reproductive organ of flowers that is composed of the stigma, style, and ovary.

Pitch: A property of a sound, determined by its frequency; the highness or lowness of a sound.

Plant extract: The juice or liquid essence obtained from a plant by squeezing or mashing it.

Plasmolysis: Occurs in walled cells in which cytoplasm, the semifluid substance inside a cell, shrivels and the membrane pulls away from the cell wall when the vacuole loses water.

Plates: Large regions of Earth's surface, composed of the crust and uppermost mantle, which move about, forming many of Earth's major geologic surface features.

Platform: The horizontal surface of a bridge on which traffic travels.

Pnematocysts: Stinging cells.

Point source: An identified source of pollution.

Pollen: Dust-like grains or particles produced by a plant that contain male sex cells.

Pollinate: The transfer of pollen from the male reproductive organs to the female reproductive organs of plants.

Pollination: Transfer of pollen from the male reproductive organs to the female reproductive organs of plants.

Pollinator: Any animal, such as an insect or bird, that transfers the pollen from one flower to another.

Pollution: The contamination of the natural environment, usually through human activity.

Polymer: Chemical compound formed of simple molecules (known as monomers) linked with themselves many times over.

Polymerization: The bonding of two or more monomers to form a polymer.

Polyvinyl acetate: A type of polymer that is the main ingredient of white glues.

Pore: An opening or space.

Potential energy: The energy of an object or system due to its position.

Precipitation: Any form of water that falls to Earth, such as rain, snow, or sleet.

Predator: An animal that hunts another animal for food.

Preservative: An additive used to keep food from spoiling.

Primary colors: The three colors red, green, and blue; when combined evenly they produce white light and by combining varying amounts can produce the range of colors.

Prism: A piece of transparent material with a triangular cross-section. When light passes through it, it causes different colors to bend different amounts, thus separating them into a rainbow of colors.

Probe: The terminal of a voltmeter, used to connect the voltmeter to a circuit.

Producer: An organism that can manufacture its own food from nonliving materials and an external energy source, usually by photosynthesis.

Product: A compound that is formed as a result of a chemical reaction.

Prokaryote: A cell without a true nucleus, such as a bacterium.

Prominences: Masses of glowing gas, mainly hydrogen, that rise from the Sun's surface like flames.

Propeller: Radiating blades mounted on a rapidly rotating shaft, which moves aircraft forward.

Protein: A complex chemical compound consisting of many amino acids attached to each other that are essential to the structure and functioning of all living cells.

Protists: Members of the kingdom Protista, primarily single-celled organisms that are not plants or animals.

Proton: A subatomic particle with a single positive charge that is found in the nucleus of an atom.

Protozoa: Single-celled animal-like microscopic organisms that live by taking in food rather than making it by photosynthesis. They must live in the presence of water.

Pulley: A simple machine made of a cord wrapped around a wheel.

Pupa: The insect stage of development between the larva and adult in insects that go through complete metamorphosis.

R

Radiation: Energy transmitted in the form of electromagnetic waves or subatomic particles.

Radicule: Seed's root system.

Radio wave: Longest form of electromagnetic radiation, measuring up to 6 miles (9.6 kilometers) from peak to peak.

Radioisotope dating: A technique used to date fossils, based on the decay rate of known radioactive elements.

Radiosonde balloons: Instruments for collecting data in the atmosphere and then transmitting that data back to Earth by means of radio waves.

Radon: A radioactive gas located in the ground; invisible and odorless, radon is a health hazard when it accumulates to high levels inside homes and other structures where it is breathed.

Rain shadow: Region on the side of the mountain that receives less rainfall than the area windward of the mountain.

Rancidity: Having the condition when food has a disagreeable odor or taste from decomposing oils or fats.

Reactant: A compound present at the beginning of a chemical reaction.

Reaction: Response to an action prompted by stimulus.

Recessive gene: A gene that produces a certain characteristic only two both copies (alleles) of the gene are present.

Recycling: The use of waste materials, also known as secondary materials or recyclables, to produce new products.

Redshift: The lengthening of the frequency of light waves toward the red end of the visible light spectrum as they travel away from an observer; most commonly used to describe movement of stars away from Earth.

Reduction: A process in which a chemical substance gives off oxygen or takes on electrons.

Reed: A tall woody perennial grass that has a hollow stem.

Reflection: The bouncing of light rays in a regular pattern off the surface of an object.

Reflector telescope: A telescope that directs light from an opening at one end to a concave mirror at the far end, which reflects the light back to a smaller mirror that directs it to an eyepiece on the side of the tube.

Refraction: The bending of light rays as they pass at an angle from one transparent or clear medium into a second one of different density.

Refractor telescope: A telescope that directs light through a glass lens, which bends the light waves and brings them to a focus at an eyepiece that acts as a magnifying glass.

Relative age: The age of an object expressed in relation to another like object, such as earlier or later.

Relative density: The density of one material compared to another.

Rennin: Enzyme used in making cheese.

Resistance: A partial or complete limiting of the flow of electrical current through a material. The common unit of measure is the ohm.

Respiration: The physical process that supplies oxygen to living cells and the chemical reactions that take place inside the cells.

Resultant: A force that results from the combined action of two other forces.

Retina: The light-sensitive part of the eyeball that receives images and transmits visual impulses through the optic nerve to the brain.

Ribosome: A protein composed of two subunits that functions in protein synthesis (creation).

Rigidity: The amount an object will deflect when supporting a weight. The less it deflects for a given amount of weight, the greater its rigidity.

River: A main course of water into which many other smaller bodies of water flow.

Rock: Naturally occurring solid mixture of minerals.

Rods: Cells in the retina that are sensitive to degrees of light and movement.

Root hairs: Fine, hair-like extensions from the plant's root.

Rotate: To turn around on an axis or center.

Runoff: Water that does not soak into the ground or evaporate, but flows across the surface of the ground.

S

Salinity: The amount of salts dissolved in water.

Saliva: Watery mixture with chemicals that lubricates chewed food.

Sand: Granular portion of soil composed of the largest soil particles.

Sapwood: The outer wood in a tree, which is usually a lighter color.

Saturated: In referring to solutions, a solution that contains the maximum amount of solute for a given amount of solvent at a given temperature.

Saturation: The intensity of a color.

Scanning tunneling microscope: A microscope that can show images of surfaces at the atomic level by scanning a probe over a surface.

Scientific method: Collecting evidence and arriving at a conclusion under carefully controlled conditions.

Screw: A simple machine; an inclined plane wrapped around a cylinder.

Scurvy: A disease caused by a deficiency of vitamin C, which causes a weakening of connective tissue in bone and muscle.

Sea cave: A cave in sea cliffs, formed most commonly by waves eroding the rock.

Second law of motion (Newton's): The force exerted on an object is proportional to the mass of the object times the acceleration produced by the force.

Sediment: Sand, silt, clay, rock, gravel, mud, or other matter that has been transported by flowing water.

Sedimentary rock: Rock formed from compressed and solidified layers of organic or inorganic matter.

Sedimentation: A process during which gravity pulls particles out of a liquid.

Seed crystal: Small form of a crystalline structure that has all the facets of a complete new crystal contained in it.

Seedling: A small plant just starting to grow into its mature form.

Seismic belt: Boundaries where Earth's plates meet.

Seismic waves: Vibrations in rock and soil that transfer the force of an earthquake from the focus into the surrounding area.

Seismograph: A device that detects and records vibrations of the ground.

Seismology: The study and measurement of earthquakes.

Seismometer: A seismograph that measures the movement of the ground.

Self-pollination: The process in which pollen from one part of a plant fertilizes ovules on another part of the same plant.

Semipermeable membrane: A thin barrier between two solutions that permits only certain components of the solutions, usually the solvent, to pass through.

Sensory memory: Memory that the brain retains for a few seconds.

Sepal: The outermost part of a flower; typically leaflike and green.

Sexual reproduction: A reproductive process that involves the union of two individuals in the exchange of genetic material.

Shear stress: An applied force to a give area.

Shell: A region of space around the center of the atom in which electrons are located; also, a hard outer covering that protects an animal living inside.

Short-term memory: Also known as working memory, this memory was transferred here from sensory memory.

Sidereal day: The time it takes for a particular star to travel around and reach the same position in the sky; about four minutes shorter than the average solar day.

Silt: Medium-sized soil particles.

Simple machine: Any of the basic structures that provide a mechanical advantage and have no or few moving parts.

Smog: A form of air pollution produced when moisture in the air combines and reacts with the products of fossil fuel combustion. Smog is characterized by hazy skies and a tendency to cause respiratory problems among humans.

Softwood: Wood from coniferous trees, which usually remain green all year.

Soil: The upper layer of Earth that contains nutrients for plants and organisms; a mixture of mineral matter, organic matter, air, and water.

Soil horizon: An identifiable soil layer due to color, structure, and/or texture.

Soil profile: Combined soil horizons or layers.

Solar collector: A device that absorbs sunlight and collects solar heat.

Solar day: Called a day, the time between each arrival of the Sun at its highest point.

Solar eclipse: An eclipse that occurs when the Moon passes between Earth and the Sun, casting a shadow on Earth.

Solar energy: Any form of electromagnetic radiation that is emitted by the Sun.

Solubility: The tendency of a substance to dissolve in some other substance.

Soluble: A substance that can be dissolved in some other substance.

Solute: The substance that is dissolved to make a solution and exists in the least amount in a solution, for example sugar in sugar water.

Solution: A mixture of two or more substances that appears to be uniform throughout except on a molecular level.

Solvent: The major component of a solution or the liquid in which some other component is dissolved, for example water in sugar water.

Specific gravity: The ratio of the density of a substance to the density of pure water.

Specific heat capacity: The energy required to raise the temperature of 1 kilogram of the substance by 1 degree Celsius.

Speleologist: One who studies caves.

Speleology: Scientific study of caves and their plant and animal life.

Spelunkers: Also called cavers, people who explore caves for a hobby.

Spiracles: The openings on an insects side where air enters.

Spoilage: The condition when food has taken on an undesirable color, odor, or texture.

Spore: A small, usually one-celled, reproductive body that is capable of growing into a new organism.

Stalactite: Cylindrical or icicle-shaped mineral deposit projecting downward from the roof of a cave. (Pronounced sta-LACK-tite.)

Stalagmite: Cylindrical or icicle-shaped mineral deposit projecting upward from the floor of a cave. (Pronounced sta-LAG-mite.)

Stamen: Male reproductive organ of flowers that is composed of the anther and filament.

Standard: A base for comparison.

Star: A vast clump of hydrogen gas and dust that produces great energy through fusion reactions at its core.

Static electricity: A form of electricity produced by friction in which the electric charge does not flow in a current but stays in one place.

Stigma: Top part of the pistil upon which pollen lands and receives the male pollen grains during fertilization.

Stomata: Pores in the epidermis (surface) of leaves.

Storm: An extreme atmospheric disturbance, associated with strong damaging winds, and often with thunder and lightning.

Storm chasers: People who track and seek out storms, often tornadoes.

Stratification: Layers according to density; applies to fluids.

Streak: The color of the dust left when a mineral is rubbed across a rough surface.

Style: Stalk of the pistil that connects the stigma to the ovary.

Subatomic: Smaller than an atom. It usually refers to particles that make up an atom, such as protons, neutrons, and electrons.

Sublime: The process of changing a solid into a vapor without passing through the liquid phase.

Substrate: The substance on which an enzyme operates in a chemical reaction.

Succulent: Plants that live in dry environments and have water storage tissue.

Sundial: A device that uses the position of the Sun to indicate time.

Supersaturated: Solution that is more highly concentrated than is normally possible under given conditions of temperature and pressure.

Supertaster: A person who is extremely sensitive to specific tastes due to a greater number of taste buds.

Supplements: A substance intended to enhance the diet.

Surface area: The total area of the outside of an object; the area of a body of water that is exposed to the air.

Surface tension: The attractive force of molecules to each other on the surface of a liquid.

Surface water: Water in lakes, rivers, ponds, and streams.

Suspension: A temporary mixture of a solid in a gas or liquid from which the solid will eventually settle out.

Swim bladder: Located above the stomach, takes in air when the fish wants to move upwards and releases air when the fish wants to move downwards.

Symbiosis: A pattern in which two or more organisms live in close connection with each other, often to the benefit of both or all organisms.

Synthesis reaction: A chemical reaction in which two or more substances combine to form a new substance.

Synthesize: To make something artificially, in a laboratory or chemical plant, that is generally not found in nature.

Synthetic: A substance that is synthesized, or manufactured, in a laboratory; not naturally occurring.

Synthetic crystals: Artificial or manmade crystals.

T

Taiga: A large land biome mostly dominated by coniferous trees.

Taste buds: Groups of taste cells located on the papillae that recognize the different tastes.

Taste pore: The opening at the top of the taste bud from which chemicals reach the taste cells.

Tectonic: Relating to the forces and structures of the outer shell of Earth.

Tectonic plates: Huge flat rocks that form Earth's crust.

Telescope: A tube with lenses or mirrors that collect, transmit, and focus light.

Temperate: Mild or moderate weather conditions.

Temperature: The measure of the average energy of the molecules in a substance.

Tendon: Tough, fibrous connective tissue that attaches muscle to bone.

Tensile strength: The force needed to stretch a material until it breaks.

Terminal: A connection in an electric circuit; usually a connection on a source of electric energy such as a battery.

Terracing: A series of horizontal ridges made in a hillside to reduce erosion.

Testa: A tough outer layer that protects the embryo and endosperm of a seed from damage.

Theory of special relativity: Theory put forth by Albert Einstein that time is not absolute, but it is relative according to the speed of the observer's frame of reference.

Thermal conductivity: A number representing a material's ability to conduct heat.

Thermal energy: Kinetic energy caused by the movement of molecules due to temperature.

Thermal inversion: A region in which the warmer air lies above the colder air; can cause smog to worsen.

Thermal pollution: The discharge of heated water from industrial processes that can kill or injure water life.

Thiamine: A vitamin of the B complex that is essential to normal metabolism and nerve function.

Thigmotropism: The tendency for a plant to grow toward a surface it touches.

Third law of motion (Newton's): For every action there is an equal and opposite reaction.

Thorax: The middle segment of an insect body; the legs and wings are connected to the thorax.

Tides: The cyclic rise and fall of seawater.

Titration: A procedure in which an acid and a base are slowly mixed to achieve a neutral substance.

Topsoil: The uppermost layers of soil containing an abundant supply of decomposed organic material to supply plants with nutrients.

Tornado: A violently rotating, narrow column of air in contact with the ground and usually extending from a cumulonimbus cloud.

Total solar/lunar eclipse: An eclipse in which our view of the Sun/Moon is totally blocked.

Toxic: Poisonous.

Trace element: A chemical element present in minute quantities.

Trace minerals: Minerals needed in relatively small quantities.

Translucent: Permits the passage of light.

Transpiration: Evaporation of water in the form of water vapor from the stomata on the surfaces of leaves and stems of plants.

Troglobite: An animal that lives in a cave and is unable to live outside of one.

Troglophile: An animal that lives the majority of its life cycle in a cave but is also able to live outside of the cave.

Trogloxene: An animal that spends only part of its life cycle in a cave and returns periodically to the cave.

Tropism: The growth or movement of a plant toward or away from a stimulus.

Troposphere: The lowest layer of Earth's atmosphere, ranging to an altitude of about 9 miles (15 km) above Earth's surface.

Trough: The lowest point of a wave. (Pronounced trawf.)

Tsunami: A large wave of water caused by an underwater earthquake.

Tuber: An underground, starch-storing stem, such as a potato.

Tundra: A treeless, frozen biome with low-lying plants.

Turbine: A spinning device used to transform mechanical power from energy into electrical energy.

Turbulence: Air disturbance that affects an aircraft's flight.

Turgor pressure: The force that is exerted on a plant's cell wall by the water within the cell.

Tyndall effect: The effect achieved when colloidal particles reflect a beam of light, making it visible when shined through such a mixture.

U

Ultraviolet: Electromagnetic radiation (energy) of a wavelength just shorter than the violet (shortest wavelength) end of the visible light spectrum and thus with higher energy than the visible light.

Unconfined aquifer: An aquifer under a layer of permeable rock and soil.

Unicellular: Living things that have one cell. Protozoans are unicellular, for example.

Unit cell: The basic unit of the crystalline structure.

Universal law of gravity: The law of physics that defines the constancy of the force of gravity between two bodies.

Updraft: Warm, moist air that moves away from the ground.

Upwelling: The process by which lower-level, nutrient-rich waters rise upward to the ocean's surface.

V

Vacuole: An enclosed, space-filling sac within plant cells containing mostly water and providing structural support for the cell.

Van der Waals' force: An attractive force between two molecules based on the positive and negative side of the molecule.

Variable: Something that can affect the results of an experiment.

Vegetative propagation: A form of asexual reproduction in which plants are produced that are genetically identical to the parent.

Velocity: The rate at which the position of an object changes with time, including both the speed and the direction.

Veneer: Thin slices of wood.

Viable: The capability of developing or growing under favorable conditions.

Vibration: A regular, back-and-forth motion of molecules in the air.

Viscosity: The measure of a fluid's resistance to flow; its flowability.

Visible spectrum: The range of individual wavelengths of radiation visible to the human eye when white light is broken into its component colors as it passes through a prism or by some other means.

Vitamin: A complex organic compound found naturally in plants and animals that the body needs in small amounts for normal growth and activity.

Volatilization: The process by which a liquid changes (volatilizes) to a gas.

Volcano: A conical mountain or dome of lava, ash, and cinders that forms around a vent leading to molten rock deep within Earth.

Voltage: Also called potential difference; a measurement of the amount of electric energy stored in a mass of electric charges compared to the energy stored in some other mass of charges. The common unit of measure is the volt.

Voltmeter: An instrument for measuring the amperage, voltage, or resistance in an electrical circuit.

Volume: The amount of space occupied by a three-dimensional object; the amplitude or loudness of a sound.

Vortex: A rotating column of a fluid such as air or water.

Waste stream: The waste materials generated by the population of an area, or by a specific industrial process, and removed for disposal.

Water (hydrologic) cycle: The constant movement of water molecules on Earth as they rise into the atmosphere as water vapor, condense into droplets and fall to land or bodies of water, evaporate, and rise again.

Water clock: A device that uses the flow of water to measure time.

Water table: The level of the upper surface of groundwater.

Water vapor: Water in its gaseous state.

Water-soluble vitamins: Vitamins such as C and the B-complex vitamins that dissolve in the watery parts of plant and animal tissues.

Waterline: The highest point to which water rises on the hull of a ship. The portion of the hull below the waterline is under water.

Wave: A means of transmitting energy in which the peak energy occurs at a regular interval; the rise and fall of the ocean water.

Wavelength: The distance between the peak of a wave of light, heat, or other form of energy and the next corresponding peak.

Weather: The state of the troposphere at a particular time and place.

Weather forecasting: The scientific predictions of future weather patterns.

Weathered: Natural process that breaks down rocks and minerals at Earth's surface into simpler materials by physical (mechanical) or chemical means.

Wedge: A simple machine; a form of inclined plane.

Weight: The gravitational attraction of Earth on an object; the measure of the heaviness of an object.

Wet cell: A source of electricity that uses a liquid electrolyte.

Wetlands: Areas that are wet or covered with water for at least part of the year.

Wheel and axle: A simple machine; a larger wheel(s) fastened to a smaller cylinder, an axle, so that they turn together.

Work: The result of a force moving a mass a given distance. The greater the mass or the greater the distance, the greater the work involved.

X

Xanthophyll: Yellow pigment in plants.

Experiment Central, 2nd edition

Xerophytes: Plants that require little water to survive.

Xylem: Plant tissue consisting of elongated, thick-walled cells that transport water and mineral nutrients. (Pronounced ZY-lem.)

Yeast: A single-celled fungi that can be used to as a leavening agent.

(49)

Life Cycles

All animals go through changes during their lives. Some simply grow larger, while others completely change their forms. This kind of change is called metamorphosis, which means "change in form."

Some insects have no metamorphosis, simply growing larger and becoming able to reproduce. Others undergo an incomplete metamorphosis, in which the immature insects are known as nymphs. Nymphs, which often live in water, resemble the adult forms, but their wings are not fully developed and they have no reproductive organs. Nymphs gradually become adults by molting, or shedding their outermost layer.

A caterpillar represents the larval stage in a complete metamorphosis. CORBIS.

Other insects go through a complete metamorphosis, in which the immature stage is called a larva. Caterpillars, for example, are the larvae of butterflies. The larva becomes a pupa, which is mostly a resting stage. Finally, the pupa emerges as a full-fledged adult, such as a butterfly. Organisms in different stages of the life cycle often live in different habitats and eat different foods.

What other organisms go through metamorphosis? Amphibians also go through a dramatic metamorphosis. You are probably familiar with the life cycle of the frog, which begins with a tadpole. You may have seen tadpoles in a pond or stream. An aquatic animal with a tail, the tadpole not only grows as it gets older, it also changes its form, growing legs, living at least partly on land, and losing its tail.

645

WORDS TO KNOW

Amphibians: Animals that live on land and breathe air but return to the water to reproduce.

Complete metamorphosis: Metamorphosis in which a larva becomes a pupa before changing into an adult form.

Control experiment: A set-up that is identical to the experiment but is not affected by the variable that affects the experimental group. Results from the control experiment are compared to results from the actual experiment.

Ecologists: Scientists who study the interrelationship of organisms and their environments.

Hypothesis: An idea in the form of a statement that can be tested by observation and/or experiment.

Incomplete metamorphosis: Metamorphosis in which a nymph form gradually becomes an adult through molting.

Larva: Immature form (wormlike in insects; fishlike in amphibians) of an organism capable of surviving on its own. A larva does not resemble the parent and must go through metamorphosis, or change, to reach its adult stage.

Metamorphosis: Transformation of an immature animal into an adult.

Molting: Shedding of the outer layer of an animal, as occurs during growth of insect larvae.

Nymph: An immature form in the life cycle of insects that go through an incomplete metamorphosis.

Pupa: A stage in the metamorphosis of an insect during which its tissues are completely reorganized to take on their adult shape.

Variable: Something that can affect the results of an experiment.

A "froglet" is one stage in the frog's life cycle. PHOTO RESEARCHERS INC.

While tadpoles eat tiny aquatic vegetation, adult frogs eat just about any small animal that flies, jumps, or crawls past and can fit in their mouths.

Why should we learn about metamorphosis? Many people are interested in the life cycles of animals. Farmers must know about insect life cycles in order to control harmful insects and encourage the helpful ones that help pollinate their plants, such as bees and butterflies. Ecologists are also interested in metamorphosis. Many amphibians are threatened with extinction due to the destruction of their habitat. Ecologists study metamorphosis to learn the needs of different stages of amphibian life cycles and better understand how to save them.

What questions do you have about life cycles? You will have an opportunity to explore life cycles in the following experiments. You will learn more about this natural phenomenon that can be so fascinating and dramatic to observe.

EXPERIMENT 1

Tadpoles: Does temperature affect the rate at which tadpoles change into frogs?

Purpose/Hypothesis **WARNING:** *Do not perform this experiment unless you have a safe, approved spot to release live frogs once experiment is completed. You should be aware that it is illegal to release or dispose of live frogs in certain areas. If you are not sure about performing this experiment, ask your science teacher.*

In this experiment, you will discover how the water temperature in which tadpoles live affects how fast they grow and become adult frogs. Tadpoles are the larval form of frogs. They hatch from eggs laid by a female frog. Tadpoles live in the water and breathe through gills, but when they become frogs or toads, they breathe air and live mostly on land. Tadpoles eat only plants, while adult frogs eat insects and even small snakes. Before you begin, make an educated guess about the outcome of this experiment based on your knowledge of tadpoles. This educated guess, or prediction, is your hypothesis. A hypothesis should explain these things:

- the topic of the experiment
- the variable you will change
- the variable you will measure
- what you expect to happen

A hypothesis should be brief, specific, and measurable. It must be something you can test through observation. Your experiment will prove or disprove your hypothesis. Here is one possible hypothesis for this experiment: "The higher the water temperature, the faster tadpoles will become frogs."

In this case, the variable you will change will be the temperature of the water, and the variable you will measure will be the number of days it

What Are the Variables?

Variables are anything that might affect the results of an experiment. Here are the main variables in this experiment:

- the temperature of the water
- the number of tadpoles in each bucket
- the age, size, and health of the tadpoles in each bucket
- the tadpoles' diet

In other words, the variables in this experiment are everything that might affect the time it takes for the tadpoles to become frogs. If you change more than one variable, you will not be able to tell which variable had the most effect on the time for the tadpoles to metamorphose.

How to Experiment Safely

Be careful when handling live animals, and treat them with respect and care. Avoid touching the tadpoles because amphibians have extremely sensitive skin. Wash your hands before and after you touch the water. If you decide to find your own tadpoles in a pond or stream, ask an adult to help you. You should be aware that it is illegal to release or dispose of live frogs in certain areas. If you are not sure about performing this experiment, ask your science teacher.

takes for the tadpoles to become frogs. You expect the tadpoles in the warmest water to develop into frogs first.

Setting up a control experiment will help you isolate one variable. Only one variable will change between the control and the experimental buckets, and that is the temperature of the water. For the control, you will use water at the air temperature outside (or at room temperature if your region is experiencing winter now). For the experimental buckets, you will have warmer and cooler water.

You will measure the number of days it takes the tadpoles to become adult frogs. You will know they are fully adult when they completely lose their tails and have fully developed legs. If warmer water results in a faster metamorphosis, your hypothesis is correct.

Level of Difficulty Difficult, because of care required with live animals.

Materials Needed

- 5 buckets or large glass jars with lids
- water to fill the containers (Allow it to sit at least overnight to let any chlorine in it evaporate.)
- a steady supply of boiled lettuce
- 5 thermometers

Steps 1 and 2: Fill the five containers each with the same amount of water. Place five tadpoles in each container.
GALE GROUP.

Container	Temperature	Days to metamorphosis
1		
2		
3		
4		
5		

Container	Day (record size each day)							
	1	2	3	4	5	6	7	8...
1								
2								
3								
4								
5								

Step 4: Recording chart for Experiment 1. GALE GROUP.

- large aquarium fish net
- about 25 tadpoles (You can order tadpoles from a biological supply company, such as those listed in the Further Readings section, or you might find them in a stream or pond.)

Approximate Budget $30 for thermometers and tadpoles.

Timetable About 4 weeks.

Step-by-Step Instructions

1. Fill each of the five containers with the same amount of water. Add a thermometer to each container.
2. Use the net to place five tadpoles in each container.
3. Place each container so that the water temperatures will be different. Leave one at room temperature. Place one outside as your

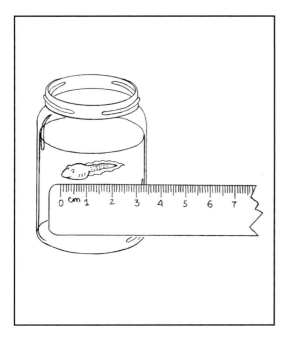

Step 7: Measure the size of the tadpoles in each container every week. GALE GROUP.

control. Place another under a lamp that will be left on constantly. Place one container in a cool, dark place, such as under a counter. Put the last one in the refrigerator. (Tadpoles in the wild often live in quite cold water.)

4. After an hour, record the water temperature in each container on a data sheet similar to the one illustrated.

5. Feed all your tadpoles about a silver-dollar-sized piece of boiled lettuce every day or every other day. Do not overfeed because the lettuce will rot. Record how much food you put in the containers each day.

6. Change the water regularly, perhaps every other day. Use water that has been allowed to sit overnight and is at the same temperature as the water you are replacing. Putting tadpoles in water that is much warmer or cooler than they are used to could kill them. If any tadpoles die for any reason, remove them as soon as possible.

7. Record the water temperature in each container each day, and describe each group of tadpoles. You may want to sketch them. Measure their size each week and record it on your data sheet.

8. After a group of tadpoles becomes frogs, which could take several weeks, record the number of days and release them into an area where it is safe and legal to do so. **You should be aware that it is illegal to release or dispose of live frogs in certain areas. If you are not sure about where to release your frogs, ask your science teacher.**

9. Continue making observations and recording data until all the tadpoles have become frogs.

Summary of Results Study the results on your chart. How many days did it take for the first group to become frogs? What was the water temperature in that container? Did tadpoles in cooler containers take longer to go through metamorphosis? Was your hypothesis correct? Summarize what you have found.

Change the Variables You can vary this experiment in several ways. For example, feed the tadpoles different amounts of food and keep the temperature of the water constant. Then you can determine how food availability impacts their growth rate. Or you might feed them different kinds of vegetation.

You can also place different amounts of water in each container or a different number of tadpoles in each container. How does that affect their growth rate? Try varying the amount of sunlight that falls on each container. How does light affect tadpole growth?

EXPERIMENT 2

Insects: How does food supply affect the growth rate of grasshoppers or crickets?

Purpose/Hypothesis **WARNING:** *You should be aware that it is illegal to release or dispose of live insects in certain areas. If you are not sure about performing this experiment, ask your science teacher.*

Insects such as grasshoppers and crickets go through an incomplete metamorphosis, where they gradually progress from eggs through several nymph stages to adulthood. In this experiment, you will explore how the amount of food available affects the growth rate of these insects from nymph to adulthood. Before you begin, make an educated guess about the outcome of this experiment based on your knowledge of insects. This educated guess, or prediction, is your hypothesis. A hypothesis should explain these things:

- the topic of the experiment
- the variable you will change
- the variable you will measure
- what you expect to happen

A hypothesis should be brief, specific, and measurable. It must be something you can test through observation. Your experiment will prove or disprove your hypothesis. Here is one possible hypothesis for this experiment: "The more food supplied to grasshoppers, the faster they will become adults."

Troubleshooter's Guide

Here are some problems that may arise during this experiment, some possible causes, and ways to remedy the problems.

Problem: All the tadpoles are going through metamorphosis at the same time.

Possible cause: The water temperatures are too similar. Find warmer and cooler places to put the jars.

Problem: Some of the tadpoles are dying.

Possible causes: They are not getting enough to eat, or the water is too warm, too cold, or too dirty. Try feeding tadpoles more or make the water a little warmer or cooler in the jars where tadpoles are dying. Also, change the water regularly.

What Are the Variables?

Variables are anything that might affect the results of an experiment. Here are the main variables in this experiment:

- the amount of food you supply
- the number of insects in each container
- the age and health of the eggs you begin with
- the temperature at which the insects are kept

In other words, the variables in this experiment are everything that might affect the time it takes the grasshoppers to develop into adults. If you change more than one variable, you will not be able to tell which variable had the most effect on the grasshoppers' growth rate.

In this case, the variable you will change will be the amount of food you feed the grasshoppers, and the variable you will measure will be the time it takes them to become adults. You expect the grasshoppers that are fed the most food will become adults first.

Only one variable will change between the control experiment and the experimental containers, and that is the amount of food you supply. For the control, you will supply a medium amount of food. For the experimental insects, you will supply a greater and a lesser amount. You will measure how many days it takes from the egg stage to the adult stage. If the insects in the containers with the most food grow fastest, your hypothesis is correct.

Level of Difficulty Difficult, because of care required with live animals.

Materials Needed

- 3 glass jars with lids
- approximately 30 grasshopper or cricket eggs (You can obtain them from a biological supply company, such as those listed under Further Readings.)
- fruit flies and a covered container to keep them in (You can also obtain fruit flies from a biological supply company.)
- measuring tape (with millimeters)

How to Experiment Safely

Always be careful with live animals and treat them with respect. Move their containers slowly. Wash your hands carefully before and after handling them. If any insects die, dispose of them. You should be aware that it is illegal to release or dispose of live insects in certain areas. If you are not sure about performing this experiment, ask your science teacher.

Approximate Budget $30, if you need to purchase insects and food.

Timetable 2 to 3 weeks.

Step-by-Step Instructions

1. Place an equal amount of eggs in each of the three jars. Label the jars "medium/control," "small amount," and "large amount."
2. Place the jars in a warm, dry place out of the direct sun.

Step 1: Place an equal amount of eggs in each of the three jars. Label as shown. GALE GROUP.

3. When the eggs hatch, record the day and time on a data chart similar to the one illustrated.

4. Provide the amount of food named on the jar labels to each group of nymphs. It will be difficult to count the fruit flies you supply, but try to record the approximate number you give to each group. Or you might vary the number of times you feed each group each day. Feed the small group only once, the control group twice, and the large group three times.

5. Every day record the growth of your insects. Measure the length of at least one insect in each group each day.

Step 5: Measure the length of at least one insect in each group each day. GALE GROUP.

6. The supply house probably provided information about how large these insects will be as adults. When the insects in any group reach that size, release them in an appropriate area. **You should be aware that it is illegal to release or dispose of live insects in certain areas. If you are not sure about where to release your insects, ask your science teacher.**

7. Continue feeding and measuring until all groups have reached adulthood.

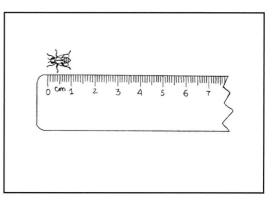

Hatching date: Control _____

Hatching date: Small Amount_____

Hatching date: Large Amount_____

Day

Jar	1 Size	2 Size	3 Size	4 Size	5 Size	6 Size	7 Size	8 Size
Control								
Small Amount								
Large Amount								

Recording chart for Experiment 2. GALE GROUP.

Summary of Results Study the results on your chart. How many days did it take your control group to reach adulthood? How many days did it take the group you fed the least? The most? Did food availability affect the growth rate of your insects? Was your hypothesis correct? Summarize what you have learned.

Change the Variables You can vary this experiment in several ways. For example, change the temperature where you keep the insects. How does heat or cold affect them? How about sunlight? Vary the number of eggs in each container. If some containers are very crowded, how does that affect the insects' growth rate? Check the labels that came with your eggs for the different kinds of food the insects eat. Does a different diet affect their growth rate?

Modify the Experiment In Experiments 1 and 2, you examined the metamorphosis of a tadpole, and the grasshopper or cricket. If it is difficult for you to obtain and care for live animals, you can simplify these experiments by drawing or constructing representations of the animals' life cycle.

First, conduct research at your local library or on the Internet of an animal that undergoes a complete metamorphosis and one that goes through an incomplete metamorphosis. You can explore the life cycle of the tadpole, grasshopper, caterpillar, or cricket. In a notebook, keep track of your research and sketch the stages of the life cycles. For example, the monarch butterfly undergoes a complete metamorphosis. You can draw the unique stages of the caterpillar life cycle as it transforms into a butterfly. You could also sculpt the changes out of modeling clay, cut out paper figures, or mold the shapes out of pipe cleaners.

Refer to your notebook and your representations to compare the life cycle of the two animals. List important features of each life stage.

Design Your Own Experiment

How to Select a Topic Relating to this Concept If you are interested in life cycles, you could study the different stages (eggs, larvae, nymphs) and the organisms' diets, habitats, sizes, forms, and activities. Perhaps you are interested in the transformation from caterpillars to butterflies. How long is each stage in the life cycle for various species? Where do they lay their eggs? What do they eat, if anything? Many butterflies, such as the monarch, migrate long distances. Where do they go? How can they fly so far, and how long do they stay there?

Maybe you are more interested in the life cycles of amphibians, such as frogs, toads, salamanders, and newts. Investigate which ones live in your area and what time of the year you could best study the different stages of their life cycles.

Check the Further Readings section and talk with your science teacher or school or community media specialist to start gathering information on animal life cycle questions that interest you.

Steps in the Scientific Method To do an original experiment, you need to plan carefully and think things through. Otherwise, you might not be

---

Troubleshooter's Guide

Here are some problems that may arise during this experiment, some possible causes, and ways to remedy the problems.

Problem: The growth rate of the insects in all the containers seemed about the same.

Possible cause: The amount you are feeding your insects is too similar. Try feeding one group several more times in a day than the other groups.

Problem: Many of the insects appear to be dying.

Possible causes: You are not feeding the insects enough, or the temperature is too cold. Try feeding more fruit flies, or check the information that came with the eggs to see if they need other kinds of food. Move them to a warmer place if the place you have been keeping them is rather cool.

The butterfly is the adult stage in the life cycle that begins as a caterpillar.
PETER ARNOLD INC.

sure what question you are answering, what you are or should be measuring, or what your findings prove or disprove.

Here are the steps in designing an experiment:

- State the purpose of—and the underlying question behind—the experiment you propose to do.
- Recognize the variables involved, and select one that will help you answer the question at hand.
- State a testable hypothesis, an educated guess about the answer to your question.
- Decide how to change the variable you selected.
- Decide how to measure your results.

Recording Data and Summarizing the Results Your data should include charts, such as the ones you did for these experiments. They should be clearly labeled and easy to read. You may also want to include photos, graphs, or drawings of your experimental setup and results.

If you have done a non experimental project, explain clearly what your research question was and illustrate your findings.

Related Projects Besides doing experiments, you could prepare a poster or model illustrating the life stages of a particular animal. Or you could research the migration patterns of a particular butterfly or study the effects of different stages of insects on agriculture. You could present your findings as a booklet, poster, or report. The possibilities are numerous.

For More Information

Carolina Biological Supply Company, 2700 York Road, Burlington, NC 27215, 1-800-334-5551. http://www.carolina.com

Frey Scientific, 100 Paragon Parkway, Mansfield, OH 44903, 1-800-225-FREY. http://www.freyscientific.com

Goor, Ron, and Nancy Goor. *Insect Metamorphosis: From Egg to Adult.* New Jersey: Simon & Schuster, 1990. Discusses both complete and incomplete metamorphoses step-by-step with full color photographs.

Kalman, Bobbie. *Animal Life Cycles: Growing and Changing.* New York: Crabtree Publishing, 2006. A simple explanation of the life cycle of different animals.

Kneidel, Sally. *Creepy Crawlies and the Scientific Method.* Golden, CO: Fulcrum Resources, 1993. A series of informative chapters on insects and other small animals, experiments, and information on keeping those animals at home or school.

Ruiz, Andres Llamas, and Francisco Arredondo. *Metamorphosis (Cycles of Life Series).* New York: Sterling Publications, 1997. Details concepts and processes of metamorphosis, focusing on frogs, butterflies, and dragonflies with colorful illustrations.

Ward's Natural Science Establishment, Inc., 5100 West Henrietta Road, PO Box 92912, Rochester, NY 14692, 1-800-962-2660. http://www.wardsci.com

50

Light Properties

Scholars wondered about the properties of light as early as 600 B.C.E. in Miletus, which was part of the Greek empire. We now know that light is a form of energy that travels through the universe in waves. All light energy exists in an electromagnetic spectrum. The visible spectrum, what we see as light, is part of the electromagnetic spectrum.

Experiments with a shutter Isaac Newton (1642–1727), a brilliant English mathematician, had just received his bachelor's degree at the University of Cambridge when the bubonic plague hit Great Britain. Because the plague spread faster in cities, Newton continued his graduate studies for two years at his countryside home. During this time, he conducted many experiments. Early in 1666, Newton darkened his room and made a small hole in his shutters. After positioning a triangular glass prism in front of this small beam of sunlight, he noticed a band of colors called a spectrum. He concluded that when the light hit the prism, it was bent, or refracted, to form many colors. He demonstrated how the colors in sunlight could be separated, then joined again to form white light.

In his work, Newton proved three of the most important characteristics of light: that it travels in straight lines, that it can be reflected, and that it can be refracted, or bent. Newton also did an experiment showing sunlight's reflection and refraction inside raindrops. He

Newton wrote about his experiments with a prism and compass in his manuscript Opticks, which was published in 1704. ARCHIVE PHOTOS.

659

This spectrum is produced by a modern diffraction grating.
PHOTO RESEARCHERS INC.

discovered that raindrops formed tiny transparent prisms that reflected and refracted the Sun to produce colorful rainbows.

Making waves In 1801, Thomas Young, a London doctor, developed a theory that light traveled in waves and presented it to the Royal Society, a prestigious group of scientists. Christian Huygens of Holland had suggested the presence of light waves in his book published in 1690, but Young would go on to prove it with his experiments in 1803.

Young used a screen with one slit. In front of that, he placed another screen with two side-by-side slits, and watched how sunlight passed through. What he saw was bands of color fanning out and meeting each other on the other side. Young realized these bands of color called interference fringes could be made only by waves of light. Up to that time it was thought that there was no form to light and that it existed everywhere. Young's experiment also showed diffraction. Diffraction occurs when an uninterruped wave of light hits an obstacle. The obstacle bends the wave into a shadow zone. This results in light and dark fringes outside the shadow's edge.

It glows in the dark Some substances produce visible light if excited by radiation, such as invisible ultraviolet light. Visible light that is produced only when the radiation source is present is called fluorescence. Certain chemicals in laundry soaps react with sunlight to produce a fluorescence that makes clothes look brighter. Visible light that is produced even after the radiation source is removed is called phosphorescence. Some plants and animals in the sea produce a phosphorescence.

Great scientists throughout history came to their conclusions about light by experimenting. Conducting some projects will enable you to become familiar with some of light's properties.

WORDS TO KNOW

Diffraction: The bending of light or another form of electromagnetic radiation as it passes through a tiny hole or around a sharp edge.

Diffraction grating: A device consisting of a surface into which are etched very fine, closely spaced grooves that cause different wavelengths of light to reflect or refract (bend) by different amounts.

Electromagnetic spectrum: The complete array of electromagnetic radiation, including radio waves (at the longest-wavelength end), microwaves, infrared radiation, visible light, ultraviolet radiation, X rays, and gamma rays (at the shortest-wavelength end).

Fluorescence: The emission of visible light from an object when the object is bombarded with electromagnetic radiation, such as ultraviolet rays. The emission of visible light stops after the radiation source has been removed.

Hypothesis: An idea phrased in the form of a statement that can be tested by observation and/or experiment.

Interference fringes: Bands of color that fan out around an object.

Light: A form of energy that travels in waves.

Phosphorescence: The emission of visible light from an object when the object is bombarded with electromagnetic radiation, such as ultraviolet rays. The object stores part of the radiation energy and the emission of visible light continues for a period ranging from a fraction of a second to several days after the radiation source has been removed.

Radiation: Energy transmitted in the form of electromagnetic waves or subatomic particles.

Reflected: The bouncing of light rays in a regular pattern off the surface of an object.

Refracted: The bending of light rays as they pass at an angle from one transparent or clear medium into a second one of different density.

Ultraviolet: Electromagnetic radiation (energy) of a wavelength just shorter than the violet (shortest wavelength) end of the visible light spectrum and thus with higher energy than the visible light.

Variable: Something that can affect the results of an experiment.

Visible spectrum: The range of individual wavelengths of radiation visible to the human eye when white light is broken into its component colors as it passes through a prism or by some other means.

PROJECT 1

Looking for the Glow: Which objects glow under black light?

Purpose/Hypothesis Fluorescence is a scientific term that refers to something (usually a chemical compound) that reacts with light energy and glows brightly. In this project, you will examine compounds that react with ultraviolet light (UV), causing the compound to glow. When certain chemicals are exposed to UV light, the molecules absorb the light energy and then release it in the form of visible light.

How to Experiment Safely

The chemicals in many detergents can irritate the skin, so avoid contact with the skin and eyes. Always use caution when handling household chemicals. Normally UV light is considered dangerous and harmful to the eyes. However, the fixture you are using emits very long wavelength UV, which is safe to use.

Level of Difficulty Easy/moderate.

Materials Needed

- UV light, also called a "black light" (fluorescent fixture with black or dark purple lightbulb)
- Wisk or Woolite brand laundry detergent
- glow-in-the-dark plastic (can be a plastic toy)
- calcite (mineral found in nature or rock stores)
- white paper
- objects to test (rocks and minerals, household detergents or cleaners, clothing, plants, etc.)

Approximate Budget $20 for black light, $5 for detergents and for calcite.

Timetable 15 minutes.

LEFT: Detergent needed for Project 1. GALE GROUP.

RIGHT: Step 2: Place a small amount of Wisk or Woolite on a piece of white paper. GALE GROUP.

detergent
white paper

Step-by-Step Instructions

1. Place the black light in a dark room and turn it on.

2. Place a small amount of Wisk or Woolite on a piece of white paper. Let the detergent dry a little and place the paper so that the light shines on it. Notice the color of the chemical. Wisk is blue/green. Woolite is green/yellow.

3. Place different objects in front of the black light, such as white socks, white or colored towels, or blue jeans. Record any color you notice. Test groups of objects such as rocks, minerals, household

Troubleshooter's Guide

Here is a problem that may arise during this project, a possible cause, and a way to remedy the problem.

Problem: None of the objects emits light.

Possible cause: The black bulb should glow a dark purple when on. If the bulb is not glowing, the light is not working. Turn the lights on in the room and unplug the black light from the wall outlet. Check to see if the lightbulb is firmly seated in its sockets on both ends. Repeat the project.

Category		
Detergents	Reacted	Color
Wisk	yes	blue green
Tide		
Woolite		
Era		
Minerals		
calcite	yes	orange / pink
gypsum		
quartz		
Flowers		
geraniums	yes	red lines in veins
roses		
four o'clocks		
Misc.		
eyeglasses	yes	green

Step 4: Sample recording chart for Project 1. GALE GROUP.

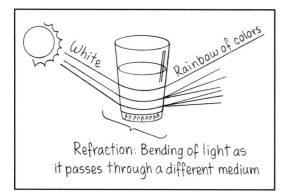

An example of light refraction using a glass of water. GALE GROUP.

A diffraction grating is a microscopically scratched plastic film that bends light as it goes around the scratched film, causing a spectrum to become visible. GALE GROUP.

detergents, flowers, fabric dyes, and plastic objects.

4. Repeat the test for each object. Record your observations.

Summary of Results Keep a record or chart of the results of the project. It's fun to discover how many things glow under UV light.

PROJECT 2

Refraction and Defraction: Making a rainbow

Purpose/Hypothesis Rainbows are a good example of refraction. Water droplets are the first step in rainbow formation. The droplets form tiny transparent prisms that reflect and refract sunlight. Refraction or bending of sunlight, or white light, makes the spectrum colors of red, orange, yellow, green, blue, and violet spread out and become visible. Refraction can be made to occur in many transparent materials, including glass, plastic, or water.

In this project, you will use a special plastic material to display the different spectrums found in colored light. The plastic material is called a diffraction grating. A diffraction grating is a microscopically scratched plastic film that bends light as it goes *around* the scratched film, causing a spectrum to become visible.

Level of Difficulty Easy/moderate.

Materials Needed

- diffraction grating (Local science and nature stores have these. They also may have toys called rainbow peepholes and rainbow makers, which contain diffraction gratings.)
- colored lightbulbs (25-watt party lights in red, blue, green, yellow, purple, and orange.)
- white lightbulb (any wattage)
- light fixture or lamp that fits lightbulbs
- colored markers

664

Approximate Budget $30: $4 to $5 for each bulb and $1 for a diffraction grating. (You might borrow colored Christmas lights.)

Timetable Approximately 30 minutes to perform and record the results.

Step-by-Step Instructions

1. Insert the white light bulb into the lamp. Plug the lamp in and turn it on.

2. Turn off all other lights and darken the room as much as possible.

3. Hold the diffraction grating approximately 0.5 inch (1.25 cm) away from your eye and look through it.

4. Notice the colors of the visible spectrum. Use the colored markers to draw the spectrum on a piece of paper and label it.

5. Turn the lights back on, shut off the lamp, and allow the bulb to cool.

6. Unplug the lamp and remove the bulb.

7. Repeat Steps 1 through 6 with each colored light.

Summary of Results Make a chart displaying the spectrums made by the different colored bulbs. Compare your results. Write a summary of your findings.

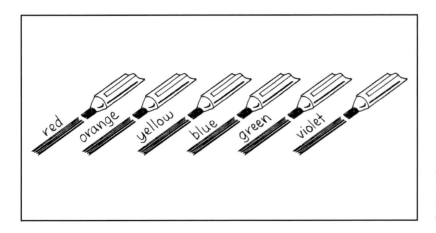

Step 4: Use the colored markers to draw the observed spectrum on a piece of paper and label it.
GALE GROUP.

What Are the Variables?

Variables are anything that might affect the results of an experiment. Here are the main variables in this experiment:

- the type of materials
- the distance from the material
- the light beam
- the distance from the ruler

In other words, the variables in this experiment are everything that might affect the passage of the light. If you change more than one variable, you will not be able to tell what had the most effect on how the material affected the light.

Step 2: Observe light reflection.
ILLUSTRATION BY TEMAH NELSON.

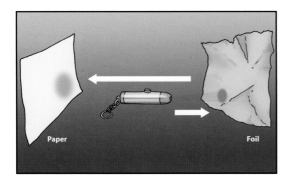

EXPERIMENT 3

Refraction: How does the material affect how light travels?

Purpose/Hypothesis In this experiment you will determine how light refracts as it interacts with different materials. You will first observe the reflection and transmission of light. Then you will determine how different materials affect light refraction. The materials you will test are plastic wrap, wax paper, a glue stick, and a glue stick wrapped in aluminum foil. Aluminum foil traps the light, reflecting it back into the material. Light transmits or passes through clear materials. As light passes through transparent materials it can refract, causing the light to bend. How much the light refracts depends upon the material.

In order to find out how light travels, you will measure the diameter of the beam of light through the materials. Also, you can see how much light is moving through the material by noting the light's intensity.

For the light source, you will use an LED to determine the path of light as it travels. An LED stands for an light emitting diode. It is a small electronic device that lights up when electricity passes through. LEDs emit a bright colored light yet consume little energy. With an LED, you can determine how and where the light travels.

Before you begin, make an educated guess about the outcome of this experiment based on your knowledge of the materials and the properties of light. This educated guess, or prediction, is your hypothesis. A hypothesis should explain these things:

- the topic of the experiment
- the variable you will change
- the variable you will measure
- what you expect to happen

A hypothesis should be brief, specific, and measurable. It must be something you can test through observation. Your experiment will prove or disprove your hypothesis. Here is one possible hypothesis for this experiment: "The glue stick wrapped in foil will cause less light to escape, leading to the strongest and narrowest beam of light."

In this case, the variable you will change will be the materials the light passes through. The variable you will measure will be the diameter and intensity of the LED beam.

Level of Difficulty Moderate.

Materials Needed

- LED, available at hardware or electronic stores
- white paper
- aluminum foil
- wax paper
- plastic wrap
- glue stick
- a ruler with exact markings
- scissors
- a dark room
- a helper

Approximate Budget $8–$12.

Timetable Approximately 45 minutes.

Step-by-Step Instructions

1. Turn off all lights and darken the room as much as possible.
2. Observe light reflection: Place aluminum foil 6 inches (15 centimeters) in front of the LED light with white paper 6 inches behind the light. Have a helper turn on the LED and make a note of the location and intensity of the light.
3. Repeat this process, replacing the aluminum foil with a piece of plastic wrap.

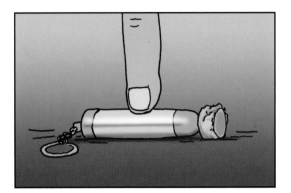

Step 3: Record the diameter of the spot and note the intensity of the light. ILLUSTRATION BY TEMAH NELSON.

Step 6: Test light refraction by holding the LED above the ruler and measuring the diameter and intensity of the beam of light. ILLUSTRATION BY TEMAH NELSON.

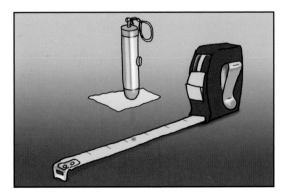

Troubleshooter's Guide

Experiments do not always work out as planned. Even so, figuring out what went wrong can be a learning experience. Here are some problems that may arise during this experiment, some possible causes, and ways to remedy the problems.

Problem: The light did not change in diameter as expected.

Possible cause: You may have moved the LED so that it was not the same from the ruler. Try having a friend place an object that is the same height as where you are holding the LED, and repeat the experiment.

Problem: The beam of light was not visible many times.

Possible cause: The room may not be dark enough. Try conducting the experiment in the evening, or block out more light from the windows.

4. Observe light transmission: Place a white piece of paper in front and in back of the aluminum foil. Record where you see the spot of light. Have a helper shine the LED toward the aluminum foil. (See illustration)

5. Observe light refraction: Hold the LED against a ¼-inch (0.64-centimeters) piece of glue stick and turn on the LED. Note the intensity of the light. Now cover the LED with a piece of aluminum foil and again turn on the LED. Record your observations.

6. Test light refraction; Hold the LED 3 inches (7.6 centimeters) above the ruler. It does not need to be exactly 3 inches (7.6 centimeters) above the ruler but you have to keep it the same distance for each material you test.

7. Shine the LED on the ruler. Measure the diameter of the beam of light and note the light's intensity.

8. Place a piece of wax paper against the LED and shine the light. Measure the diameter of the spot on the paper. Record the data.

9. Repeat the process, replacing the wax paper one at a time with plastic wrap, ¼-inch (0.64-centimeter) piece of glue stick, and a ¼-piece (0.64-centimeters) of glue stick wrapped in foil. Each time, record the diameter of the spot and note the intensity of the light.

Summary of Results Take a look at your data and notes. Was your hypothesis correct? When the light was directed at the glue stick, how did it differ with and without the aluminum foil? Was there one or more materials that caused the light to lose intensity? What material led to the beam of light having the largest diameter? Write a paragraph on your findings.

Change the Variables There are many variables you can change in this experiment. For example, you can try passing the light through a variety of materials that are only solids, such as different metals. Or you can turn the light on in front of various liquids. You can also dye the same liquid, such as water, to measure how color plays a factor in light transmission. You can also change the type of light you are using.

Design Your Own Experiment

How to Select a Topic Relating to this Concept There are many aspects of the properties of light you can study, either as a project or as an experiment. One aspect you may want to study might be reflection. If you choose reflection, one question might be: How can I see into a puddle past my reflection? Check the Further Readings section for this topic, and talk with a teacher or with a librarian before finalizing your choice.

Steps in the Scientific Method To do an original experiment, you need to plan carefully and think things through. Otherwise, you might not be sure what question you're answering, what you are or should be measuring, or what your findings prove or disprove.

Here are the steps in designing an experiment:

- State the purpose of—and the underlying question behind—the experiment you propose to do.
- Recognize the variables involved, and select one that will help you answer the question at hand.
- State a testable hypothesis, an educated guess about the answer to your question.
- Decide how to change the variable you selected.
- Decide how to measure your results.

Recording Data and Summarizing the Results In the two properties of light projects, your data might include drawings or photographs. If you exhibit your project, you need to limit the amount of information you offer, so viewers will not be overwhelmed by detail. Make sure the beginning question, the variable you measured, the results and your conclusions about light are clear. Viewers and judges will want to see how each experiment was set up. You might want to take a detailed photo at each stage. Label your photos clearly. Have colorful tables and charts ready with information and results.

Related Projects Your project does not have to be an experiment that investigates or answers a question. It can also be a model, such as Newton's original experiment with window shutters and a prism. Setting up such a model would be fun, and you would learn how this concept works.

For More Information

Burnie, David. *Light.* London: Dorling Kindersley, 1992. Includes a chapter on how Newton split light and other interesting aspects of this phenomenon with great photos and illustrations.

Davidson, Michael W. et al. "Light and Color; *Molecular Expressions.* http:// micro.magnet. fsu.edu/primer/lightandcolor/index.html (accessed on January 18, 2008).

Hamilton, Gina L. *Light: Prisms, Rainbows, and Colors.* Chicago: Raintree, 2004.

51

Magnetism

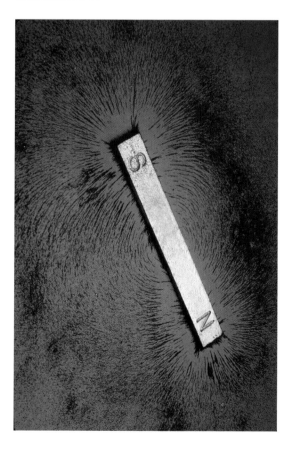

The pattern of the iron filings in this demonstration shows the magnetic field of the bar magnet. PHOTO RESEARCHERS INC.

One of the most mysterious phenomena we witness every day is magnetism, a fundamental force of nature caused by the motion of electrons in an atom. You put a note on a refrigerator door. You watch the speedometer in a car tell you how fast you are travelling. You listen to a tape of recorded music. All of these depend on magnetism, but how do these things work? How does the simple physics of the magnet make so much possible?

Magnetism is a matter of alignment What turns an ordinary piece of iron into a magnet? A large iron bar actually contains millions of "mini-magnets," small magnetized areas called domains. Each has a north pole and a south pole. If the poles of the iron's domains are aimed in all different directions, their magnetic forces act against one another and cancel each other out. When all of the domains are facing the same way, the bar becomes a magnet because it now has a single, strong magnetic field, a space in which its magnetic force can be observed.

How can we get all the domains facing the same way? This can be achieved by repeatedly rubbing the bar with one pole of another magnet in the same direction. Once the bar is magnetized, its magnetic field will exert enough force on the domains in nearby iron filings to temporarily magnetize them. Each filing has its own north and south poles, and those poles are attracted to or repelled by the magnet's poles. (Remember that unlike poles attract and like poles repel.)

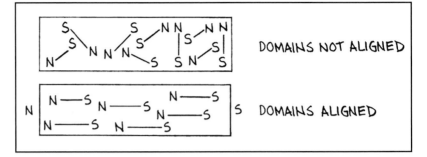

When a metal's domains face in all different directions, it has no overall magnetism. When they are lined up, as illustrated, they create a strong magnetic field. GALE GROUP.

Hans Christian Oersted studied the relationship between electricity and magnetism. PHOTO RESEARCHERS INC.

The position of the domains in such a magnet is not permanent, however. Striking or jarring the bar will literally knock its domains out of alignment, and the bar will lose its magnetism. Even as time passes and the magnet sits in a drawer, it will slowly lose its magnetism as the domains shift back to their original positions. One way to preserve a magnet is to keep it in a magnetic circuit, in which each domain is held in place by the direction of the next domain. Placing a steel plate across the poles of a horseshoe magnet will complete the circuit: all the domains in the circuit will point in the same direction and will tend to remain that way.

In the first experiment you will create a magnet and then test the effects on the magnet's strength of heat, cold, jarring, and rubbing with another magnet.

Electricity can also produce magnetism
Electrical current flowing through a wire produces a magnetic field. If the wire is wound into a coil, it will produce a stronger magnetic field, similar to that of a bar magnet: each end of the coil will become a magnetic pole. This effect was discovered by Danish physicist Hans Christian Oersted (1777–1851). He noticed that electric current disturbed the normal functioning of magnetic compasses.

WORDS TO KNOW

Alignment: Adjustment in a certain direction or orientation.

Alloy: A mixture of two or more metals with properties different from those metals of which it is made.

Circuit: The complete path of an electric current including the source of electric energy.

Control experiment: A setup that is identical to the experiment but is not affected by the variable that affects the experimental group.

Domain: Small regions in iron that possess their own magnetic charges.

Electron: A subatomic particle with a mass of about one atomic mass unit and a single electrical charge that orbits the nucleus of an atom.

Electromagnetism: A form of magnetic energy produced by the flow of an electric current through a metal core. Also, the study of electric and magnetic fields and their interaction with charges and currents.

Hypothesis: An idea in the form of a statement that can be tested by observation and/or experiment.

Insulated wire: Electrical wire coated with a non-conducting material such as plastic.

Magnetic circuit: A series of magnetic domains aligned in the same direction.

Magnetic field: The space around an electric current or a magnet in which a magnetic force can be observed.

Magnetism: A fundamental force in nature caused by the motion of electrons in an atom.

Terminal: A connection in an electric circuit; usually a connection on a source of electric energy such as a battery.

Variable: Something that can affect the results of an experiment.

Electromagnetism is a form of magnetic energy produced by the flow of an electric current through a metal core. It has many applications in our modern technology. Stereo speakers are one of the most common applications. Electrical signals pass through a coil, creating a varying magnetic field that pushes and pulls on another magnet attached to the speaker. This causes the paper speaker cone to move back and forth to produce sound. Some metals, including iron, can be made into electromagnets strong enough to lift tons of scrap steel. One advantage of electromagnets is that they can be turned on and off with the flip of a switch.

In the second experiment, you will create a small electromagnet using an electric current and you will test the effect on the magnet when the strength of the current is varied.

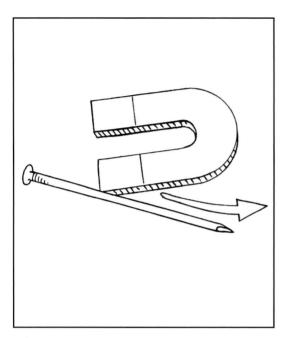

The "keeper" placed across the positive and negative poles of this horseshoe magnet create a magnetic circuit that holds the domains in place and stops the magnet from losing its strength.

GALE GROUP.

EXPERIMENT 1

Magnets: How do heat, cold, jarring, and rubbing affect the magnetism of a nail?

Purpose/Hypothesis In this experiment, you will first test the effect of rubbing a bar magnet on a steel or iron nail. The bar magnet should align the domains in the iron so that the nail becomes magnetized. You will then measure the effect of four actions upon the nail's magnetic strength—heating, cooling, rubbing with a magnet in the opposite direction, and striking with a hammer. Each of the four actions will be tested on a different magnetized nail. Before you begin, make an educated guess about the outcome of this experiment based on your knowledge of magnetism. This educated guess, or prediction, is your hypothesis. A hypothesis should explain these things:

- the topic of the experiment
- the variable you will change
- the variable you will measure
- what you expect to happen

A hypothesis should be brief, specific, and measurable. It must be something you can test through observation. Your experiment will prove or disprove whether your hypothesis is correct. Here is one possible hypothesis for this experiment: "Rubbing a magnetized nail with the opposite pole of the bar magnet that was used to magnetize it, striking or dropping it, and raising or lowering its temperature will decrease the strength of its magnetic field."

In this case, the variables you will change are the four actions you will take on identically magnetized nails, and the variable you will measure is the resulting strength of the nail's magnetic field. You expect that all four actions will reduce the nail's magnetic strength.

Level of Difficulty Easy/moderate.

Materials Needed

- bar magnet
- 5 steel or iron nails about 3 inches (7.5 centimeters) long (iron is preferable; steel is an alloy containing other metals that cannot be magnetized)
- hammer
- 1 cup of hot tap water
- 1 cup of cold tap water with ice added
- 10 staples (separated and unused)
- 10 steel paper clips
- 10 plastic-coated paper clips
- small wooden block
- safety glasses

Approximate Budget Less than $10 for the magnet. (Try to borrow the hammer and safety glasses, if you do not have them.)

Timetable About 30 minutes.

Step-by-Step Instructions

1. Rub one pole of the bar magnet lengthwise down one nail fifty times, always in the same direction.
2. Test the nail for magnetism by touching its point to a staple, then to a steel paper clip, then to a coated paper clip.
3. Observe and record on your data chart which objects the nail can lift. Carefully set the nail aside. Keep it several inches away from the other nails.
4. Repeat this procedure with three other nails, rubbing them the same number of times in the same direction with the same pole of the bar magnet. The magnetic strength of the nails should be almost the same. If one is significantly weaker, rub it with the magnet until the

What Are the Variables?

Variables are anything that might affect the results of an experiment. Here are the main variables in this experiment:

- type of metal in the nails
- the size of the nails
- the strength of the bar magnet used
- the number of times the nail is rubbed with the bar magnet
- the direction in which the nail is rubbed with the bar magnet
- the actions performed on the nails (striking, heating, etc.)

In other words, the variables in this experiment are anything that might affect the magnetic strength of the nails. If you change more than one variable for each nail, you will not be able to tell which variable had the most effect on the resulting magnetic strength of the nail.

A fifth nail will be magnetized and tested without any action performed on it. This control experiment lets us know that any changes we see in magnetism result from the actions and not from some unseen factor.

How to Experiment Safely

Safety glasses must be worn any time you are striking metal on metal. Do not strike the nail with great force, and be sure to rest the nail on the wooden block so it does not bend or snap when hit. Do not lift the hammer more than 6 inches (15 centimeters) from the block. (See illustration.)

	Trial #1			Action
	staples	paper clips	coated paper clips	
NAIL #1				hot
NAIL #2				cold
NAIL #3				rubbing
NAIL #4				jarring
NAIL #5				(control)

Step 4: Data chart for Experiment 1. GALE GROUP.

Step 7d: Rest the shaft of the nail flat on the block. GALE GROUP.

strength of its field is similar to the others. Your data chart should look like the illustration.

5. To establish your control experiment, test the remaining nail for magnetism. If this nail picks up any of the test objects, it has somehow been magnetized. Do not be surprised if the nail does have a very weak magnetic field. Just the movements of nails against one another in a box can align a small percentage of the domains in the metal. To prove that rubbing the first four nails with the bar magnet caused them to become magnegtized, however, you must see a significant difference between their magnetic strength and that of the control nail.

6. Now rub the control nail the same number of times in the same direction. Check to be sure it is magnetized, record the results, and carefully set it aside away from the other nails.

7. Perform one action on each nail. (Remember not to disturb the control nail.)

a. Place the first nail in hot water and leave it for ten minutes.

b. Place the second nail in the ice water and leave it for ten minutes.

c. Rub the third nail with the same pole of the magnet used earlier, but in the opposite direction, twenty-five times.

d. With everyone present wearing safety goggles, place the shaft of the fourth nail flat on the wooden block and strike it firmly three or four times. (Do not lift the head of the hammer any more than 6 inches [15 centimeters].)

8. Test the magnetic strength of each nail and note any changes on your chart.

9. Finally, check the control nail to make sure that nails do not lose their magnetic strength simply by sitting unused for several minutes. Record the strength of the control nail in the appropriate row on your chart.

Summary of Results Compare your data from the four tests. Determine which of the actions demagnetized the nails and which did not. Check your findings against the predictions you made in your hypothesis. Which actions did you accurately predict would demagnetize the nails? Which actions did not have the effect you expected? Summarize your results in writing.

Change the Variables By altering your variables, you can make this experiment the basis of a series of interesting and informative investigations into magnetism. For example, how fast does magnetic strength weaken? Can we preserve a magnet longer by refrigerating it? Are the effects

Troubleshooter's Guide

This experiment is fairly straightforward. You should encounter little difficulty if you use the listed materials. When you are doing experiments with magnetism, results can be difficult to measure precisely. To compare the strengths of magnets, test their lifting power several times and average the results to achieve a greater degree of accuracy.

Here are some problems that may arise during the experiment, some possible causes, and ways to remedy the problems.

Problem: All of the nails are strongly magnetized to start with.

Possible cause: They may have been exposed to a strong magnetic field prior to the experiment. Demagnetize them by striking each several times with the hammer. (It is not necessary to strike with great force. Remember to wear safety glasses and place the nails flat on a wooden block so they will not bend or snap.)

Problem: The nails will not magnetize.

Possible causes:

1. The nails are made of a metal or alloy that cannot be magnetized. Use iron or steel nails. (Iron is preferable.)

2. Your bar magnet is too weak. Check its strength and replace it if necessary.

3. You are changing the direction of the stroke as you rub the magnet on the nail, or you are accidentally switching poles as you rub the nail. Either mistake will sweep the nail's domains in different directions. Follow this procedure carefully.

What Are the Variables?

Variables are anything that might affect the results of an experiment. Here are the main variables in this experiment:

- the type of nail used
- the number of batteries attached to the circuit, which is directly proportional to the current
- the type and gauge of wire used
- the shape and weight of the test objects used

In other words, the variables in this experiment are everything that might affect the magnetic field strength of the electromagnet. If you change more than one variable, you will not be able to tell which variable had the most effect on the magnetic strength.

Steps 1 to 3: Set-up of nail and D-cell battery. GALE GROUP.

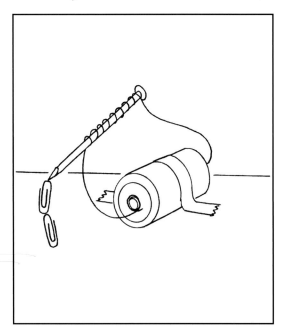

of demagnetization always reversible, or can domains be put permanently out of order?

EXPERIMENT 2

Electromagnets: Does the strength of an electromagnet increase with greater current?

Purpose/Hypothesis In this experiment, you will create an electromagnet and test the effect of varying levels of electric current on the strength of the magnetic field. You will increase the current by adding batteries to the circuit— the path of the electric current through a wire attached to the terminals of a source of electric energy. Before you begin, make an educated guess about the outcome of this experiment based on your knowledge of electromagnets. This educated guess, or prediction, is your hypothesis. A hypothesis should explain these things:

- the topic of the experiment
- the variable you will change
- the variable you will measure
- what you expect to happen

A hypothesis should be brief, specific, and measurable. It must be something you can test through observation. Your experiment will prove or disprove whether your hypothesis is correct. Here is one possible hypothesis for this experiment: "The strength of an electromagnet's magnetic field will increase when the current applied to the electromagnet is increased."

In this case, the variable you will change is the electrical current, and the variable you will measure is the resulting strength of the magnetic field of the electromagnet. You expect that a higher current will result in a higher magnetic field strength.

Level of Difficulty Easy/moderate.

Materials Needed

- 2 feet (0.6 meter) of insulated, 16 to 18 gauge solid copper wire
- 3 fresh D-cell batteries
- iron or steel nail (iron is preferable)
- electrical tape
- 10 staples (separated and unused)
- 10 steel paper clips
- 10 plastic-coated paper clips
- magnetic compass
- wire strippers

Approximate Budget Less than $15 for wire, batteries, and electrical tape. (Try to borrow the wire strippers and compass, if necessary.)

Timetable 15 to 20 minutes.

Step-by-Step Instructions

1. Secure one of the D-cell batteries to a flat surface using a strip of electrical tape.
2. Coil the insulated copper wire ten or more times around the nail, starting at one end of the nail and working toward the other. Leave about 2 inches (5 centimeters) of straight wire at each end.

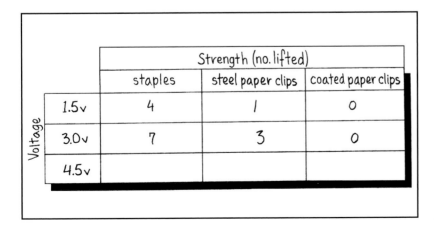

Voltage	Strength (no. lifted)		
	staples	steel paper clips	coated paper clips
1.5v	4	1	0
3.0v	7	3	0
4.5v			

Step 6: Sample data chart for Experiment 2. GALE GROUP.

Troubleshooter's Guide

When doing experiments with magnetism, results can be difficult to measure precisely. To compare the strengths of magnets, test their lifting power several times and average the results to achieve a greater degree of accuracy.

Here is a problem that may arise during the experiment, some possible causes, and ways to remedy the problems.

Problem: The nail does not show any magnetism.

Possible causes:

1. A connection is loose. Check your connections, especially where the copper wire meets the battery terminals. Secure them with electrical tape if necessary.

2. The nail is made of a metal or alloy that does not magnetize. Use an iron nail.

3. You are using uninsulated wire, causing the current to travel across the coil and disrupt the magnetic field. Use insulated wire.

4. Your batteries are dead. Check them with a flashlight and replace them if necessary.

3. Strip the insulation off both ends of the wire. Hold one end to the positive terminal on the battery, and the other end to the negative terminal.

4. Check the nail for a magnetic field by holding it over the compass. Does the compass needle always point along the same direction on the nail? Which end of the coil forms the north pole of the magnetic field, the one leading to the positive terminal or the one leading to the negative terminal?

5. Use the magnet to lift as many staples as possible. Repeat with the steel paper clips and with the coated paper clips.

6. Record on your data chart the number lifted each time. Your chart should look like the illustration.

7. Increase the voltage applied to the electromagnet by adding another D-cell battery to the circuit. This will double the electrical current. Secure the batteries firmly together with electrical tape, making sure the positive terminal of one is touching the negative terminal of the other.

8. Repeat the test of the magnet's lifting power and record your observations on the chart.

9. Finally, repeat the tests once more with three batteries. This will triple the current. Do not use more than three D-cell batteries! Do not use any other type of battery without first asking your teacher.

Summary of Results Your data from Steps 6, 8, and 9 should be recorded on a chart. This chart should contain the information that will show whether your hypothesis is correct. Did changes in current strength affect the magnetic strength? You can increase the clarity of your results by converting the data into graph form. Summarize your results in writing.

Change the Variables To further explore the topic of electromagnetism, you can vary this experiment in the following ways:

- Use a different type of nail, such as copper or aluminum, or a heavier iron or steel nail
- Try a heavier gauge copper wire
- Vary the shape and weight of the items you try to pick up

One variation you must avoid is adding more than three batteries to the circuit or using a kind of battery other than D-cell. This can create enough electric current to be dangerous.

Design Your Own Experiment

How to Select a Topic Relating to this Concept If you look carefully around your house, you will discover that magnets play a hidden role in much of the technology we use today. You can investigate other uses of magnets and develop interesting ideas for experiments and demonstrations. Remember that magnetic particles make tape recordings and computer diskettes function. Magnets are at work in every electric motor you see. Magnetism also affects natural phenomena, such as the aurora borealis (northern lights) and the migratory patterns of birds.

The electromagnet is especially useful in the scrap yard because it can be easily switched on and off. PHOTO RESEARCHERS INC.

Check the Further Readings section and talk with your science teacher of school or community media specialist to start gathering information on magnetism questions that interest you. Remember that any experiment involving electricity should use no more than three 1.5-volt batteries, and any experiment proposal should be approved by your teacher.

Steps in the Scientific Method To do an original experiment, you need to plan carefully and think things through. Otherwise, you might not be sure what question you are answering, what you are or should be measuring, or what your findings prove or disprove.

Here are the steps in designing an experiment:

- State the purpose of—and the underlying question behind—the experiment you propose to do.

- Recognize the variables involved, and select one that will help you answer the question at hand.

- State a testable hypothesis, an educated guess about the answer to your question.

- Decide how to change the variable you selected.

- Decide how to measure your results.

Recording Data and Summarizing the Results In the experiments included here, and in any experiments you develop, try to display your data in accurate and interesting ways. When presenting your results to those who have not seen the experiment performed, showing photographs of the various steps can make the process more interesting and clear.

Related Projects Simple variations on the two experiments in this section can prove valuable and informative. The magnetic field created by an electromagnet has poles just like a permanent magnet. How could you discover which end of the coil is north and which is south? How does reversing the positive and negative contacts on the coil affect the field? What happens if you put an electromagnet coil around an already magnetized nail? Does it increase the strength of the field?

For More Information

The Exploratorium. "Snacks about Magnetism." *The Exploratorium Science Snacks.* http://www.explo ratorium.edu/snacks/iconmagnetism.html (accessed on February 19, 2008). A number of short experiments on magnetism.

Gillett, Kate, ed. *The Knowledge Factory.* Brookfield, CT: Copper Beech Books, 1996. Provides some fun and enlightening observations on questions relevant to this topic, along with good ideas for projects and demonstrations.

The Interactive Plasma Physics Education Experience! *Electricity and Magnetism.* http://ippex.pppl.gov/interactive/electricity/ (accessed on February 19, 2008). Information and animations on magnetism, and how it relates to electricity.

Macaulay, David and Neil Ardley. *The New Way Things Work.* Boston: Houghton Mifflin, 1998. Detailed description of how machines work, including those that use electricity and magnetism.

Ray, C. Claibourne. *The New York Times Book of Science Questions and Answers.* New York: Doubleday, 1997. Addresses both everyday observations and advanced scientific concepts on a wide variety of subjects.

University of Maryland, Department of Electrical and Computer Engineering. *Gallery of Electromagnetic Personalities.* http://www.ece. umd.edu/~taylor/ frame1.htm (accessed on February 19, 2008). Brief biographies of the people who make contributions to magnetism and electromagnetism.

Materials Science

We live in a world filled with materials. There are materials that people have created, such as plastics, and others that come from nature, like wood. Our clothes, furniture, dishes, music players, sports equipment, and homes are all made of materials. Materials are a part of medicine in the threads for stitches and artificial hearts. Materials are key to space exploration in the astronaut's spacesuits and the metals used in the spacecraft. The materials that make up packaging keep our food fresh and safe from harmful microorganisms. Materials science is the study of all these materials to better understand and use them.

By understanding the properties, materials scientists can find ways to improve existing materials and develop new ones.

Following nature's lead The story of Velcro began when an electrical engineer, George de Mestral, noticed how burrs were sticking to his dog's fur. An up-close look at the burr's under a microscope showed him that the burr's had natural hooks that were sticking to the fur. That led him to develop Velcro, a material that fastens with hooks on one side and loops on the other.

The development of Velcro is an example of biomimetics. The science of developing materials inspired by nature is called biomimetics. Many organisms create materials with such amazing properties that scientists have long tried to mimic them for manmade materials. For example, scientists have long studied the silk a spider produces. Spider silk is so light and strong that if a thread of spider silk was the same weight as a thread of steel, the silk would be stronger. Spider silk can also stretch a long way without breaking.

A material that could be manufactured having the same properties as spider silk would be useful for humans.

All types of materials There are several ways to categorize materials, and some materials can fall under more than one category. Different types of materials are:

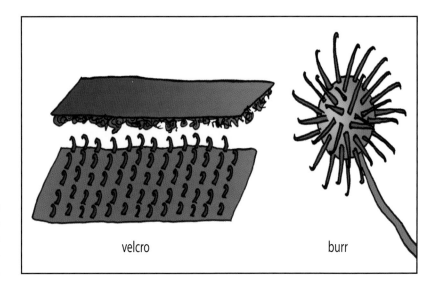

velcro

burr

Electrical engineer, George de Mestral, noticed that burrs have natural hooks, leading to the development of Velcro. ILLUSTRATION BY TEMAH NELSON.

- Metals: These materials include metals or mixtures of metals.

- Polymers: Polymers are long chains of repeating smaller units. Examples of polymers include plastic bottles, nylon, and polyester.

- Textiles: Any type of cloth, yarn, or fabric is a textile.

- Ceramics: Glass, cement, and pottery all fall under ceramics, which is any material that is not metal and not organic (from living organisms).

- Semiconductors: Material that have electrical properties in-between a conductor and insulator.

- New materials: Developments in science and technology are leading to new materials by mixing two or more materials together (composites) or by manipulating particles in current materials.

Material properties With so many materials, there are a lot of material properties. Some properties can change with heat, cold, pressure, or other conditions. When developing and finding the best-suited materials, a few common properties that scientists look at include:

Spider silk is so light and strong that if a thread of spider silk was the same weight as a thread of steel, the silk would be stronger. (C) LAYNE KENNEDY/ CORBIS.

- Strength: There are different types of measuring strengths for materials. Tensile strength is one commonly used measure of strength. Tensile strength measures the point at which a material will break when it is pulled. For materials that are pulled or stretched frequently, such as plastic bags, having a high tensile strength is an important feature. Compressional strength is another category, referring to the strength of a material when weight is pushing down or compressing the material. Materials where compressional strength is important include steel and concrete.

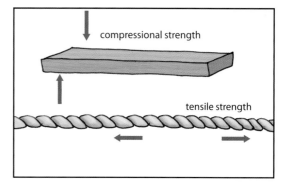

There are different types of measuring strengths for materials: tensile strength and compressional strength. ILLUSTRATION BY TEMAH NELSON.

- Toughness: The toughness of a material is the amount of energy needed to break a material. A plastic spoon that easily snaps into two pieces would have far less toughness than a strip of wood that you can't break.
- Heat: Thermal properties relate to heat and include how well a material can hold, insulate, or conduct heat. Some materials, such as winter fabrics for the outdoors, are selected for their ability to insulate, not allowing heat to pass—either out or into the body. Flammability is a measure of how quickly a materials lights on fire and is a common test for many household materials.
- Electrical: How well a material conducts electricity is a measure of its conductivity. Materials chosen for their ability to conduct electricity (electrons) include metals such as copper and silver. Other materials, such as rubbers and plastics, are selected because they do not conduct electricity.
- Chemical: A material's chemical properties are a measure of how the material will chemically change or react with other substances. When iron rusts, for example, that is a chemical change as the iron reacts with oxygen.
- Biodegradable: Materials made of natural biological materials that are broken down by natural processes are called biodegradable. Materials made from primarily from plants—such as wool, corn, wood, and cotton—are examples of materials that could be biodegradable.

Materials science is an interdisciplinary field. Professionals who work to develop materials could specialize in chemistry, engineering, or

WORDS TO KNOW

Biodegradable: Capable of being decomposed by biological agents.

Biomimetics: The development of materials that are found in nature.

Conductivity: The ability of a material to carry an electrical current.

Control experiment: A setup that is identical to the experiment, but is not affected by the variable that acts on the experimental group.

Electricity: A form of energy caused by the presence of electrical charges in matter.

Flammability: The ability of a material to ignite and burn.

Hypothesis: An idea in the form of a statement that can be tested by observation and/or experiment.

Insulator: A material through which little or no heat energy will pass.

Polymer: Chemical compound formed of simple molecules (known as monomers) linked with themselves many times over.

Tensile strength: The force needed to stretch a material until it breaks.

Variable: Something that can affect the results of an experiment.

physics. In the experiments below, you will investigate two types of materials. As you conduct the experiments, consider what questions you have about materials and what you would like to explore.

EXPERIMENT 1

Testing Tape: Finding the properties that allow tape to support weight.

Purpose/Hypothesis How would you develop a tape that supports a lot of weight? There are a variety of properties that make tape support weight. One property is the adhesive on the tape. Some tapes have an adhesive that bonds tightly to an object while others are developed with a relatively weak adhesive.

Another property of material strength is how much the tape can withstand tearing when it is pulled. This is called tensile strength. The higher the material's tensile strength, the more pressure it can take before breaking.

In this experiment, you will measure how a variety of tapes support weight to determine the properties of the tapes. You will first examine how each tape tears. You can then add an increasing amount of weight supported by the tape. Water will be the weight: One cup of water weighs approximately 8 ounces (0.24 milliliters). By measuring when the tape can no longer hold the weight, you can draw conclusions about the properties of the strongest tape.

To begin this experiment make an educated guess, or prediction, of what you think will occur based on your knowledge of material science and tapes. This educated guess, or prediction, is your hypothesis. A hypothesis should explain these things:

- the topic of the experiment
- the variable you will change
- the variable you will measure
- what you expect to happen

A hypothesis should be brief, specific, and measurable. It must be something you can test through further investigation. Your experiment will prove or disprove whether your hypothesis is correct. Here is one possible hypothesis for this experiment: "The more difficult a tape is to tear, the more weight it will support."

In this experiment the variable you will change will be the type of tape, and the variable you will measure will be the amount of weight the tape can hold before it breaks.

Level of Difficulty Easy/moderate.

Materials Needed

- 5 small paper bags, lunch bags work well
- funnel
- scissors
- 2-liter soda bottle
- measuring cup
- water
- ruler
- 4 to 5 different types of tapes, including Duct, packing, and masking (clear

What Are the Variables?

Variables are anything that might affect the results of an experiment. Here are the main variables in this experiment:

- the type of bag
- the bottle
- the type of tape
- the amount of tape used

In other words, variables in this experiment are everything that might affect the amount of weight the tape can hold. If you change more than one variable, you will not be able to tell which variable impacted the tape's strength.

Materials needed for Experiment 1. ILLUSTRATION BY TEMAH NELSON.

How to Experiment Safely

If you use the scissors to cut the bottle or bag, be careful. Check with an adult that you can stick tape to the wall. This experiment can be messy. If you have an outside area with a flat wall you may want to set up the experiment outside.

household tape and painter's tape are other types)
- large container (to catch falling water)

Approximate Budget $10.

Timetable 30 minutes

Step-by-Step Instructions

1. For each tape, tear off a piece about 6 inches (15 centimeters) using your hands. Note how difficult each tape is to rip crosswise. If you have to use scissors to tear the tape, write that down in a chart.
2. For each tape, tear the piece lengthwise and note how difficult each tape is to rip.
3. Tear a new piece of the first tape one inch less than the width of the bag and stick it on the bag with half the width of the tape on the bag.
4. Stick the bag on the wall and set the empty bottle in the bag. The bottle should be slightly higher than the bag. You may need to cut the top of the bottle or the bag with the scissors.
5. Set the large container underneath the bag/bottle and place the funnel in the bottle.
6. Carefully add ¼ cup (about 2 ounces) of water to the bottle, being careful not to drip any water on the bag. Continue adding water in ¼ cup increments, remembering to note how much water you are adding. When the tape can no longer support the bottle, write down the amount of weight the tape held.
7. Repeat Steps 3–6 with each of the tapes, using a new, dry bag in each set-up. Note your results.

Step 6: Carefully add ¼ cup (about 2 ounces) of water to the bottle. When the tape can no longer support the bottle, write down the amount of weight the tape held. ILLUSTRATION BY TEMAH NELSON.

Summary of Results Look at your chart. You may want to graph the results with the amount of water on the y-axis and the tape on the x-axis.

Did the tapes break at different weights? How did the ease or difficulty of tearing the tape relate to the tapes ability to hold weight? Consider other properties of the material that helped it withstand weight. If you were developing a tape that was stronger than the strongest tape you tested, what properties would you use? Write a summary of your results.

Change the Variables You can vary this experiment in several ways, depending on the goal of the material you want. If you want to continue testing strength, you can test the tape strength from another direction. You can also change the temperature, test the strength at both colder and warmer temperatures. If you wanted to focus on one tape, you could keep the weight the same and examine how the dimensions of the tape play a role in its strength.

EXPERIMENT 2

Developing Renewables: Can a renewable packing material have the same qualities as a non-renewable material?

> ## Troubleshooter's Guide
>
> Below are some problems that may arise during this experiment, some possible causes, and some ways to remedy the problem.
>
> **Problem:** The bag broke before barely any weigh was added.
>
> **Possible cause:** You may have dribbled some of the water on the bottom of the paper bag, which could have caused it to tear. Using a new, dry bag, repeat the test.
>
> **Problem:** The tape kept peeling off the wall.
>
> **Possible cause:** The surface may have a coating that is difficult to adhere to. Try to find a smooth, non waxy flat surface, and repeat the experiment.
>
> **Problem:** The bottle was filled with water and the tape did not break.
>
> **Possible cause:** That is a strong tape. If another bottle of any sort fits in the bag, insert it into the bottle and continue adding weight (water). You can also try using a larger paper bag that holds two bottles.

Purpose/Hypothesis Developing and testing renewable material is a major area of material science. In general, renewable materials cause less harm to the environment than the counterpart materials. There are many issues to consider when developing a renewable material. For a renewable material to replace a non-renewable, it needs to show similar qualities as what it is meant to replace. Cost and manufacturing are two other issues involved in material development.

In this experiment, you will work to develop a renewable packing material that can replace a non-renewable material. Packing peanuts are commonly made out of a form of polymer, such as Styrofoam, which can take hundreds of years to degrade. Properties that make Styrofoam a popular packing material include its lightness (it does not add weight to a

What Are the Variables?

Variables are anything that might affect the results of an experiment. Here are the main variables in this experiment:

- the type of manufactured peanut
- the item being tested
- the amount of material tested
- the height the egg is dropped

In other words, the variables in this experiment are anything that might affect the protective properties of the corn-based material. If you change more than one variable, you will not be able to tell which variable had the most effect on material's qualities.

package) and its protective qualities. Styrofoam packing peanuts cushion objects to protect them from breaking.

In this experiment you will focus on only matching the material's qualities. You will produce and test renewable packing peanuts, made from corn. Corn-based packing peanuts dissolve in water. The goal is to produce a renewable material that has comparable qualities to the non-renewable packing peanut. You will vary the amount of water in your material before you test its protective qualities. By dropping a hard-boiled egg on both the renewable and non-renewable materials you can determine how they compare.

Before you begin, make an educated guess about the outcome of the experiment based on your knowledge of renewables and material science. This educated guess, or prediction, is your hypothesis. A hypothesis should explain these things:

- the topic of the experiment
- the variable you will change
- the variable you will measure
- what you expect to happen

A hypothesis should be brief, specific, and measurable. It must be something you can test through observation. Your experiment will prove or disprove your hypothesis. Here is one possible hypothesis for this experiment: "Materials made from corn will have the same protective qualities as the Styrofoam packing peanuts."

In this case, the variable you will change will be the main component of the material, and the variable you will measure will be the protective quality of the material.

Level of Difficulty Moderate.

Materials Needed

- Styrofoam packing peanuts, approximately 1 cup
- yardstick
- measuring cup

- tablespoon
- hard boiled eggs, at least 4 to possibly 12
- 3 bowls, all the same size and shape
- microwave
- 2 microwave-safe mixing bowls
- spoon
- water
- cornstarch

How to Experiment Safely

When you use the microwave, make sure the bowl is microwave-safe. Cornstarch can clog a garbage disposal so ask an adult how to dispose of it.

Approximate Budget $5; assuming you can find Styrofoam packing peanuts in the household or school.

Timetable 1 hour.

Step-by-Step Instructions 1.) Making the corn-based packing material:

1. Pour 1 cup of cornstarch into the microwave-safe bowl. Add 4 tablespoons of warm water and stir.
2. Heat the bowl in the microwave for about 10 seconds.
3. Continue stirring the mixture. It should be the consistency of a thick paste. You may want to put it back in the microwave for another two to five seconds at a time. This is Material 1.
4. Repeat Steps 1–3, using a new bowl and adding 5 tablespoons of water to the cornstarch. This is Material 2.
5. Shape each of the corn paste into shapes that match the shape and size of the Styrofoam materials, keeping the two materials separate.

2.) Testing the materials:

1. Set a yardstick against the wall; you may need to tape it or have a helper hold it.
2. Pour 1 cup of the Styrofoam peanuts into bowl 1. The peanuts should cover the bottom of the bowl and be at least 1-inch (2.5 centimeters) higher than bowl. The exact amount you use does not matter, as long as all the bowls have the same amount.

Step 1:5 Shape each of the corn paste into shapes that match the shape and size of the Styrofoam materials, keeping the two materials separate. ILLUSTRATION BY TEMAH NELSON.

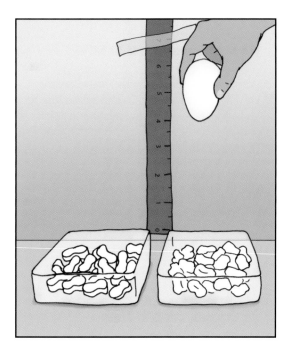

Step 2:5 Test how high you can drop the egg into the Styrofoam peanut bowl before the shell cracks. ILLUSTRATION BY TEMAH NELSON.

3. Pour 1 cup (or the matching amount) of the corn peanuts from Material 1 into the second clean bowl. Pour 1 cup (or the matching amount) of the corn peanuts from Material 2 into the third clean bowl.

4. Test how high you can drop the egg from in the Styrofoam peanut bowl before the shell cracks. Start at 6 inches and continue dropping the egg at 1-inch increments until you see or hear a crack. Note the height.

5. Drop a new hardboiled egg in the Material 1 bowl, starting at the same height you noted for the Styrofoam material. If the egg cracks, lower a new egg 1-inch and drop it again. Continue lowering the egg in 1-inch increments until the egg does not crack, using a new egg every time. If the egg does not crack, continue raising the egg in 1-inch increments until it cracks. Note the height.

6. Repeat this same process for Material 2, using new eggs.

7. When you are done with the experiment, slowly pour water over the corn packing material and watch it dissolve.

Summary of Results How do the three materials compare to each other in terms of protecting the egg from cracking? If one material provided a far better cushion look at the materials and consider why. When producing the two corn-based packing materials, which of the materials was easier to make and shape? Which provided more of a cushion? Write a paragraph summarizing the challenges and testing of the renewable packing materials. You can hypothesize how you would improve upon the renewable material and other tests you would conduct.

Change the Variables You can vary this experiment. Try using different types of packing materials to test the renewable against. How does the corn-based material compare to bubble materials, for example? You can also add different ingredients to the corn-based material, such as a few drops of oil.

Design Your Own Experiment

How to Select a Topic Relating to this Concept
Materials are all around you. Consider if there is one item that you have seen change materials over time. Look around you at all the different objects in your house and school and see what properties interest you about these materials.

Check the Further Readings section and talk with your science or engineering teacher to learn more about the properties of different materials. As you consider possible experiments, make sure to discuss them with your science teacher or another adult before trying them.

Steps in the Scientific Method To do an original experiment, you need to plan carefully and think things through. Otherwise, you might not be sure what question you are answering, what you are or should be measuring, or what your findings prove or disprove.

Here are the steps in designing an experiment:

- State the purpose of—and the underlying question behind—the experiment you propose to do.
- Recognize the variables involved and select one that will help you answer the question at hand.
- State your hypothesis, an educated guess about the answer to your question.
- Decide how to change the variable you selected.
- Decide how to measure your results.

Recording Data and Summarizing the Results In any experiment you conduct, you should look for ways to clearly convey your data. You can do this by including charts and graphs for the experiments. They should be clearly labeled and easy to read. You may also want to include photographs and drawings of your experimental setup and results, which will help others visualize the steps in the experiment. You might decide to

Troubleshooter's Guide

Experiments do not always work out as planned. Even so, figuring out what went wrong can definitely be a learning experience. Here are some problems that may arise during this experiment, some possible causes, and ways to remedy the problems.

Problem: The corn paste keeps crumbling when it is shaped into a peanut.

Possible cause: You may not have added enough water or mixed the water in thoroughly. Try again, microwaving before you stir and using your fingers to make sure the mixture is smooth.

Problem: There was no noise but the eggs had a crack in them many times.

Possible cause: The eggs might have started with small cracks. Before you drop the eggs, inspect each one thoroughly to make sure it is uncracked, and repeat the tests.

conduct an experiment that lasts several months. In this case, include pictures or drawings of the results taken at regular intervals.

If you are preparing an exhibit, you may want to display your results, such as any experimental setup you designed. If you have completed a nonexperimental project, explain clearly what your research question was and illustrate your findings.

Related Projects There are numerous possible experiments and projects you can undertake related to materials science. For example, you can investigate how the materials for one sports item, such as skis or a tennis racquet, have changed over time. What properties set a professional, expensive tennis racquet apart from an everyday, less-expensive racquet? How have materials affected the sport?

You can look at one property of clothing, such as waterproofing, weight, or insulation. Or you can experiment with recently developed fabrics, such as polyester or materials that are lightweight and warm. Does the warmth of a fabric relate to its weight? You could also test materials made from nature against similar, manmade materials.

For More Information

BBC. *The Science of Sport.* http://www.bbc.co.uk/worldservice/sci_tech/ features/science_of_sport (accessed April 24, 2008). Information on the role of science and materials in sports.

Gardner, Robert. *Science Projects about Chemistry.* Hillside, NJ: Enslow Publishers, 1994. Describes many science projects, including separating and identifying substances and detecting unknown solids.

Mueller, Tom. "Biomimetics: Design by Nature." *National Geographic.com.* April 2008. Available online at http://ngm.nationalgeographic.com/2008/ 04/biomimetics/tom-mueller-text (accessed April 24, 2008).

Peacock, Graham. *Materials.* New York: Thomson Learning, 1994. Basic activities on a range of materials.

Polymer Science Learning Center, University of Southern Mississippi. *The MacroGalleria.* http://pslc.ws/macrogcss/maindir.html (accessed on April 14, 2008). Detailed site on all aspects of polymers, from studying them to everyday applications.

Memory

When you recall a particularly memorable event, think about what you remember. For example, what if you went to a great waterpark several years ago. You likely will remember your family or friends who you went with. You probably recall the rides, something you ate, and the thrill of the ride. But do you remember what you wore that day? What about where you parked or what you drank?

Our brain processes so much information throughout a day—or event—that it picks and chooses what to file. The ability to store, retain, and recall information is memory. If someone had asked you on the way home from the hypothetical waterpark what you drank that day, it likely would have still been filed in your memory. And if every day you thought about what you drank at the waterpark, you would probably be able to recall it two years later. Where and how memories are stored tells a lot about how humans learn. Understanding memory can also lead researchers to help people retain their memories.

Types of memory Memory is generally organized into three categories, depending upon the length of time it stays in the brain.

- Sensory memory: Most of what we senses that gives us a picture of the scene around us is known as sensory memory. Sensory memory is fleeting, the brain can hold onto the information for seconds before it becomes lost. When you are taking a walk and spot a dog run by or a crack in the sidewalk, those scenes are sensory memory.
- Short-term memory: When sensory memory moves into a longer form of storage it becomes short-term memory. This is also known as working memory. When you remember a shopping list, this is short term memory. Working memory allows us to link the past to the present.
- Long-term memory: Once a memory is here, it is stored for days or decades. There are different types of long-term memory. One

short term

to do list
go shopping
walk
call Jane
buy bread

sensory

long term

There are three types of memory: sensory, short term, and long term. ILLUSTRATION BY TEMAH NELSON.

type is how we remember to tie our shoes or ride a bike. This type of long-term memory records skills and facts that we have learned. The other type of long-term memory is the memory related to an episode or experience (this is called episodic memory). This is how we remember the sights, sounds, and emotions of an event years after it happened.

How the filing system works The brain is made up of several different parts, which each have distinct functions. One area of the brain that plays an important role in memory is the hippocampus. The hippocampus, located deep inside the brain, is where new memories are formed. It is also important in directing the storage of memories to different parts of the brain.

The hippocampus works with another part of the brain, the cerebral cortex. The cerebral cortex is the outer layer of the brain that is often linked to higher learning and processing information. It is also called the grey matter. Researchers theorize that memories are stored in different parts of the cerebral cortex.

Memory problems Memory can falter or be harmed in several ways. Forgetting where you put your books or a math formula is common. But when memory is truly lost, it is called amnesia. Because the brain stores and processes memory, if the brain is harmed it can cause amnesia. In some cases, such as a stroke or car accident, memories will return. In other cases, such as Alzheimer's disease, memories may be permanently lost. Alzheimer's is a disease that affects the hippocampus and as a result, affects the formation and storage of memories.

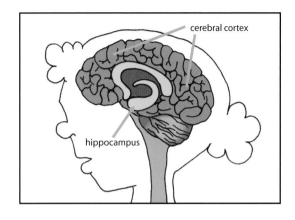

The hippocampus works with another part of the brain, the cerebral cortex. ILLUSTRATION BY TEMAH NELSON.

The major cause of amnesia in people who are not elderly is from some form of brain damage. Damage to different parts of the brain can lead to different types of amnesia. In one form of amnesia, a person cannot form new memories but the person can recall childhood memories. In another form of amnesia, a person will not be able to recall memories right before the injury but all other memories remain intact.

When people remember an event that never happened or change the way it actually occurred it is called a false memory. False memories are not

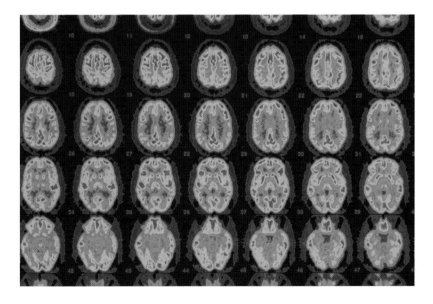

PET scans comparing Alzheimer's sufferer's brain with healthy brain. The red color shows maximum, healthy blood flow, the yellow-green indicates less blood flow, while dark green and purple-blue areas indicate no flow. JONATHAN SELIG/COLLECTION/ GETTY IMAGES.

WORDS TO KNOW

Acronym: A word or phrase formed from the first letter of other words.

Amnesia: Partial or total memory loss.

Cerebral cortex: The outer layer of the brain.

Control experiment: A setup that is identical to the experiment but is not affected by the variable that will be changed during the experiment.

False memory: A memory of an event that never happened or an altered memory from what happened.

Hippocampus: A part of the brain associated with learning and memory.

Hypothesis: An idea in the form of a statement that can be tested by observation and/or experiment.

Long-term memory: The last category of memory in which memories are stored away and can last for years.

Memory: The process of retaining and recalling past events and experiences.

Mnemonics: Techniques to improve memory.

Sensory memory: Memory that the brain retains for a few seconds.

Short-term memory: Also known as working memory, this memory was transferred here from sensory memory.

Variable: Something that can affect the results of an experiment.

---

due to brain damage. They can occur when memories or suggestions are "planted" to a person, or when the brain is trying to make sense of a complex scene. In false memories people can truly believe the event occurred as they remember it.

Keeping memory sharp Using what you have learned and stored in your memory is a way to keep it available. When people don't use skills or knowledge for long periods of time, it can be hard for the brain to recollect it.

There are also many ways to make memories "stick." Mnemonics (pronounced "ne-mon-ics") are techniques or devices that help people retain memories. Different people have different mnemonic techniques that work for them. An examples of a visual mnemonic technique links an image to the item to be remembered.

Creating a memorable acronym or phrase is another mnemonic device. An acronym is a word or phrase formed from the first letter of another word or name. "Roy G. Biv" is a well used acronym for the order of the colors in white light: red, orange, yellow, green, blue, indigo, and violet. "My Dear Aunt Sally" uses the first letter of each word to call to mind the math rule: multiply and divide before you add and subtract. Setting numbers or facts to song is another common memory technique.

EXPERIMENT 1

Memory Mnemonics: What techniques help in memory retention?

Purpose/Hypothesis One of the most famous mathematical concepts is pi (pronounced "pie"). Pi (π) equals the distance around a circle (its circumference) divided by the distance across the circle (its diameter). Pi is a constant, meaning it is always the same number no matter what the size of the circle. And pi is a number that never ends. In shorthand, pi is commonly memorized as 3.14. Some people might know it is 3.14159. But the decimal of pi goes on forever, and there is no pattern to the numbers. Computers have calculated pi to over a trillion decimal places! And people have contests memorizing as many as they can.

In this experiment, you can use pi to measure how different mnemonic devices help people remember up to 12 digits of pi. You can use two different mnemonics: Music, images, and repeating in patterns are three options. Because people have different abilities to memorize, it will help to find at least three people in each group so that you can find an average.

The first group will set the numbers of pi to a song. The second group will relate patterns of numbers to images. The third group will be the control. This group will not use a mnemonic. All the groups will have the same amount of time to look at and memorize the number. The next day, you will measure how many numbers of pi people in each group remembered. You will need to ask each person separately so one person does not influence another. (If finding a lot of people is difficult you can select one mnemonic devices and a control.)

Before you begin, make an educated guess about the outcome of this experiment based on your knowledge of memory and mnemonics. This educated guess, or prediction, is your hypothesis. A hypothesis should explain these things:

What Are the Variables?

Variables are anything that might affect the results of an experiment. Here are the main variables in this experiment:

- the participants
- events or noise occurring in the background
- the amount of time given to participants
- the number to memorize

In other words, the variables in this experiment are everything that might affect the ability of the participants to memorize pi. If you change more than one variable, you will not be able to tell which variable had the most effect on memory.

Pi equals the distance around a circle (its circumference) divided by the distance across the circle (its diameter).
ILLUSTRATION BY TEMAH NELSON.

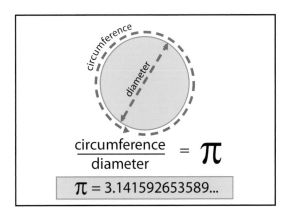

$$\frac{\text{circumference}}{\text{diameter}} = \pi$$

$$\pi = 3.141592653589\ldots$$

How to Experiment Safely

There are no safety hazards in this experiment.

- the topic of the experiment
- the variable you will change
- the variable you will measure
- what you expect to happen

A hypothesis should be brief, specific, and measurable. It must be something you can test through observation. Your experiment will prove or disprove whether your hypothesis is correct. Here is one possible hypothesis for this experiment: "The people who use music will recall the most digits of pi, compared to the other mnemonic device and the control."

In this case, the variable you will change is the mnemonic device, and the variable you will measure is the amount of numbers the participants can recall. The participants who do not use a mnemonic device will serve as the control. If the people who set the numbers to song recall more digits on average than all other groups, you will know your hypothesis is correct.

Level of Difficulty Moderate/difficult (because of the time and participants involved).

Materials Needed

- the number pi (below)
- paper and pencil
- watch or timer
- participants, at least three in each group for a minimum of nine, with the more tested the stronger the experiment (if finding participants is difficult, you can select one mnemonic device to test. Participants will need to be available 20 minutes on Day 1 and about five minutes on Day 2)

Approximate Budget $0.

Timetable Approximately two hours over two days. The time will increase if participants in each group are tested separately or if each group is gathered on separate days. Each participant (group of participants) should have 20 minutes to remember the digits in pi on Day 1 and you

Step 1: Think of a song you and the participants will know and set the 12 decimal places of pi to its tune. ILLUSTRATION BY TEMAH NELSON.

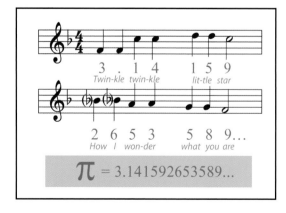

will need several minutes with each participant on Day 2. It does not matter what day each group is gathered, as long as the following day you test their recall.

Step-by-Step Instructions

1. Think of a song you and the participants will know and set the 12 decimal places of pi to its tune. (See illustration.) The song can be as simple as "Happy Birthday to You" or a song that has a set rhythm.

2. Gather the first group of participants. Tell them you are conducting a memory experiment and have them all sing the song with the "pi" lyrics. Give them 20 minutes to sing the song.

3. Consider the second mnemonic device and come up with images for groups of numbers. The images can tell a story. For example, one set of images could be about a day at school where you are getting back a big math test. You look at the test and happily see you got 14 out of 15 correct (1415); the date on the calendar is September 26 (926); on a desk is a set of colored pencils, five of them are red, three are green, and five are orange (535); the window in the classroom has 8 out of the 9 windows dirty (89). Whatever the story or images are, sketch or print images that relate to each group of numbers.

4. Gather the second group of participants. After telling them you are conducting a memory experiment have them look at and say the numbers related to each image. Allow them to continue looking at the images and saying the numbers for 20 minutes.

5. For the control group, tell participants you are conducting a memory experiment and show them the numbers of pi, up to 12 decimal places. Ask them to simply repeat the number and try to memorize it over the next 20 minutes.

6. The day after working with Group 1, ask each participant individually in Group 1

Step 3: Come up with images for groups of numbers. For example, one set of images could be about a day at school where you are getting back a big math test. ILLUSTRATION BY TEMAH NELSON.

Step 6: Make a note of how many numbers each person remembered. ILLUSTRATION BY TEMAH NELSON.

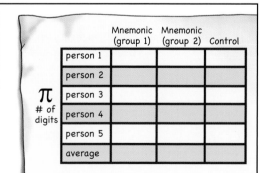

π # of digits	Mnemonic (group 1)	Mnemonic (group 2)	Control
person 1			
person 2			
person 3			
person 4			
person 5			
average			

Troubleshooter's Guide

Here are some problems that may arise during this experiment, some possible causes, and ways to remedy the problems.

Problem: The people in each group differed widely in how many numbers they recalled.

Possible causes: The ability to memorize and retain information can differ among people. You may need a larger sample size to get a better average. If possible, increase your sample size to five people in each group and repeat the experiment. When you are calculating averages, do not use the highest and lowest numbers. Average only the three middle numbers for each group. There are generalities to the way people learn and memorize, but individuals have different learning styles. If possible, increase your sample size to five people in each group and repeat the experiment. When you are calculating averages, do not use the highest and lowest numbers. Average only the three middle numbers for each group.

Problem: The people who put the numbers to lyrics could not recall as expected.

Possible causes: Participants may not have been familiar with the song or tune. Find a song or tune each participant in the song group knows well, and set the pi numbers to that. Repeat the experiment.

to recite as many numbers of pi as they can recall. Start to hum the tune and ask again. Make a note of how many numbers each person remembered.

7. The day after working with Group 2, ask each participant individually to recite as many numbers of pi as they can recall. Show them the images you used. Note how many numbers each person recalled.

8. Repeat the same test for the control group one day after working with the control participants.

Summary of Results Average the number of digits each group recalled. (To calculate the average, add up the number of digits participants in each group remembered and divide by the total number of digits. If there were three participants and you tested 12 decimal places, the total number of digits would be 36. If there were four participants, the total digits would be 48.) Was your hypothesis correct? Could one group that used mnemonics recall the numbers of pi significantly better than the other group? How did the mnemonic groups compare to the control. Were there one or two participants who were especially good at recalling the numbers? Consider why certain mnemonic devices may help people with memory recall. Write a paragraph summarizing your findings and explaining whether they support your hypothesis.

Change the Variables Here are ways to vary this experiment:

- Use different types of mnemonic devices, such as associating each number with a letter or object.
- Test the type of people, using the same memorizing device. Will children show better memory retention than adults?
- Change what is memorized; use a group of words or science terms, such as the names of the bones in our skeleton.

EXPERIMENT 2

False Memories: How can memories be influenced?

Purpose/Hypothesis Sometimes, the brain can lead people to remember things that did not actually occur. This is called false memory. One way a false memory can form is if a memory is "planted" or suggested to the person who is recalling the memory. In this experiment, you will test how false memories can be created.

You will tell several helpers that you want to find out if you can recreate a crime scene from their description. Set-up a scene in which there is activity and color: A person wearing colorful clothing and holding a bag comes into the room and places two to three items in the bag. The person will be wearing a large, colorful band-aid or other item on one hand. The "witnesses" will watch the scene. By asking some witnesses a leading question that suggests the band-aid was on the opposite hand, you can determine if each witness will retell the scene with the false memory.

Before you begin, make an educated guess about the outcome of this experiment based on your knowledge of false memory. This educated guess, or prediction, is your hypothesis. A hypothesis should explain these things:

- the topic of the experiment
- the variable you will change
- the variable you will measure
- what you expect to happen

A hypothesis should be brief, specific, and measurable. It must be something you can test through observation. Your experiment will prove or disprove your hypothesis. Here is one possible hypothesis for this experiment: "False memories can form from a misleading suggestions."

In this case, the variable you will change will be the planting of the memory, and the variable you will measure will be asking or not asking a leading question. You expect that when you ask a misleading question, you implant a false memory.

What Are the Variables?

Variables are anything that might affect the results of an experiment. Here are the main variables in this experiment:

- the length of time witnesses are watching the scene
- background noise and activity
- the questions

In other words, the variables in this experiment are everything that might affect the witnesses memory.

How to Experiment Safely

There are no safety hazards in this experiment.

Level of Difficulty Easy/moderate.

Materials Needed

- 6 witnesses, you can have more but try not to have less than 4
- 1 helper
- bright shirt or other clothing for the helper
- bag or purse
- pen and notebook
- colorful accessory to place on helper's arm (large band aid works well)

Approximate Budget $0.

Timetable Approximately 30 minutes, depending upon the number of participants.

Step-by-Step Instructions

1. Gather all your witnesses and tell them you want to see if they can recreate the scene and suspect for an experiment you are doing on forensics.
2. Have the helper put the colorful band aid in a prominent place on the right arm before entering the room.
3. Have the helper enter the room, place several small room items in the bag and leave.
4. Ask your witnesses not to talk about the scene and question each witness individually in a separate room.
5. Ask the first witness a series of questions: For example: What did the suspect take? In what order were the items taken? What color hair did the suspect have? What color clothes was s/he wearing? At the end of your questioning, ask: What color band-aid was the suspect wearing on his/her left arm?
6. Write down all the answers and repeat the answers, clearly stating the color of the band aid on the left arm, if the witness did not correct you.
7. Repeat these questions for half of the witnesses.
8. Repeat the questions for the other half of the witnesses, except in place of the misleading question ask directly: What arm was the band-aid on? What color was the band aid?

9. When everyone is back together talk about what people remembered. Bring up the fact, if true, that some of the witnesses said the band aid was on the left arm. Do they still remember it that way?

Step 3: Have the helper enter the room, place several small room items in the bag and leave. ILLUSTRATION BY TEMAH NELSON.

Summary of Results Did the witnesses who were asked directly to recall the band aid remember it more accurately? Did the witnesses recall the color more than the placement? Were there certain memories that all the people recalled? When the witnesses were told that others remembered the placement of the band aid on a different arm, did they revise their memory? Write a summary of your results.

Change the Variables You can vary this experiment in several ways.

- Try varying the ages of the "witnesses." Are younger people more likely to accept a false memory than adults?
- Change the activity of the helper, to test how a more or less active scene will affect false memories.
- Change the amount of time of the scene.

Design Your Own Experiment

How to Select a Topic Relating to this Concept Memory is such a fundamental part of our lives that studying it is important. You might decide to research the different forms of memories and what causes events to become memorable. Consider the ways that you use the different types of memory on a daily basis. When you instinctually step over a hole in the sidewalk, consider how your memory compares to what a small child would do? You might also what to investigate how memories are retained.

Check the Further Readings section and talk with your science teacher to gather information on memory questions that interest you. You might also want to consider talking with someone who is a physician or involved in brain research.

Steps in the Scientific Method To do an original experiment, you need to plan carefully and think things through. Otherwise, you might not be sure

Troubleshooter's Guide

There should be no major problems with this experiment. Recall can vary depending upon the person. The more people you conduct this experiment on, the better the chance you will have clear results.

what question you are answering, what your are or should be measuring, or what your findings prove or disprove.

Here are the steps in designing an experiment:

- State the purpose of—and the underlying question behind—the experiment you propose to do.
- Recognize the variables involved, and select one that will help you answer the question at hand.
- State a testable hypothesis, an educated guess about the answer to your question.
- Decide how to change the variable you selected.
- Decide how to measure your results.

Recording Data and Summarizing the Results It's always important to write down data and ideas you gather during an experiment. Keep a journal or record book for this purpose. If you keep notes and draw conclusions from your experiments and projects, other scientists could use your findings in their own research.

Related Projects Memory-related projects or experiments can go in many different directions. For example, you might conduct experiments on what leads a sensory memory to transfer into a long-term memory. You might investigate what techniques help you or your classmates memorize facts or formulas. You could investigate how factors that relate to influencing memory. You could also experiment with memory in animals, such as cats, dogs, and insects. Do certain animals have longer memories than others? For a research project, you could also conduct a research project on memory loss: the types of amnesia and causes.

For More Information

DiSpezio, Michael A. *How Bright Is Your Brain?: Amazing Games to Play with Your Mind.* New York: Sterling Pub. Co, 2004. Games and simple activities that explore the brain.

The Exploratorium. *Memory.* http://www.exploratorium.edu/memory (accessed on May 19, 2008). Articles and webcasts from a museum exhibit.

"Memory Matters." *KidsHealth.* http://www.kidshealth.org/kid/health_problems/brain/memory.html (accessed on May 21, 2008). Clear information on memory and the brain.

Murphy, Pat, et al. *The brain explorer: puzzles, riddles, illusions, and other mental adventures.* New York: H. Holt, 1999 Brain-based experiments and activities.

PBS. "3-D Brain Anatomy." *The Secret Life of the Brain.* http://www.pbs.org/wnet/brain/3d (accessed on May 21, 2008). A three dimensional tour of the brain.

Microorganisms

In 1675, Anton van Leeuwenhoek (1632–1723), a Dutch merchant with an interest in science, looked through a microscope at a drop of stagnant water. He had originally built a simple microscope to examine textile threads for the draperies he made. Eventually, as a result of his scientific investigations, he built a more powerful microscope that could magnify objects 200 times. Under such a microscope, van Leeuwenhoek saw that the dirty water was full of tiny living creatures. Before his discovery, the smallest living creatures known were tiny insects. He called the life forms he looked at animalcules, but they would later become known as protozoa and bacteria. Other scientists would also find different life forms under the microscope and give them specific names. In time, the term microorganisms would be used to describe all microscopic forms of life.

Connecting bacteria to disease Van Leeuwenhoek's animalcules had an active life, scurrying around by means of small whip-like tails or by expelling streams of fluid. The bacteria he observed were quieter. They mostly lay about and multiplied. It was Louis Pasteur (1822–1895), a French chemist, who pieced together the connection between disease and these microorganisms.

In the 1850s, while Pasteur was a professor and dean at the University of Lille in France, he helped a man who wanted to know why some of his sugar-beet juice, which was being distilled for alcohol, was going bad. What Pasteur discovered were rodlike organisms in the bad batches. They were bacteria, which multiply quickly. In his experiment, he found that heat killed these microorganisms.

Pasteur applied his theory to the wine industry and showed wine growers in his hometown

Microorganisms come in a wide range of shapes but are too tiny to see with the naked eye.
PHOTO RESEARCHERS INC.

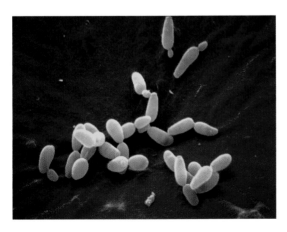

Louis Pasteur discovered the link between disease and bacteria. LIBRARY OF CONGRESS.

Penicillin mold growing in a culture. PHOTO RESEARCHERS INC.

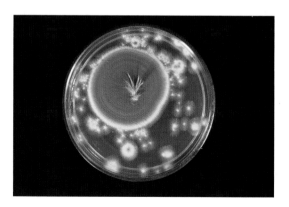

that bad-tasting wine occurred when bacteria fell into wine as it was being bottled. Pasteur advised them how to heat bottled wine just enough to kill bacteria. This method, known as pasteurization, is still used in the wine and milk industries.

Between 1865 and 1870, Pasteur also discovered what was killing off France's silkworms. Under a microscope, he saw microorganisms infecting the sick silkworms as well as the leaves they were eating. After Pasteur recommended that the infected silkworms and leaves be destroyed, the unaffected ones thrived. These incidents supported Pasteur's germ theory of disease, that microorganisms cause diseases. He advanced the field of bacteriology, the study of different groups of bacteria.

These little guys do a lot Tiny microorganisms are basically everywhere—in the air, in your body, in your cat's or dog's fur, and in the soil. Bacteria are the smallest single-celled organisms. To help us see them, today's microscopes can magnify subjects up to 2,000 times. That's ten times stronger than the microscope van Leeuwenhoek developed, which was quite an accomplishment for his time. We usually group all microorganisms together as disease-carrying germs, but many are important to life functions.

Microorganisms are categorized into five major groups: bacteria, such as salmonella; algae, such as blue-green algae; fungi, such as yeast; protists, such as amoebas; and viruses, such as chickenpox. Microorganisms are essential in the production of antibiotics, pickles, cheeses, and alcoholic beverages. Yeasts, which are in the fungi group, are used in bread and cheese making. The fungi group includes a mold called penicillin, which is an antibiotic. Bacteria, protozoa, and fungi feed on dead, decaying organisms, such as the organic material placed into composters.

We cannot see microorganisms with the naked eye unless they multiply. Conducting some experiments will put us in touch with these amazing living creatures.

EXPERIMENT 1

Microorganisms: What is the best way to grow penicillin?

Purpose/Hypothesis Penicillin is a microscopic mold that grows on fruit. It looks green and powdery and is shaped like a small paint brush when viewed under a microscope. The word, *penicillin,* in fact, means "small brush" in Latin. Early writing was often done with a small, fine-pointed brush, and the English words pen and pencil are also derived from this Latin word.

In this experiment, you will determine the best growing conditions for the penicillin mold. You will place one set of fruit in a warm location and another set in a cool location. The difference in the amount of mold that grows will tell you whether temperature affects penicillin growth.

To begin the experiment, use what you know about mold growth to make an educated guess about the effect of temperature. This educated guess, or prediction, is your hypothesis. A hypothesis should explain these things:

- the topic of the experiment
- the variable you will change
- the variable you will measure
- what you expect to happen

A hypothesis should be brief, specific, and measurable. It must be something you can test through observation. Your experiment will prove or disprove whether your hypothesis is correct. Here is one possible hypothesis for this experiment: "Penicillin mold will grow more rapidly and produce more visible mold under warm conditions."

What Are the Variables?

Variables are anything that might affect the results of an experiment. Here are the main variables in this experiment:

- the type and age of the fruit
- the amount of bruising of the fruit
- temperature of the environment
- amount of light reaching the fruit
- humidity of the environment

In other words, the variables in this experiment are everything that might affect the growth of penicillin mold on the fruit. If you change more than one variable, you will not be able to tell which variable had the most effect on mold growth. Citrus fruits are the best source for this mold, so only citrus fruit will be used.

A moldy lemon (a small inset shows how mold looks under a microscope). GALE GROUP.

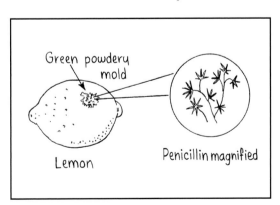

WORDS TO KNOW

Animalcules: Life forms that Anton van Leeuwenhoek named when he first saw them under his microscope; they later became known as protozoa and bacteria.

Bacteria: Single-celled microorganisms that live in soil, water, plants, and animals and that play a key role in the decaying of organic matter and the cycling of nutrients. Some are agents of disease.

Bacteriology: The scientific study of bacteria, their characteristics, and their activities as related to medicine, industry, and agriculture.

Colony: A mass of microorganisms that have been bred in a medium.

Control experiment: A set-up that is identical to the experiment but is not affected by the variable that affects the experimental group.

Cultures: Microorganisms growing in prepared nutrients.

Germ theory of disease: The belief that disease is caused by germs.

Hypothesis: An idea phrased in the form of a statement that can be tested by observation and/or experiment.

Lactobacilli: A strain of bacteria.

Medium: A material that contains the nutrients required for a particular microorganism to grow.

Microbiology: Branch of biology dealing with microscopic forms of life.

Microorganisms: Living organisms so small that they can be seen only with the aid of a microscope.

Pasteurization: The process of slow heating that kills many bacteria and other microorganisms.

Penicillin: A mold from the fungi group of microorganisms; used as an antibiotic.

Protists: Members of the kingdom Protista, primarily single-celled organisms that are not plants or animals.

Protozoa: Single-celled animal-like microscopic organisms that live by taking in food rather than making it by photosynthesis. They must live in the presence of water.

Variable: Something that can affect the results of an experiment.

In this case, the variable you will change is the temperature of the environment, and the variable you measure is the amount of visible mold that grows.

Level of Difficulty Easy/moderate.

Materials Needed

- 2 cotton balls or small sponges
- 2 oranges, about equally ripe
- 2 lemons, about equally ripe

- 2 clear plastic bags (gallon size)
- bowl
- twist ties
- water
- use of a refrigerator
- microscopes and slides are optional

Approximate Budget $2 for fruit and bags.

Timetable 20 minutes to set up, and one or two weeks to complete.

Step-by-Step Instructions

1. Bruise the fruit by rubbing it on the floor and dropping it. This helps the mold to invade the tough skin of the fruit.
2. Place the fruit in a bowl for one to three days. Leave the bowl out in the open where it will come into contact with mold in the air.
3. In one bag place one orange, one lemon, and one moist cotton ball. (The moist cotton ball raises the humidity.)
4. Repeat Step 3 for the other bag.
5. Tie each bag closed with a twist tie.
6. Place one bag in the refrigerator and the other in a warm place.
7. Every day, record any changes you observe.
8. After two weeks, open the bags and examine the fruit.
9. If you have access to a microscope, smear a small sample of mold on a slide and view it.

Summary of Results Compare the mold growth in each plastic bag. The bag in the warmer place should show considerably more growth because mold thrives in warm environments. Photograph your final results or draw a picture of what grew.

Change the Variables You can conduct several similar experiments by changing the variables. For example, you can vary humidity by varying

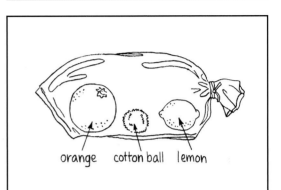

Steps 3 and 4: Place one orange, one lemon, and one moist cotton ball in clear plastic bag. GALE GROUP.

Step 8: After 2 weeks, open the bags and examine the fruit for mold. GALE GROUP.

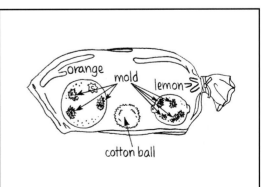

Troubleshooter's Guide

Here is a problem that may arise during this experiment, a possible cause, and a way to remedy the problem.

Problem: Neither bag showed any mold growth after two weeks.

Possible cause: There was not enough humidity present in the bags. Remoisten the cotton balls and allow the experiment to run for an additional two weeks.

the number of soaked cotton balls or sponges. You could also change the fruit. Remember, if you change more than one variable at a time, you will not be able to tell which variable had the most effect on mold growth.

Modify the Experiment This experiment examines the best temperature for mold growth. You can add to this experiment by measuring other environmental conditions that could affect mold growth. Factors you can examine include light and air. From what you know about how organisms live and grow, make a hypothesis about how light and air will affect the amount of mold that will grow on the fruit.

Follow Steps 1 and 2 in the experiment, adding four more oranges and four lemons. Prepare four addition bags containing an orange, lemon, and moist cotton ball. You should have six bags. In addition to placing bag 1 in the refrigerator and bag 2 in a warm place: Place bag 3 in a drawer or other dark area and bag 4 in a well-lit area, such as by a window; Wrap plastic wrap around each of the two fruits in bag 5 and leave bag 6 in a room temperature environment. The plastic wrap will seal the fruit from air.

After two weeks examine the fruit in all the bags. Make a chart of each of the environments and note or draw the amount of mold growth in each setting. Was your hypothesis correct? You can measure mold growth on each of these environments separately using different fruits.

EXPERIMENT 2

Growing Microorganisms in a Petri Dish

Purpose/Hypothesis Microbiologists often breed microorganisms in large quantities called colonies. For this experiment you will prepare the medium needed to grow colonies of microorganisms.

In this experiment you will change the source of the microorganisms. You will prepare the same medium for all samples. This medium is rich in nutrients needed by most microorganisms. You will then obtain microorganisms from different sources and observe their growth in the medium.

To begin the experiment, use what you know about the source of microorganisms to make an educated guess about whether different types will grow in the same medium. This educated guess, or prediction, is your hypothesis. A hypothesis should explain these things:

- the topic of the experiment
- the variable you will change
- the variable you will measure
- what you expect to happen

A hypothesis should be brief, specific, and measurable. It must be something you can test through observation. Your experiment will prove or disprove whether your hypothesis is correct. Here is one possible hypothesis for this experiment: "Different kinds of microorganisms can be obtained in many places, and all will thrive in a nutrient-rich medium to produce visible growth that varies in amount, color, and texture."

In this case, the variable you will change is the source of the microorganisms, and the variable you measure is the amount, color, and texture of the visible growth that appears.

Level of Difficulty Moderate. (This experiment requires special attention to cleanliness. Sterile conditions are ideal but almost impossible to obtain without training and special equipment.)

Materials Needed

- 6 petri dishes and lids (If petri dishes are not available, use small bowls and clear plastic wrap.)
- 1 package unflavored gelatin
- ¼ cup (60 milliliters) sugar
- 1 tablespoon (15 milliliters) salt
- 1 tablespoon (15 milliliters) pork or beef, finely ground
- 1½ quart (1.5 liter) pot with a cover
- 1 quart (1 liter) water
- tongs

Approximate Budget $10 for petri dishes and food products.

What Are the Variables?

Variables are anything that might affect the results of an experiment. Here are the main variables in this experiment:

- the type of medium
- the temperature of the environment
- the humidity of the environment
- the amount of light reaching the petri dishes
- the sources of the microorganisms

In other words, the variables in this experiment are everything that might affect the type and growth of microorganisms. If you change more than one variable, you will not be able to tell which variable had the most effect on the amount, color, and texture of the visible growth.

How to Experiment Safely

This experiment requires boiling hot water to cook gelatin and to sterilize the equipment. Ask an adult to help you when using the stove or when handling boiling water.

Steps 1 and 2: When the water is boiling, use tongs to submerge the petri dishes into the water for 1 minute. GALE GROUP.

Timetable 90 minutes to prepare, and one to two weeks for results.

Step-by-Step Instructions

1. In the pot, boil one quart of water.
2. When the water is boiling, use tongs to submerge the petri dishes into the water for one minute.
3. Remove the petri dishes from the water. Place on the counter or table. Place the lids on top to keep the inside clean. Allow them to cool.
4. Follow directions on the package to prepare gelatin.
5. Add sugar, salt, and finely ground meat.
6. Bring gelatin to quick boil and remove from the heat.

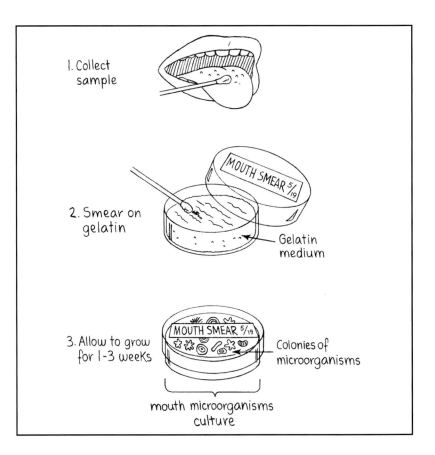

1. Collect sample
2. Smear on gelatin — Gelatin medium
3. Allow to grow for 1-3 weeks — Colonies of microorganisms

mouth microorganisms culture

Steps 10 to 12: Example of collecting microorganisms from the inside of the mouth. Be sure to collect samples from five different sources. GALE GROUP.

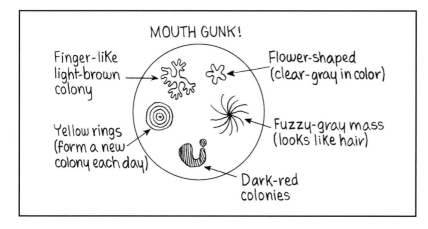

MOUTH GUNK!

Finger-like light-brown colony

Flower-shaped (clear-gray in color)

Yellow rings (form a new colony each day)

Fuzzy-gray mass (looks like hair)

Dark-red colonies

Step 15: Examples of microorganism colonies from mouth samples in petri dish after two weeks. GALE GROUP.

7. Cover and cool for three to five minutes.

8. Ask an adult to help you fill the six petri dishes halfway with the gelatin medium. Cover each dish immediately.

9. Cool one hour before moving.

10. To collect microorganisms from the environment, gently wipe a surface with a cotton swab. Here are some suggestions for samples: doorknob, arm, inside of mouth, floor, used cup, leftover food, dirt. Wipe five different surfaces—one for each of five petri dishes.

11. Gently rub each used swab on the gelatin in a dish. Do not touch more than one swab to a dish. You will not be able to see the microorganisms on the cotton swab. Trust that something is there.

12. Mark each dish with the date and the source of the sample. Cover each dish and seal it with tape.

13. For a control experiment, leave one petri dish untouched. Label it "control" and seal it.

14. Keep the petri dishes together in a dark, warm area. Allow dishes to sit one to three weeks.

15. After the petri dishes show fuzzy gray mounds or slimy blobs, make a drawing of the microorganisms.

16. Do not open dishes or handle any microorganisms. Throw them away after the experiment.

Summary of Results Because of the complexity and variety of microorganisms, you cannot identify specific species. However, you should draw and describe your findings to share with others. Write a summary. Did colonies of microorganisms develop in all of your petri dishes? Were

Troubleshooter's Guide

Here is a problem that may arise during this experiment, a possible cause, and a way to remedy the problem.

Problem: The microorganisms are not growing.

Possible cause: The conditions they need to grow are not in place. If after two weeks no growth is evident, try leaving the dishes in a warmer environment.

they different in color and texture? Did any growth appear in the control dish? Don't be surprised if it did. Even the air contains microorganisms. Were you able to support your hypothesis?

Change the Variables After you have determined and recorded the amount, color, and texture of growth from various sources, repeat the experiment and change the amount of light or the temperature or the humidity. Do some microorganisms grow more or less than before? Do they appear different from before? Remember, if you change more than one variable at a time, you will not be able to tell which variable had the most effect on growth.

Design Your Own Experiment

How to Select a Topic Relating to this Concept Microorganisms are everywhere. They are covering your body at this very moment, so you do not have to look far to find them. An experiment with microorganisms could include topics such as culturing or identifying their characteristics.

Check the Further Readings section and talk with your science teacher or school or community media specialist to start gathering information on microorganism questions that interest you. As you consider possible experiments, be sure to discuss them with your science teacher or another knowledgeable adult before trying them. Some of the microorganisms or procedures might be dangerous.

Steps in the Scientific Method To do an original experiment, you need to plan carefully and think things through. Otherwise, you might not be sure what question you are answering, what you are or should be measuring, or what your findings prove or disprove.

Here are the steps in designing an experiment:

- State the purpose of—and the underlying question behind—the experiment you propose to do.
- Recognize the variables involved, and select one that will help you answer the question at hand.
- State a testable hypothesis, an educated guess about the answer to your question.

- Decide how to change the variable you selected.
- Decide how to measure your results.

Recording Data and Summarizing the Results The most important part of the experiment is the information gathered from it. Scientists working 400 years ago made discoveries in science that still help us today. In the fruit experiment, you cannot save the fruit to display or stop the decaying process with refrigeration. The results need to be recorded in drawings, photos, or notes. All these pieces of information you gathered then should be summarized into a conclusion or result.

Related Experiments Microbes are simple organisms with simple needs, such as air (in some cases not even air), water, warm temperatures, and food. By putting microorganisms on a petri dish and adding a drop of different chemical cleaners, you can find out what substances keep them from growing. If it is safe, you may want to use that chemical when you wash. That's the idea behind antibacterial soaps.

For More Information

American Museum of Natural History. "The Microbe Size-O-Meter." *Meet the Microbes!* http://www.amnh.org/nationalcenter/infection/01_mic/01d_size 01.html (accessed on March 2, 2008). A look at the sizes of different microorganisms relative to familiar objects.

"Bacteria cam." *Cells alive!* http://www.cellsalive.com/cells/bactcell.htm (accessed on March 2, 2008). Bacteria cell structure and images of real-time bacteria growing.

Dashefsky, H. Steven. *Microbiology: 49 Science Fair Projects.* Austin, TX: Tab Books, 1994. Outlines science projects that are well-suited for this topic.

Lang, S. *Invisible Bugs and Other Creepy Creatures That Live With You.* New York: Sterling Publishers, 1992. Describes different microorganisms, their functions, and purpose.

"Penicillin: The true story?" *Timeline Science.* http://www.timelinescience.org/ resource/students/pencilin/pencilin.htm (accessed on March 2, 2008). A brief history of the many people who helped develop the antibiotic penicillin.

Mixtures and Solutions

Most of the substances we see around us are mixtures, combinations of different elements or compounds. The components of some mixtures—such as sandy water, which consists of grains of sand suspended in water—can easily be separated or will naturally settle. Others, such as salty water, form more permanent mixtures. How can we separate different kinds of mixtures into their component parts?

Mixtures that settle—separate out naturally—are called suspensions. Sandy water is a good example of a suspension. Stirring will mix the sand and the water, but over time, the denser sand will fall to the bottom of the container, and a clear layer of water will appear above it.

A mixture whose parts remain stable and remain mixed over time is called a solution. Solutions commonly consist of a solid solute that is dissolved in a liquid solvent. The molecules of the solute are evenly dispersed and very small. Salt water, lemon juice, and antifreeze are all solutions. These mixtures will remain mixed even when left standing for a long time.

A third type of mixture is a colloid, in which relatively large molecules of one substance remain mixed and stable due to electric charge repulsions. This repulsion occurs because colloidal particles contain an equal number of positive and negative ions (charged atoms), but the negative ions form a layer surrounding the particle. Thus, the particles are electrically neutral but still tend to repel one another to spread out evenly through the

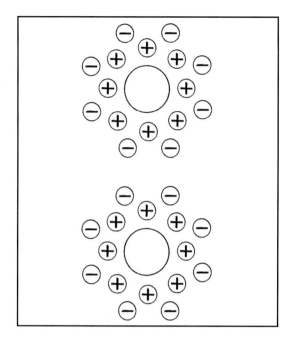

Although colloidal particles are electrically neutral, they possess an outer layer of negative ions and so repel one another. GALE GROUP.

dispersing medium. Milk, gelatin, clay, and smoke are all colloids that combine solids, liquids, and gases in different ways.

How mixtures can be separated It is often necessary to separate mixtures into their component parts. Separating a suspension can be fairly simple. Suppose you lose a ring in a bucket of sandy water. Once the denser sand and the ring have settled to the bottom of the bucket, you can carefully pour off the clear water into another container. This process is known as decanting. Next, you can pour the soupy mixture of sand, water, and your ring into a strainer large enough to let the sand and water pass through. This process, known as filtration, will separate the ring from the other components of the suspension. Another means of separating mixtures is the centrifuge, which spins the mixture at high speeds until the more-dense particles are forced outward by centrifugal force and separate from the less-dense solvent.

Separating a solution is more difficult. For example, filtering salt out of seawater is possible only with extremely high pressure and very precise "molecular" filters. However, there are other ways to separate pure water from seawater. Raising the temperature of the solution until the water boils, capturing the steam and then cooling it until it condenses will yield pure liquid water and solid solute. This process is called distillation. Another process is called evaporation, which allows the vaporized water to escape, yielding only the solute.

Colloids can also be separated into their component parts. When a colloid is heated, the repelling force between the colloidal particles is no longer great enough to keep the heated particles from bouncing into each other and bonding together. They gradually form clumps and settled out of the mixture. Causing colloidal particles to gather is called coagulation. It can be seen clearly in milk, which forms clumps of fat, called curds, when heated.

Knowing how to separate mixtures into their component parts is crucial in both science and everyday life. Removing spaghetti from a pot of boiling water is not easy without filtration. Coagulation allows ionic or electrostatic cleaners to remove dust and soot from the air we breathe. A centrifuge is used to separate blood into its vital parts without

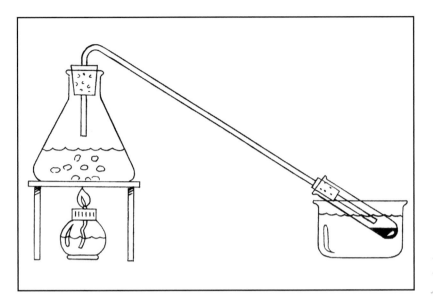

Distillation uses boiling and condensing to separate a solute from water. GALE GROUP.

damaging them. In the first experiment, you will identify various mixtures as suspension or solutions by applying different separation techniques.

Although liquid colloids can often behave just like suspensions, there is a simple method for distinguishing between them. A light beam passing through a solution will not encounter any particles large enough to deflect it, and thus will not be visible. Colloidal particles are not dissolved and can be quite large compared to the particles in a suspension. A light beam passing through a colloid will be visible as it is dispersed by these particles. This phenomenon is called the Tyndall effect. In the second project, you will use the Tyndall effect to distinguish a colloidal mixture from a solution.

A light beam passing through a colloid will be visible, while one passing through suspension will not. This phenomenon is called the Tyndall effect. PHOTO RESEARCHERS INC.

EXPERIMENT 1

Suspensions and Solutions: Can filtration and evaporation determine whether mixtures are suspensions or solutions?

Purpose/Hypothesis In this experiment, you will attempt to separate the component parts of

WORDS TO KNOW

Centrifuge: A device that rapidly spins a solution so that the heavier components will separate from the lighter ones.

Coagulation: The clumping together of particles in a mixture, often because the repelling force separating them is disrupted.

Colloid: A mixture containing particles suspended in, but not dissolved in, a dispersing medium.

Control experiment: A set-up that is identical to the experiment but is not affected by the variable that affects the experimental group.

Decanting: The process of separating a suspension by waiting for its heavier components to settle out and then pouring off the lighter ones.

Distillation: The process of separating liquids from solids or from other liquids with different boiling points by a method of evaporation and condensation, so that each component in a mixture can be collected separately in its pure form.

Electric charge repulsion: Repulsion of particles caused by a layer of negative ions surrounding each particle. The repulsion prevents coagulation and promotes the even dispersion of such particles through a mixtures.

Evaporation: The escape of liquid vapor into the air, yielding only the solute.

Filtration: The use of a screen or filter to separate larger particles that cannot slip through from smaller ones that can slip through the filter's openings.

Hypothesis: An idea in the form of a statement that can be tested by observation and/or experiment.

Ion: An atom or group of atoms that carries an electrical charge—either positive or negative—as a result of losing or gaining one or more electrons.

Mixtures: Combinations of different elements or compounds.

Solute: The substance that is dissolved to make a solution and exists in the least amount in a solution, for example sugar in sugar water.

Solution: A mixture of two or more substances that appears to be uniform throughout.

Solvent: The major component of a solution or the liquid in which some other component is dissolved, for example water in sugar water.

Suspension: A temporary mixture of a solid in a gas or liquid from which the solid will eventually settle out.

Tyndall effect: The effect achieved when colloidal particles reflect a beam of light, making it visible when shined through such a mixture.

Variable: Something that can affect the results of an experiment.

several mixtures using two different methods. The result of each method will determine the nature of the mixture. One mixture will consist of sand in distilled water, and the other will be lemon juice in distilled water. Before you begin, make an educated guess about the outcome of this experiment based on your knowledge of mixtures. This educated guess, or prediction, is your hypothesis. A hypothesis should explain these things:

- the topic of the experiment
- the variable you will change
- the variable you will measure
- what you expect to happen

A hypothesis should be brief, specific, and measurable. It must be something you can test through observation. Your experiment will prove or disprove whether your hypothesis is correct. Here is one possible hypothesis for this experiment: "A solid mixed into a liquid may be separated by filtration if the mixture is a suspension, such as sand in water, or by evaporation if the mixture is a solution, such as lemon juice in water."

In this case, the variable you will change is the component mixed with water, and the variable you will measure is ability of a specific method to separate the components. You expect that filtration will separate the sand, thus showing it is a suspension, and evaporation will separate the lemon juice, thus showing it is a solution.

What Are the Variables?

Variables are anything that might affect the results of an experiment. Here are the main variables in this experiment:

- the type of mixtures tested
- the purity of the mixed components
- size of the openings in the filter
- the temperature of the mixture

In other words, the variables in this experiment are everything that might affect the ability of a component to be separated from a mixture. If you change more than one variable, you will not be able to tell which variable had the most effect on the separation.

You will also set up a control experiment of pure water, with no substances mixed into it, to which you will apply the same methods of separation for comparison.

Level of Difficulty Moderate, because of the time involved and the care required when using a heat source.

Materials Needed

- 2 small saucepans, about 5 inches (12.5 centimeters) in diameter
- heat source (stove or a Bunsen burner)
- 4 clear 1-quart (1-liter) wide-mouth bottles
- 6 lemons
- 3 cups distilled water
- 1 cup (225 grams) of sand
- knife
- tablespoon
- funnel
- 3 conical paper coffee filters
- large wooden cutting board

Approximate Budget Less than $5, assuming a Bunsen burner or a stove is available.

How to Experiment Safely

This experiment involves heat and boiling liquid. These steps should be performed with adult supervision and with proper protection, including potholders. Do not substitute other mixtures for those in this experiment without consulting your teacher. Many substances can ignite or give off toxic fumes when heated.

Timetable The first stage of this experiment requires at least 1 hour for set-up, filtration, and partial evaporation by boiling. The second stage, evaporation without boiling, may take several hours or days, depending upon how much liquid remains in the saucepans.

Step-by-Step Instructions

1. Carefully cut the lemons in half and squeeze their juice into a bottle. Do not remove any solid particles or seeds from the juice. Add 1 cup of distilled water and set the bottle aside.

2. Pour 1 cup of distilled water into another bottle and stir in 3 tablespoons of sand.

3. In a third bottle, place 1 cup of distilled water. This will be your control experiment.

4. Filter the lemon juice. Place a coffee filter inside the funnel, hold the funnel over a bottle, and slowly pour the lemon juice into the funnel. The liquid that passes through the filter should appear uniform but will not be clear. Discard the used filter and clean the funnel and bottle, rinsing them with distilled water.

5. Prepare a chart on which you will record your observations. Your chart should look something like the illustration.

6. Stir each of the three samples, making sure to clean the spoon or stirrer after each one. Note the appearance of each sample on your chart.

7. Allow the mixtures to settle for several minutes. In the next column on your chart, note any change in appearance.

8. Line the funnel with another coffee filter and place it over the opening of the fourth bottle. Pour the mixture of water and sand into the funnel. Allow the liquid to filter into the bottle. Note any change in appearance on your chart. (See illustration.)

9. Pour the lemon-juice mixture into a saucepan and place the saucepan on the heat source. Do not leave this sample unattended. Observe the sample as it evaporates. Do not allow the liquid to evaporate completely!

10. When only a few tablespoons of the liquid remain, remove the saucepan from the heat and place it carefully on the wooden cutting board. (Remember to turn off the heat source when not using it and to be cautious around the saucepan, which will cool slowly.)

Appearance After				
		Stirring	Filtering	Evaporation
Mixture	lemon/ water	cloudy w/ visible particles		
	sand/ water	cloudy		
	control (water)	clear		

Step 5: Sample data chart for Experiment 1. GALE GROUP.

11. Repeat step 9 with your control liquid (the distilled water sample) in the second saucepan.

12. Place both saucepans in a safe place. Do not cover them. The liquids must continue to evaporate for you to see any dissolved solids. This final evaporation may take hours or even days, depending on how much liquid is left.

13. Check the samples periodically. Once the liquid in the lemon juice has completely evaporated, note on your chart whether any visible solids have been left behind on the surface of the saucepan. Also monitor your control experiment. It should leave no significant solid residue in the pan. If it does, then your results cannot prove your hypothesis.

Summary of Results Examine your results and determine whether your hypothesis is true. If a solid in a mixture is removed by your filtration method, then it was in suspension, and not in solution. If a solid is not removed by filtration

Step 8: Pour the mixture slowly and carefully into the funnel, as it may not drain quickly through the coffee filter. GALE GROUP.

Troubleshooter's Guide

Here is a problem that may arise during this experiment, a possible cause, and a way to remedy the problem.

Problem: The sand and water sample will not pass through the filter.

Possible cause: The sand is preventing the water from passing through the funnel. Set the apparatus aside and allow time for the water to filter slowly through the sand and the filter. This may take awhile.

but is removed by evaporation, then the solid was in solution. Compare your results for the control, the sand mixture, and the lemon mixture. Write a summary of your findings.

Change the Variables You can conduct similar experiments by changing the variables. For example, try different mixtures. Do not use any solvent other than water. Compare your results for mixtures using salt, flour, gelatin, bouillon cubes, or effervescent antacid tablets. You can also experiment with the effect of temperature. Some solids, such as sugar, will dissolve more easily when the water is hot than when it is cool.

PROJECT 2

Colloids: Can colloids be distinguished from suspension using the Tyndall effect?

Purpose/Hypothesis In this project, you will demonstrate how the Tyndall effect can be used to show that a mixture that looks like a solution is actually a colloid.

Level of Difficulty Moderate.

Materials Needed

- flashlight
- black construction paper
- tape
- 5 pint (0.25 liter) heavy cream
- lemon juice
- 12-ounce (0.33-liter) soda
- 1 quart (1 liter) distilled water
- 5 teaspoon measuring spoon
- 5 clear glass jars

Approximate Budget $10 to $15. (Most materials may be found in the average household.)

Timetable Less than 1 hour.

Step-by-Step Instructions

1. Pour 1 cup of distilled water into each jar. Add 0.5 teaspoon of heavy cream to the first jar and stir vigorously. Clean the spoon with distilled water.

2. Add 0.5 teaspoon of lemon juice, salt, and soda to the second, third, and fourth jars respectively. Remember to stir each one and to wash the spoon to avoid mixing the samples. The fifth jar, the control, should contain only distilled water.

3. Curl a sheet of construction paper into a cone, leaving a 1-inch (2.5-centimeter) diameter opening. Tape the cone to the flashlight so it narrows the beam through the small opening.

4. Darken the room or an area of the room. (Total darkness is not necessary or safe.) Set the control jar of distilled water on a flat, clear surface. Shine the light through the jar from one side and observe that the light does not illuminate the water itself.

5. Try shining the light through the milk mixture. If the path of the beam is visible in the liquid, the mixture is a colloid. If the beam is not visible, the mixture is a solution.

6. Repeat Step 5 with the other mixtures.

7. If you find it difficult to determine when the light beam is being scattered, construct a shield to block other illumination from reaching the jar. Curl a sheet of construction paper into a tube. Cut an opening at the front through which you can observe, and a hole at the side through which you can shine the light beam. Place the tube over the jar and repeat Steps 4 and 5 to see the difference between a light beam when it is scattered and when it is not scattered.

8. Create a chart to show the results of your demonstration, noting which mixtures are colloids and which are solutions.

Step 7: Construct a shield to block other illumination from reaching the jar. GALE GROUP.

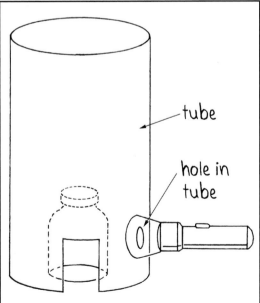

tube

hole in tube

	water/cream	water/lemon	water/salt	water/soda	control
appearance in normal light:					
appearance in Tyndall Effect test:					
colloid? y/n:					

Step 8: Data chart for Project 2.
GALE GROUP.

Summary of Results Remember that those who view your results may not have seen the project demonstrations performed, so you must present the information you have gathered in as clear a way as possble. Illustrations can show viewers the steps involved in determining whether a mixture is a solution or a colloid.

Design Your Own Experiment

How to Select a Topic Related to this Concept The nature of mixtures can provide topics for fascinating experiments and projects. Try measuring the changes that occur in the temperature at which water boils and when salt is added to it. You might test other methods of purification. Can you construct a simple centrifuge to separate suspensions? Can you purify salt water by freezing as well as by boiling? Finding the answers to these questions can become the basis for simple yet informative projects.

Check the Further Readings section and talk with your science teacher or school or community media specialist to start gathering information on mixture questions that interest you. Remember to check with a knowledgeable person before experimenting with unfamiliar materials.

Steps in the Scientific Method To do an original experiment, you need to plan carefully and think things through. Otherwise, you might not be sure what question you are answering, what you are or should be measuring, or what your findings prove or disprove.

Here are the steps in designing an experiment:

- State the purpose of—and the underlying question behind—the experiment you propose to do.

- Recognize the variables involved, and select one that will help you answer the question at hand.

- State a testable hypothesis, an educated guess about the answer to your question.

- Decide how to change the variable you selected.

- Decide how to measure your results.

Recording Data and Summarizing the Results In the experiments included here and in any experiments you develop, you can try to display your data in more accurate and interesting ways. For example, in the colloid project, you could redesign the demonstration to show the light-beam test simultaneously for all of the jars.

Remember that those who view your results may not have seen the experiment performed, so you must present the information you have gathered in as clear a way as possible. Including photographs or illustrations of the steps in the experiment is a good way to show a viewer how you got from your hypothesis to your conclusion.

Related Projects The isolation of substances in mixtures is an important and challenging part of chemistry. Other methods besides those described here can provide ideas for projects and experiments. For example, mixtures of two solids can be separated by using magnetism. Mixtures of two liquids that have different boiling points can be separated using distillation. Investigate these methods in the books listed in Further Readings, and try incorporating them into other projects.

Troubleshooter's Guide

This project is fairly simple, so not many problems should arise. However, when doing experiments involving mixtures, be aware that a number of unseen variables—such as temperature and impurity of substances—can affect your results. When mixing substances for a demonstration or experiment, you must keep the mixing containers and utensils clean. Even tiny impurities in a mixture can drastically alter your results. Any experiment you perform must be carefully designed to avoid letting unknown variations change the outcome and lead you to an incorrect conclusion.

Here is a problem that may arise during this project, some possible causes, and ways to remedy the problem.

Problem: All of the mixtures appear to scatter the light beam.

Possible causes:

1. Too much light is reaching the back, top, or sides of the jar. Try isolating the jars by constructing the light shield described in step 7.

2. Your samples have become corrupted. Prepare new samples, making sure to clean the spoon between each mixture.

For More Information

Andrew Rader Studios. "Mixture Basics." *Rader's Chem4kids.com* http://www.chem4kids.com/files/matter_mixture.html (accessed on February 18, 2008). Information on the chemistry of mixtures.

BBC. "Mixtures."Mixtures. *Schools. Science: Chemistry.* http://www.bbc.co.uk/ schools/ks3bitesize/science/chemistry/elements_com_ mix_6.shtml (accessed on February 18, 2008). Basic information on the chemistry of mixtures.

Gillett, Kate, ed. *The Knowledge Factory.* Brookfield, CT: Copper Beech Books, 1996. Provides some fun and enlightening observations on questions relevant to this topic, along with good ideas for projects and demonstrations.

Kurtus, Ron. "Mixtures." *School for Champions.* http://http://www.school-for-champions.com/chemistry/mixtures.htm (accessed on February 18, 2008). Basics of mixtures versus compounds.

Ray, C. Claibourne. *The New York Times Book of Science Questions and Answers.* New York: Doubleday, 1997. Addresses both everyday observations and advanced scientific concepts on a wide variety of subjects.

Wolke, Robert L. *What Einstein Didn't Know: Scientific Answers to Everyday Questions.* Secaucus, NJ: Birch Lane Press, 1997. Contains a number of entries relevant to mixtures and solutions.

56

Mountains

If you were to view Earth from up high, you would see a planet covered with mountains. A mountain is an area that rises above its surrounding area and has a peak. It is estimated that about one-fifth of the Earth's land contains mountains. There are even more mountains underwater. Mountains are an important source of our freshwater. They contain unique animals, plants, and ecosystems where many peoples make their homes and livelihood. Mountains also are a source of recreation and striking beauty.

Mountain stretches and peaks There is no defined height a landform needs to be before it is called a mountain. In general, a mountain is taller than a hill. Mountains exist in ranges, a chain of mountains that are next to one another. A mountain range can stretch for a few miles to thousands of miles. The height of a mountain is typically measured by how far it reaches above sea level.

The longest mountain range in the world is the Andes. This chain of mountains in South America runs for approximately 4,500 miles (7,242 kilometers). The Rocky Mountains are North America's longest mountain range. This series of mountains extends about 3,000 miles (4,828 kilometers), running from Alaska through Canada to New Mexico. There is a point in Colorado where the "Rockies" reach over 14,440 feet (4,401 meters).

The Rockies are high, but the tallest mountains are located in Asia. Mount Everest is the world's tallest mountain. Located along Nepal and Tibet, Mt. Everest has a peak that reaches more than 29,000 feet (8,839 meters). That's over 5 miles (8 kilometers)!

Tip-top formation Mountains all take shape from chunks of rock. The majority of mountains formed from the movement of Earth's crust (the outer layer of the Earth). Scientists have divided the crust into seven large sections or plates that fit together like an eggshell. There are also many smaller plates.

Mount Everest is the world's tallest mountain. © ALISON WRIGHT/CORBIS.

The plates can shift, overlap, or move against each other in what is called plate tectonics. The movement of the plates can push the crust upward, forming a mountain.

How the plates move determines the shape of the mountain. For example, fold mountains occur when plates push against each other. The crust buckles or "folds," much like wrinkles, as it lifts. As the folding continues, the mountains continue to grow higher and can take on ridge-like shapes. A fault-block mountain forms along a fault (a crack in the crust). The crust on one side of the fault moves apart from the crust on the other side. One side of the crust is forced upwards in an incline position, leaving one side of the mountain with a steep side and the other having a sloping side.

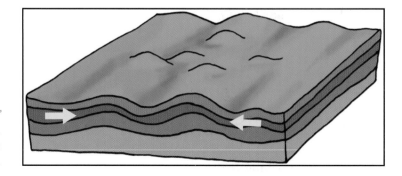

The crust buckles or "folds," much like wrinkles, as it lifts. ILLUSTRATION BY TEMAH NELSON.

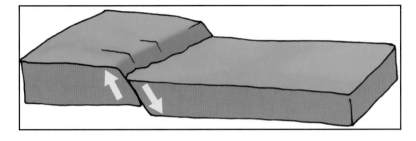

One side of the crust is forced upwards in an incline position, leaving one side of the mountain with a steep side and the other having a sloping side. ILLUSTRATION BY TEMAH NELSON.

Mountains are continuously changing shape due to natural weathering and erosion. In general, the taller the mountain, the younger it is. Rain, wind, and mountain rivers can erode (wear down) and move small bits of rocks on the mountain. Waterfalls, which often occur in mountains, will erode rocks. Over time, a sharp peak can become rounded and the mountain shape will change.

Life on a mountain Mountains ecosystems generally share some climate rules. The higher you go up a mountain, the colder it becomes. Air molecules near the surface are packed together. As warm air rises above ground the air molecules begin to cool down. The more the air rises, the colder it gets. With more space for the air molecules to move around, the air becomes less dense (fewer air molecules in a certain area). Air higher in the atmosphere is often referred to as thinner.

The cold air means mountain tops are cold. Mountains can also capture a lot of precipitation. Precipitation that falls in the form of rain on land will often be snow on the colder mountain top.

Mountains can also affect the environment surrounding it. A large mountain can block the wind and rain on one side. It can also cause large shadows, which can lead to less plant and animal life. Rain flowing down a mountain is the source of freshwater rivers.

Mountains are home to a diverse range of unique animals and plants. What lives on a mountain depends primarily upon where the mountain is located. The relative warmth makes life more

MODIS image illustrating the dramatic rainshadow effect of the Andes Mountains in South America on rainfall and vegetation. At left is Chile, which appears quite lush, while Argentina (right) appears dry and brown. © NASA/CORBIS.

WORDS TO KNOW

Crust: The hard outer shell of Earth that floats upon the softer, denser mantle.

Ecosystem: An ecological community, including plants, animals and microorganisms, considered together with their environment.

Erosion: The process by which topsoil is carried away by water, wind, or ice action.

Fault mountain: A mountain that is formed when Earth's plates come together and cause rocks to break and move upwards.

Fold mountain: A mountain that is formed when Earth's plates come together and push rocks up into folds.

Hypothesis: An idea in the form of a statement that can be tested by observation and/or experiment.

Leeward: The side away from the wind or flow direction.

Mantle: Thick dense layer of rock that underlies Earth's crust and overlies the core.

Mountain: A landform that stands well above its surroundings; higher than a hill.

Precipitation: Any form of water that falls to Earth, such as rain, snow, or sleet.

Rain shadow: Region on the side of the mountain that receives less rainfall than the area windward of the mountain.

Tectonic plates: Huge flat rocks that form Earth's crust.

Variable: Something that can affect the results of an experiment.

plentiful at the bottom areas of the mountains. Some cultures live around or near the lower areas of mountains. Mountains in warmer climates, such as North America, are home to bears, lions, and cougars.

At higher altitudes, goats, sheep, and smaller animals live. Birds, such as the eagle and condor, can also fly and live in high mountain areas.

In the following experiments, you will explore more about mountain formation and about how mountains affect the surrounding climate.

EXPERIMENT 1

Mountain Plates: How does the movement of Earth's plates determine the formation of a mountain?

Purpose/Hypothesis Some mountains are created by the movement of tectonic plates. When these plates come together they can change the make-up of Earth's surface features. Several elements are involved in affecting the features of a mountain, including the force with which the plates come together, the makeup of the Earth's rocky outer crust, and the angle the plates meet. Mountains are often formed by folds or fault break movements. In a fold mountain, the movement of two plates forces rocks upwards into folds. Some rocks are brittle and will not fold or bend. A fault mountain occurs from a break or fracture in the plates.

In this experiment you will create a simulation of plate movements and observe the flexibility of the terrain when plates collide in different ways. Plates can collide at even heights, uneven heights, and at angles. A strip of paper will represent a relatively flexible outer crust. A broom straw or spaghetti noodle will represent a hard and brittle outer crust. Which type of crust and movement will result in a fold versus a fault (a break)?

To begin your experiment, use what you know about mountains and plate movement to make an educated guess about the formation of mountains. This educated guess, or prediction, is your hypothesis. A hypothesis should explain these things:

- the topic of the experiment
- the variable you will change
- the variable you will measure
- what you expect to happen

A hypothesis should be brief, specific, and measurable. It must be something you can test through observation. Your experiment will prove or disprove whether your hypothesis is correct. Here is one possible hypothesis for this experiment: "The plates which are even heights and with the paper will create a fold when they collide."

In this case, the variables you will change, one at a time, are the type of crust and the angle with which the plates come together. The variable you will measure is the shape of the mountain that forms when the plates meet. If

What Are the Variables?

Variables are anything that might affect the results of the experiment. Here are the main variables in this experiment:

- the terrain
- the height of the plates
- the thickness of the paper
- the length of the paper
- the force with which the plates move

In other words, the variables in this experiment are everything that might affect the movement of the terrain. If you change more than one variable at a time, you will not be able to tell which variable had the most effect on the mountain formation.

How to Experiment Safely

There are no safety concerns in this experiment.

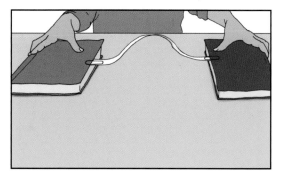

Step 4: Slowly slide the books toward each other.
ILLUSTRATION BY TEMAH NELSON.

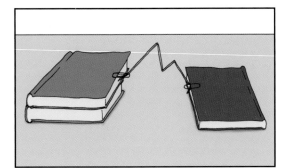

Step 7: Repeat Steps 4–6, using a piece of straw.

ILLUSTRATION BY TEMAH NELSON.

Summary of Results: Use sketches to observe how plates' heights and movements affect the formation of a mountain.

ILLUSTRATION BY TEMAH NELSON.

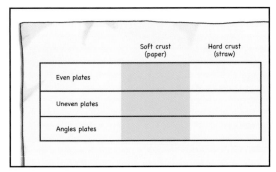

the paper forms a folded shape you will know your hypothesis is correct.

Level of Difficulty Easy to Moderate.

Materials Needed

- 6 or more hard bound books, 2 of which are the same height
- 2 large paper clips
- Strong tape, about 4 inches
- Several pieces of broom straws (spaghetti noodles will also work)
- 1, 8 × ½ inch strip of paper, the weight of copy paper

Approximate Budget $5.

Timetable Approximately 30 minutes.

Step-By-Step Instructions

1. Tape a paperclip to the center of each of the two books that are the same width.
2. Lay the books flat on a table or desk about 7 inches (18 centimeters) apart. Have the sides with the paper clips face each other. The books are now representing your plates.
3. Insert the ends of the paper strip into each of the paper clips.
4. Slowly slide the books toward each other. The strip of paper is an area of Earth's crust. Sketch a picture or make a note of what happens to the crust when the plates move toward each other.
5. Stack the books so that one stack is higher than the other, keeping the books with the paper clips on top. Repeat Steps 2–4.
6. Change the plates so that they are the same height. Repeat Steps 2–4 again, this time moving the plates at an angle as they come together.
7. Repeat Steps 4–6, using a broom handle or spaghetti noodle as the "crust" on these trials.

Summary of Results Use your sketches and observations to determine how plates' heights and movements as well as crust makeup, affects the formation of a mountain. Is a brittle crust more likely to form a fold or a fault? Which existing mountain ranges do your sketches represent? How is the shape of a mountain affected when the plates move towards each other at an angle? Write a paragraph showing your results.

Change the Variables You can change one of the variables and repeat this experiment. You can change the force with which the plates move and observe how this affects the movement of the crust? You can also alter the crust by adding gravel or fabric between the plates.

EXPERIMENT 2

Mountain Formations: How does the height of the mountain have an affect on desert formation?

Troubleshooter's Guide

Experiments do not always work out as planned. Below are some problems that may arise during this experiment, some possible causes, and ways to remedy the problems.

Problem: The paper does not form dips.

Possible cause: If the paper only arches and does not create valleys your paper may be too thick. Try using a thinner paper and repeat the experiment.

Problem: The noodle keeps breaking before the plates move together.

Possible cause: The noodles you are using may be too brittle. You can try steaming the noodles for a minute, or pluck some straws from a broom handle. Repeat the experiment.

Purpose/Hypothesis The formation of mountains can affect the surrounding climate and terrain (surface features) of the mountain area. Mountains are often found near deserts, because mountains often obstruct the airflow and ultimately rain in reaching the land bordering the leeward side of a mountain. How the mountain affects the surrounding terrain depends upon several factors, including the height of the mountain and the climate.

In this experiment you will be looking at how warm moist air and mountain height affect the formation of a desert. Warm air, which contains moisture, rises into the atmosphere. As it rises, it cools and the moisture ultimately falls as a form of precipitation.

Rain clouds often lose most of their moisture before the clouds completely cross the mountain range. In the case of tall mountain ranges, the precipitation can fall on one side of the mountain. The other side or, leeward side receives little to no rain, thus creating a dessert. This effect, called "rain shadow," can produce a desert behind the mountain.

In your experiment, you will create a flow of warm water to simulate the warm air rising and crossing the mountain range. You can observe how the warm air reacts in cool air, which is cool water placed in a dish with

What Are the Variables?

Variables are anything that might affect the results of the experiment. Here are the main variables in this experiment:

- the width of the mountain
- the temperature of the water

In other words, the variables in this experiment are everything that might affect the size of the air that moves over the mountain. If you change more than one variable, you will not be able to tell which variable had the most effect on mountain formation.

"mountains." You will then change the height of the mountain. Does the height of the mountain have an affect on how much of the warm "air" is able to cross to the other side?

To begin your experiment use what you know about mountains and deserts to make an educated guess about mountain formation. This educated guess, or prediction, is your hypothesis. A hypothesis should explain these things:

- the topic of the experiment
- the variable you will change
- the variable you will measure
- what you expect to happen

A hypothesis should be brief, specific, and measurable. It must be something you can test through observation. Your experiment will prove or disprove whether your hypothesis is correct. Here is one possible hypothesis for this experiment: "The height of a mountain has the greatest effect on if a desert is formed on the leeward side of the mountain."

In this case, the variable you will change is the height of the mountain, and the variable you will observe is the how great the mass of air is that moves over the mountain. If the mass is less with the taller mountain, you will know your hypothesis is correct.

Step 6: Slowly pour the half a cup of hot water into the cup placed in the corner.
ILLUSTRATION BY TEMAH NELSON.

Level of Difficulty Easy to Moderate.

Materials Needed

- 9 × 13 glass baking dish
- 2 lbs of modeling clay
- food coloring (red)
- glass measuring cup
- paper cups
- yard stick
- hot and cold water

Approximate Budget $8.

Timetable Approximately 1 hour.

Step-By-Step Instructions

1. Use the modeling clay to create a "mountain range" in the middle of the baking dish. Your first range should be approximately 1.5 inches (3.8 centimeters) wide and reach half way up the baking dish. Stretch the mountains to either side of the glass dish.

2. Poke 10 holes in the sides of the cup near the bottom, no higher than the depth of the baking dish.

3. Fill the baking dish with cold water to about a half-inch from the top.

4. Add three drops of red food coloring to one-half cup of hot water.

5. Place the paper cup, with holes, in the corner of one side of the dish.

6. Slowly pour the half a cup of hot water into the cup placed in the corner. This is your "warm air mass."

7. Observe if the water rises and crosses the mountain, or sinks and is unable to cross the mountain. Record your observations on a chart. Note about how much of the mass cross the mountain.

8. Empty the water from the baking dish.

9. Build a new mountain, this one should reach almost the top of the dish. Leave enough space so that water could still flow over the mountain, but not over flow the dish.

10. Fill the baking dish with cold water until the mountain range is covered.

11. Add three drops of red food coloring to one-half cup hot water.

12. Place the paper cup, with holes, in the corner of one side of the dish.

13. Slowly pour the one-half cup of cold water into the cup placed in the corner. This is your warm airflow.

14. Observe if the water rises and crosses the mountain, or sinks and is unable to cross the mountain. Record your observations on the chart. Note about how much of the mass crosses the mountain.

How to Experiment Safely

Be sure to use a pot holder and a measuring cup with a handle for the warm water.

Steps 7 and 14: Observe if the water rises and crosses the mountain. ILLUSTRATION BY TEMAH NELSON.

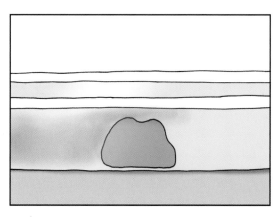

Troubleshooter's Guide

Not all experiments work exactly as planned. Sometimes, what seems like a "mistake" will turn into a new learning experience. Below is a problem that may arise during this experiment, some possible causes, and some ways to remedy the problems.

Problem: The cloud spreads out too much in the water to see where it moves.

Possible cause: There may not be enough of a difference in the water temperatures. Your water may not have been hot or cold enough. Try the experiment again, making the hot water hotter and the cold water colder.

Problem: It is too hard to measure how much of the cloud is moving.

Possible cause: There may be too much water for your size dish. Try decreasing the amount of water you use to make your cloud, using a quarter of a cup, and try the experiment again.

Summary of Results Examine your data on the different between how the warm water crossed over the low and high mountain range. Was your hypothesis correct? Consider how warm air might behave the same or different than the warm water. You might want to draw a picture of the results of your experiment and write a brief summary.

Change the Variables Here are some ways you can vary this experiment:

- Build the mountain range out of rocks or pebbles, for a jagged mountain that is not as solid.
- Build a mountain range with variation in its heights.
- Conduct the experiment in different environmental conditions.

Design Your Own Experiment

How to Select a Topic Relating to this Concept If you have ever gone mountains climbing, hiking, or skiing, or visited a mountain, you have most likely come across some unique properties to mountains. You may have questions and ideas for experiments based on your experience. Did you come across any interesting animals or plants? Was it a rocky or grassy mountain? Are there mountain ranges that you are interested in, either locally or in other countries? If so, consider what type of mountain it is, its features, and life.

Check the Further Readings section and talk with your science teacher or school or community media specialist to gather information on mountain questions that interest you.

Steps in the Scientific Method To do an original experiment, you need to plan carefully and think things through. Otherwise, you might not be sure what question you are answering, what you are or should be measuring, or what your findings prove or disprove.

Here are the steps in designing an experiment:

- State the purpose of—and the underlying question behind—the experiment you propose to do.

- Recognize the variables involved, and select one that will help you answer the question at hand.
- State a testable hypothesis, an educated guess about the answer to your question.
- Decide how to change the variable you selected.
- Decide how to measure your results.

Recording Data and Summarizing the Results Make drawings, graphs, and charts to display your information for others. You might also draw conclusions about your findings. Which type of mountain seems to be the most common in your region? Why might that be?

Related Projects If you are interested in mountains and want to discover more of their uses in your daily life, you might investigate how mountains erode over time, or mountains change the terrain in other ways aside from desert formation. You may want to conduct a research project on cultures that depend on mountains and the mountain life they use. You could also investigate extreme mountain climbing, how climbers prepare for the thinner atmosphere and other challenges.

For More Information

Cox, Shirley. *Earth Science.* Vero Beach, FL: Rourke Publications, Inc., 1992. Chapters include how to choose geology projects.

GMB Services. *RocksForKids.* http://www.rocksforkids.com (accessed February 7, 2008). Information on rock formation, identification, and collection.

Knapp, Brian. *Mountain.* Danbury, CT: Grolier, 1992. Describes mountains and their makeup. Some chapters include experiments.

The Mountain Institute. *Learning about Mountains.* http://www.mountain.org/education/index.html (accessed on April 18, 2008). Comprehensive information about mountains, including formation, life, and weather.

Parker, Steve. *The Earth and How It Works.* North Bellmore, NY: Marshall Cavendish, 1993. Outlines a variety of projects and experiments that examine Earth's composition.

U.S. Geological Survey. *Geologic Provinces of the United States: Rocky Mountains.* http://geomaps.wr.usgs.gov/parks/province/rockymtn.html (accessed on April 15, 2008). Information on features and geology of the Rocky Mountains.

U.S. Geological Survey. *Rocks and Minerals Site Contents.* http://wrgis.wr.usgs.gov/parks/rxmin/index.html (accessed February 7, 2008). Provides information on rocks and minerals.

57

Nanotechnology

Nanotechnology is a relatively new field of science that makes more headlines every year. It is a field that focuses on the small—the extremely small. In nanotechnology, people manipulate atoms and molecules to make new things. Those things can be materials or devices.

Throughout history, people have made new things from altering or combining substances that already exist. But nanotechnology works the opposite way. In nanotechnology, researchers develop a substance from the small to the large by manipulating the basic building blocks of matter. The result could be miniature materials or devices that have completely unique properties.

Science of the small The basic building blocks of nanotechnologies are atoms and molecules. All substances are made up of molecules. A drop of water, for example, is made up of millions of water molecules. If you were to keep dividing the drop into smaller droplets, you would end up with one molecule. That one water molecule would have the same properties as the drop of water.

Molecules are made of atoms held together by chemical bonds. The water molecule consists of two hydrogen atoms and an oxygen atom. Diamonds are made up of a molecule of carbon atoms bonded together. Salt is made of the sodium chloride molecule, which is one sodium atom bonded to one chloride atom.

Atoms and molecules are so small that a new prefix was coined to measure them: nano. The prefix "nano" comes from the Greek word for dwarf. Nano represents one billionth and so one nanometer is one-billionth of a meter. That's about the size of one strand of the width of your hair split into about 50,000 pieces! It's also about the size of ten hydrogen atoms. Things on the nanoscale are generally between 1 and 100 nanometers. Proteins in our bodies, viruses, and some particles in the air are nanosized.

A drop of water, for example, is made up of millions of water molecules. ILLUSTRATION BY TEMAH NELSON.

Seeing the small In order to work on the nanoscale, researchers needed to be able to see images of atoms and molecules. In 1981, the development of a powerful microscope allowed people to visualize the nanoscale on metals. Called the scanning tunneling microscope (STM), the microscope magnifies images of the shapes of atoms on the metal's surface. Micro-scopes soon followed that allowed researchers to see images of atoms and molecules on other materials.

Nanotechnology is not about simply mak-ing devices smaller. The field uses the fact that nanosize materials can have different properties than their larger counter-parts. Color, hardness, melting point, and conductivity are all some of the properties that can change as the material become nanosized. One phys-ical characteristic that can lead to these changes is the increased ratio of the surface area to volume.

Surface area is all the area that is on the outside—surface—of the material. Volume is the amount of three-dimensional space taken up by a material. As a material shrinks, its surface area increases compared to its volume, In the nanosize, this ratio can increase dramatically, which can lead to different reactions. Gold nanoparticles, for example, can appear a reddish color and turn liquid at room temperature.

Things on the nanoscale are generally between 1 and 100 nanometers. ILLUSTRATION BY TEMAH NELSON.

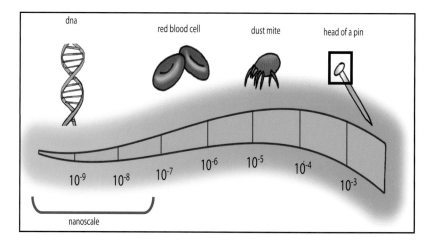

It is the arrangement of the atoms and molecules that gives materials its properties. Diamonds and the lead of pencils (graphite) are both made of up carbon molecules. In diamonds, the arrangement and bonds of the carbon atoms make it hard and clear. Graphite is dark and relatively soft. If researchers can pluck individual atoms and decide how to arrange them, they can determine the property of the material. One nanoscale material that was discovered in 1991 is also made of pure carbon. Carbon nanotubes are threads of carbon and the arrangement of its carbon makes it light, flexible, and stronger than steel.

A nano-world of technologies There are high hopes that research in nanotechnology will translate into many products and devices that will help people. The technology will affect a wide range of fields, including transportation, sports, electronics, and medicine. Some of the current and future possibilities of nanotechnology includes:

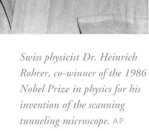

Swiss physicist Dr. Heinrich Rohrer, co-winner of the 1986 Nobel Prize in physics for his invention of the scanning tunneling microscope. AP PHOTO.

- Medicine: Researchers are working to develop nanorobots to help diagnose and treat health problems. Medical nanorobots, also called nanobots, could someday be injected into a person bloodstream. In theory, the nanobots would find and destroy harmful substances, deliver medicines, and repair damage.

- Sports: Nanotechnology has been incorporated in outdoor fabrics to add insulation from the cold without adding bulk. In sports equipment, nanotech metals in golf clubs make the clubs stronger yet lighter, allowing for greater speed. Tennis balls coated with nanoparticles protect the ball from air, allowing it to bounce far longer than the typical tennis ball.

- Materials Science: Nanotechnology has led to coatings that make fabric stain proof and paper water resistant. A car bumper developed with nanotechnology is lighter yet a lot harder to dent than conventional bumpers. And nanoparticles added to surfaces and paints could someday make them resistant to bacteria or prevent dirt from sticking.

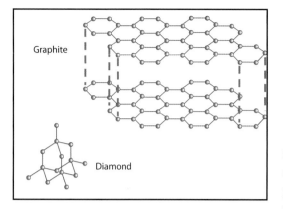

Graphite

Diamond

Diamonds and the lead of pencils (graphite) are both made of up carbon molecules. The arrangement and bonds of the carbon atoms cause the differences. ILLUSTRATION BY TEMAH NELSON.

- Electronics: The field of nano-electronics is working on miniaturizing and increasing the power of computer parts. If researchers could build wires or computer processing chips out of molecules, it could dramatically shrink the size of many electronics.

Guarding the nano-future Much like other new technologies, nanotechnology has raised concerns and ethical questions. If devices become nanosize, people would not be able to see them. There is some concern these "invisible" devices could cause harm.

If nanobots are developed, researchers would want them to self-replicate like the cells in our body. These nanobots could potentially do many amazing things, such as pull trash apart into its microscopic molecules. But one question is what happens if there is a problem. What if nanorobots programmed to disassemble trash started taking apart other items? And what if these nanorobots multiplied endlessly?

So far, nanobots are only theoretical and years in the future. The field of nanotechnology promises many future benefits, and people are working to develop guidelines that will help us deal with potential problems.

EXPERIMENT 1

Nanosize: How can the physical size affect a material's properties?

Purpose/Hypothesis As materials become smaller, the surface area to volume ratio changes. Materials that are microscopic and nanosized have a much higher surface area to volume ratio compared to the same material you can see. Because you cannot see nano materials, in this experiment you will measure how the surface area to volume ratio changes the melting and freezing point of water. By freezing the water into large and small ice cubes, you can measure the surface area to volume ratio of each, and determine how long each size takes to melt and freeze.

For a cube, the surface area is the area of the six square. The area of one square is the length × the width, which are the same in a cube. The surface area (S) of the cube is the area of one side multiplied by six. If the length and width are represented by "a," then $S = 6 \times a \times a$.

The volume (V) of a cube is $a \times a \times a$. For a cube, the ratio of surface area to volume is then S/V, or 6/a (6:a).

WORDS TO KNOW

Atom: The smallest unit of an element, made up of protons and neutrons in a central nucleus surrounded by moving electrons.

Bond: The force that holds two atoms together.

Control experiment: A set-up that is identical to the experiment but is not affected by the variable that will be changed during the experiment.

Hypothesis: An idea in the form of a statement that can be tested by observation and/or experiment.

Molecule: The smallest particle of a substance that retains all the properties of the substance and is composed of one or more atoms.

Nanobots: A nanoscale robot.

Nanometer: One-billionth of a meter.

Nanotechnology: Technology that involves working and developing technologies on the nanometer (atomic and molecular) scale.

Scanning tunneling microscope: A microscope that can show images of surfaces at the atomic level by scanning a probe over a surface.

Surface area: The total area of the outside of an object.

Variable: Something that can affect the results of an experiment.

Volume: The amount of space occupied by a three-dimensional object.

Before you begin, make an educated guess about the outcome of the experiment based on your knowledge of surface area to volume ratio and water. This educated guess, or prediction, is your hypothesis. A hypothesis should explain these things:

- the topic of the experiment
- the variable you will change
- the variable you will measure
- what you expect to happen

A hypothesis should be brief, specific, and measurable. It must be something you can test through observation. Your experiment will prove or disprove your hypothesis. Here is one possible hypothesis for this experiment: "The cubes with the smaller surface area to volume ratio will melt and freeze faster."

In this case, the variable you will change will be the surface area to volume ratio, and the variable you will measure will be the time it takes

What Are the Variables?

Variables are anything that might affect the results of an experiment. Here are the main variables in this experiment:

- the size of the ice cubes
- the material of the ice tray
- the material the ice melts on
- the temperature of the freezer
- the room temperature

In other words, the variables in this experiment are everything that might affect the melting and freezing of the ice.

How to Experiment Safely

There are no safety issues in this experiment.

Step 1: Pour water into at least three of the cubes in both the large and small ice cube trays.

Step 4: Place two large ice cubes on one plate, and two mini ice cubes on the second plate.
ILLUSTRATION BY TEMAH NELSON.

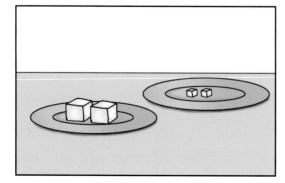

for the ice to freeze and melt. You expect a shorter freezing and melting time for the smaller ice than the larger ice cubes.

Level of Difficulty Easy/moderate (there is simple math involved).

Materials Needed

- conventional, large ice cube trade
- mini ice-cube tray (available at party stores)
- 2 plates
- freezer
- clock with minute hand
- toothpicks or other small pointy object
- ruler with centimeters

Approximate Budget $5.

Timetable Approximately 3 hours.

Step-by-Step Instructions

1. Pour water into at least three of the cubes in both the large and small ice cube trays.
2. Place the trays in the freezer. Time for 30 minutes and poke each with a toothpick. If one set of ice cubes are frozen, note the time and leave them both in the freezer. Check back every five minutes until both sets are frozen and note the time for each. If neither ice cube tray is frozen solid, leave the trays in the freezer and check back every five minutes.
3. When all the ice cubes are frozen solid, remove them from the trays. On one of the large and mini ice cubes, use the ruler to measure the dimension for a side of each. Round off the measurement and note.
4. Place two large ice cubes on one plate, and two mini ice cubes on the second plate. Make sure the ice cubes are not

touching. Set the plates aside and wait at least 30 minutes.

5. Continue checking on the cubes at regular intervals. Note when the two small cubes and the two large cubes have completely melted.

Summary of Results Was your hypothesis correct? Did the mini cubes melt and freeze faster than its larger counterpart? Rounding off the measurements, you can calculate the surface area and volume of the large cube and the small cube. How do the different surface area to volume ratios relate to the melting and freezing point?

Change the Variables If you want to vary this experiment, you can freeze water and melt the cubes in extreme size differences. How would a pan of water compare to an ice cube? You can also change the substance and look at surface area to volume ratios in solid substances, such as salt or sugar.

> ## Troubleshooter's Guide
>
> This experiment is straightforward and you should not have any major issues. The freezing time may vary from the protocol depending upon the temperature of the freezer and the size of the cubes. The melting time will also vary depending upon the size of the cubes.

EXPERIMENT 2

Nanosize Substances: How can the physical size affect the rate of reaction?

Purpose/Hypothesis One reason that nanosize substances may behave differently than the macrosize is due to the rate of reaction. Nanosize substances have a larger surface area compared to its larger counterpart. In this experiment, you will look at how increasing the surface area of a substance can affect its rate of reaction. You can use an antacid tablet and water. When antacid tablets react with water, the reaction produces carbon dioxide. In an enclosed container the carbon dioxide gas will push on the container and force its "top" into the air.

You can compare the rate of reaction between a whole antacid tablet and two varying sizes of the crushed tablet. One tablet will be broken into chunks and the other will be crushed, which will result in more surface area. Before you begin, make an educated guess about the outcome of the experiment based on your knowledge of surface area to volume ratio and water. This educated guess, or prediction, is your hypothesis. A hypothesis should explain these things:

What Are the Variables?

Variables are anything that might affect the results of an experiment. Here are the main variables in this experiment:

- the size of the ice cubes
- the brand of antacid tablet
- the size of the antacid tablet
- the amount of water
- the temperature of the water

In other words, the variables in this experiment are everything that might affect the rate at which the reaction occurs.

- the topic of the experiment
- the variable you will change
- the variable you will measure
- what you expect to happen

A hypothesis should be brief, specific, and measurable. It must be something you can test through observation. Your experiment will prove or disprove your hypothesis. Here is one possible hypothesis for this experiment: "The greater the surface area, the faster the rate of reaction."

In this case, the variable you will change will be the surface area, and the variable you will measure will be the time it takes for the carbon dioxide to pop the top.

Level of Difficulty Easy.

Materials Needed

- 6 antacid tablets
- 2 pieces of paper
- spoon or any hard object

Step 4: Quickly, snap on the top. ILLUSTRATION BY TEMAH NELSON.

- 3 film canisters (35 mm film) with lids that fit on the inside (as opposed to snap on the outside of the canister); you could also use 1 canister and rinse it out after each use
- watch with minute hand
- helper
- outside area or clear, inside area than can get messy

Approximate Budget $5.

Timetable Approximately 15 minutes.

Step-by-Step Instructions

1. Fill all three canisters half full with water that is about room temperature. (If you only have one canister, fill a cup with

water and allow it to get to room temperature before pouring it in the canister.)

2. Go to the area where you want to set the canister down to time the reaction. As soon as you place the tablet in the canister, have your helper begin timing.

3. Drop a whole antacid tablet in the canister. (Your helper should start timing now.)

4. Quickly, snap on the top and set the canister down with the top on the bottom.

5. When the reaction occurs and the canister flies into the air, make a note of the time.

6. Place the second tablet on a piece of paper. Use a hard object, such as a book, to break the tablet into chunks. Carefully, drop the chunks into the second canister. Start timing! Firmly, place the top on the canister, flip it so the top is on the bottom and note the reaction time. Repeat this step with a crushed tablet. You will need to fold the paper and pour the crushed antacid into the container.

7. Repeat each of the trials. If one reaction time is far off from the same tablet size, you may want to repeat the trial a third time until you can get repeatable results.

Summary of Results Look at the reaction times for each of the three tablets with different surface areas. How does the amount of surface area relate to the reaction time?

Was your hypothesis correct? Write a summary of your results, including how this experiment relates to nanostructures and substances.

Change the Variables Here are some ways you can vary this experiment:

- Change the temperature of the water.
- Change the amount of water.
- Use a different substance to measure the rate of reaction, such as sugar and dissolving rates.

How to Experiment Safely

Step back quickly when you put the top on the canister so that it does not hit you. This experiment can be messy. If possible, work outside or in an area that is easy to clean.

Step 6: Place the second tablet on a piece of paper. Use a book to break the tablet into chunks. ILLUSTRATION BY TEMAH NELSON.

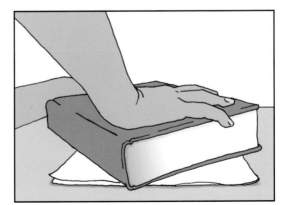

Troubleshooter's Guide

Below is a problem that you may have during this experiment and a way to remedy the problem.

Problem: The times for the two trials that were the same surface area were not at all close.

Possible cause: You may have used different water temperatures. Warmer water can speed up a reaction. Try setting aside a large container of water. Wait for the water to come to room temperature and then use this water for all your trials.

Design Your Own Experiment

How to Select a Topic Relating to this Concept Nanotechnology is a wide and growing field that may be incorporated in materials and technologies you use. Most likely, it could be in a car you use, sunscreen, or even clothes you wear. You may want to look up products that were developed with nanotechnology and see if the products are familiar or readily available.

Check the Further Readings section and talk with your science teacher to start gathering information on questions that interest you about nanotechnology.

Steps in the Scientific Method To do an original experiment, you need to plan carefully and think things through. Otherwise, you might not be sure what questions you're answering, what you are or should be measuring, or what your findings prove or disprove.

Here are the steps in designing an experiment:

- State the purpose of—and the underlying question behind—the experiment you propose to do.
- Recognize the variables involved, and select one that will help you answer the question at hand.
- State a testable hypothesis, an educated guess about the answer to your question.
- Decide how to change the variable you selected.
- Decide how to measure your results.

Recording Data and Summarizing the Results Think of how you can share your results with others. Charts, graphs, and diagrams of the progress and results of the experiments are very helpful in informing others about an experiment.

Related Projects To experiment in nanotechnology, you can find products that are made using nanotechnology and compare those products to others. Some papers and clothing have a nanotech surface. Aside from surface area to ratio, you can experiment with other properties that make nanosize materials different than their larger counterparts.

There are also many research projects you can do in nanotechnology. You can conduct a project on the major breakthroughs in the field or focus on one breakthrough, such as microscopes. You can also investigate the development and consequences of nanotechnology products in a certain field, such as medicine or sports equipment. Ethical issues and questions in the field of nanotechnology is another area of research.

For More Information

Darling, David. *Beyond 2000: Micromachines and Nanotechnology.* Parsippany, NJ: Dillon Press, 1995.

Johnson, Rebecca L. *Nanotechnology.* Minneapolis: Lerner Publications, 2006.

Lawrence Hall of Science, University of California, Berkeley. *Nanozone.* http://www.nanozone.org (accessed on May 17, 2008). Information, graphics, activities and videos on nanoscience.

Northwestern University. "History of Nano Timeline." *Discover Nano* http://www.discovernano.northwestern.edu/whatis/History/# (accessed on May 17, 2008). Interactive timeline traces the history of nanotechnology from pre-eighteenth century to modern day.

Science Museum in London. *Nanotechnology: small science, big deal.* http://www.sciencemuseum.org.uk/antenna/nano/index.asp (accessed on May 19, 2008). Information and an online game about nanotechnology from a science exhibit.

The University of Wisconsin. "What is a Nanotechnologist?" *Intro to Nanotechnology* http://mrsec.wisc.edu/Edetc/technologist/index.html (accessed on May 17, 2008). Profiles of professionals in nanotechnology that explains what they do.

58

Nutrition

The foods you eat affect whether you pay attention in class, how much energy you have for sports, and even whether you feel happy or sad. In fact, your meals and snacks affect how every cell in your body works. How do we know? Nutrition is the science of how the body uses nutrients to grow and function effectively. Nutrients are nourishing substances that the body needs. For example, the heart needs certain nutrients to help it pump blood. Our kidneys need nutrients to help rid our bodies of harmful wastes. Not surprisingly, deficiencies in certain nutrients can cause disease.

Real men eat fruit Hardly anyone gets scurvy anymore, but this disease was common a few centuries ago, especially among the first explorers and the crews on their ships. No one knew what caused scurvy. People with it felt weak. Their gums, noses, and mouths bled, and their muscles ached. When the ship of French explorer Jacques Cartier became icebound on the St. Lawrence River in Montreal in 1535, 25 men became ill and died. Cartier was visited by local Native Americans. He mentioned his feelings of weakness and the bleeding symptoms of his men. The Native Americans went into the woods, brought back pine needles and bark from a tree, and told Cartier to boil them in water. Cartier and his men drank the tea and recovered.

We now know the pine needles contained vitamin C, a substance also present in fruits and vegetables. Fruits and vegetables were rarely eaten on ships at that time. Storing them was a problem, and they were expensive to buy.

In 1747, James Lind, a Scottish doctor, knew that many British sailors were dying from scurvy, but he had read a report that fruits and vegetables helped prevent the disease. The sailors recovered quickly when Lind added citrus fruit juices to their diet, so Lind suggested this remedy to the British navy. Still, it took several decades before this remedy was taken seriously. Eventually, scurvy was all but eliminated.

JAMES LIND (1716-1794)

Dr. James Lind suggested eating citrus fruits to prevent scurvy. BETTMANN ARCHIVE.

Eating healthy foods helps people stay healthy. KELLY A. QUIN.

Eat right to stay healthy It was not until the early 1900s that scientists began to understand how nutrient deficiencies affect the body. The body cannot make all the substances it needs, but those missing substances are found in food. Before we realized this, however, these substances were often removed from food.

In the early 1900s, many foods were being processed. When rice processors removed the bran layers from whole rice to make white rice, they did not realize they were also removing a substance that was necessary for the body to function well. In regions where rice was the main food, a deficiency in this substance was causing a disease called beriberi. In 1911, Polish researcher Casimir Funk isolated this substance and discovered a type of chemical compound called an amine. He linked it with the Latin word *vita,* meaning "life," and the new term vitamin was created. The vitamin in bran was named thiamine, a B vitamin that helps the body obtain energy from carbohydrates.

As they learned more, scientists concluded that eating a variety of foods that are not processed, such as meats, fish, and fresh fruits and vegetables, helps our bodies stay healthy. And taking extra vitamins does not hurt either.

The necessary nutrients Besides vitamins, what are the other main substances your body needs to work well? One is carbohydrates, which give your body energy. They are present in starches, including potatoes, rice, bread, peas, and beans. They are also in milk and fruit, as well as in fiber from grains and vegetables. Your body uses carbohydrates to manufacture the zip you need to win a race or hit a home run.

Fats are necessary, too. Fats that come from olive oil, yogurt, nuts, and cheese help you grow and make your skin smooth. Fats also cushion body organs, keep your body warm, and help you absorb vitamins. Extra fats are stored under the skin and become another source of energy when needed.

Minerals, another kind of essential nutrient, help build bones and soft tissues. They act as regulators, keeping your blood pressure stable and your heart rate steady. They also keep your bones and teeth tough and help you digest your food. The six main minerals your body requires are calcium, magnesium, phosphorus, potassium, sodium, and sulfur. These minerals can be found in dairy products, fruit, vegetables, and meats. Other minerals, just as important but needed in smaller quantities, are known as trace elements. Some of the more important ones are iron, fluorine, iodine, and zinc.

Peas and beans are good sources of carbohydrates. GRANT HEILMAN.

Your body needs help making cells as you grow and replacing cells that become worn out. That's where proteins come in. Besides helping to build new cells, proteins trigger and speed up reactions within your body. Proteins also help form antibodies that ward off infections. Soybeans, beef, fish, beans, eggs, peas, and whole wheat are sources of protein.

You might not think that water would be an important nutrient, but it is. Nutrients can be carried to where they are needed only in watery solutions.

Good nutrition is essential for good health. Eating a variety of fresh, nonprocessed foods helps prevent diseases and sickness and gives you energy to work, think, and play. The projects that follow will help you analyze what you are actually eating on a day-to-day basis.

PROJECT 1

Energizing Foods: Which foods contain carbohydrates and fats?

Purpose/Hypothesis This project will help you analyze a typical meal to discover which foods provide the energy we need for our day-to-day activities. You will test for fats and for starches. Fats supply energy and are stored in the body for times when energy levels are low, such as when you exercise or miss a meal. The starches in carbohydrates also provide energy.

WORDS TO KNOW

Amine: An organic compound derived from ammonia.

Amino acid: One of a group of organic compounds that make up proteins.

Antibody: A protein produced by certain cells of the body as an immune (disease-fighting) response to a specific foreign antigen.

Antigen: A substance that causes the production of an antibody when injected directly into the body.

Beriberi: A disease caused by a deficiency of thiamine and characterized by nerve and gastrointestinal disorders.

Carbohydrate: A compound consisting of carbon, hydrogen, and oxygen found in plants and used as a food by humans and other animals.

Fat: A type of lipid, or chemical compound used as a source of energy, to provide insulation and to protect organs in an animal body.

Inorganic: Not containing carbon; not derived from a living organism.

Metabolism: The process by which living organisms convert food into energy and waste products.

Mineral: An inorganic substance found in nature with a definite chemical composition and struc-

ture. As a nutrient, it helps build bones and soft tissues and regulates body functions.

Nutrient: A substance needed by an organism in order for it to survive, grow, and develop.

Nutrition: The study of the food nutrients an organism needs in order to maintain well-being.

Organic: Containing carbon; also referring to materials that are derived from living organisms.

Protein: A complex chemical compound that consists of many amino acids attached to each other that are essential to the structure and functioning of all living cells.

Scurvy: A disease caused by a deficiency of vitamin C, which causes a weakening of connective tissue in bone and muscle.

Thiamine: A vitamin of the B complex that is essential to normal metabolism and nerve function.

Trace element: A chemical element present in minute quantities.

Translucent: Permits the passage of light.

Vitamin: A complex organic compound found naturally in plants and animals that the body needs in small amounts for normal growth and activity.

How to Experiment Safely

Be careful not to get the iodine in your eyes. Ask an adult to help you use the iodine.

Level of Difficulty Easy.

Materials Needed

- iodine with dropper
- brown paper bags cut into 10 or more 4-inch (10-centimeter) squares

- clear glass dinner plate
- a typical meal (For example, a lunch consisting of a turkey and Swiss cheese sandwich with tomato, lettuce, and mayonnaise; milk; potato chips. Or a dinner of hamburger, pasta salad, corn bread, milk, and cake with icing)

Approximate Budget $2 for iodine; other supplies from meals.

Timetable 1 hour; this project can be repeated after each meal to determine eating trends.

Step-by-Step Instructions

1. Create two 1 teaspoon-sized samples of each food, such as two samples of turkey, two of Swiss cheese, two of bread, and so on.
2. To test the foods for fat, rub a food sample on a square of brown paper. Remove the food sample, and allow the paper to dry.
3. Hold the paper up to the light and notice if it is translucent (if you can see light through it). Describe your observations on a data chart. Make a plus sign under a Fats heading for those foods that leave a translucent stain.

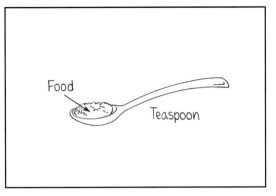

Step 1: Create two 1 teaspoon-sized samples of each food. GALE GROUP.

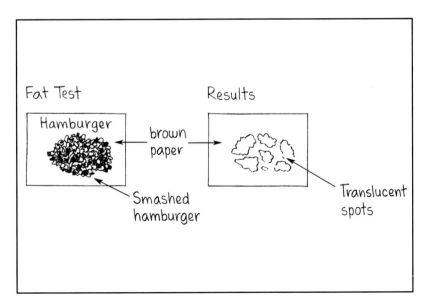

Steps 2 and 3: To test the foods for fat, rub a food sample on a square of brown paper. Remove the food sample, and allow the paper to dry. GALE GROUP.

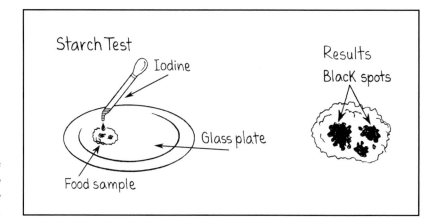

Steps 4 and 5: Test food samples for starch by dripping four to five drops of iodine onto the food. GALE GROUP.

Troubleshooter's Guide

Here is a problem that may arise during this project, a possible cause, and a way to remedy the problem.

Problem: Apples or pears do not stain black with iodine.

Possible cause: These fruits contain cellulose, which is plant starch. Iodine turns black with more soluble, digestible starches, such as wheat, rice, and beans.

4. To test for starch, place a food sample on the glass dinner plate. Drip four to five drops of iodine onto the food. Allow 15 minutes for the iodine to penetrate.

5. On your data chart, make a plus sign under a Starch heading for foods that turn black from the iodine.

6. Repeat Steps 2 through 5 for each kind of food. Place each sample in a different spot on the paper and on the plate.

Summary of Results Analyze your results. Figure out how many foods in your meal contain starch and/or fat. Consider what this says about the healthfulness of the meal and of your diet in general.

PROJECT 2

Nutrition: Which foods contain proteins and salts?

Purpose/Hypothesis This project will help you identify proteins and salts, nutrients needed for cell repair and daily maintenance. Proteins, present in every cell, are known as body builders. They help you grow and replace cells. Salts are minerals that your body uses to maintain water balance.

Level of Difficulty Moderate. This experiment requires the purchase of two chemicals and the supervision of an adult.

Materials Needed

- silver nitrate (a salt-indicator solution, which can be purchased from science supply catalogs)
- Biuret solution (a protein-indicator solution, also available from science supply catalogs)
- glass test tubes or glass cups
- test tube rack
- food from one meal
- water
- goggles
- rubber gloves

Approximate Budget $20 for the silver nitrate and Biuret solutions, depending on the quantity. The silver nitrate can be purchased as a crystal and dissolved in water.

Timetable 1 hour.

Step-by-Step Instructions

1. Create ¼-teaspoon-size samples of each type of food from your meal.
2. Set test tubes in rack.
3. For the protein test, put a food sample into a test tube and add 10 drops of Biuret solution.
4. Wait 10 minutes. If the blue Biuret solution turns lavender, the sample contains protein. Record the result on a data chart.
5. For the salt test, put a food sample into a test tube and fill tube halfway with water. Shake gently. Add 10–20 drops of silver nitrate solution.

How to Experiment Safely

Ask an adult to help you with this project. Wear goggles or other eye protection and protective gloves when handling silver nitrate. Be careful with the silver nitrate, as it stains the skin.

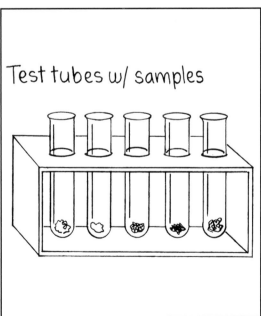

Step 3: Place a food sample into each test tube. GALE GROUP.

Troubleshooter's Guide

Here is a problem that may arise during this experiment, a possible cause, and a way to remedy the problem.

Problem: None of my foods tested positive for salt.

Possible cause: Insignificant amounts of salt may be present. Make a test tube sample of salt and water. Add silver nitrate to see if the solution turns white. If not, the silver nitrate may be contaminated.

6. Watch to see if the clear silver nitrate forms a milky white precipitation in the water. If so, salt is present. Record your results.
7. Repeat Steps 3 through 6 for each food sample, recording all your results on the data sheet.

Summary of Results After testing a typical meal, analyze your results. How many samples contained protein or salt? Do you see any pattern? Write a paragraph summarizing your findings.

PROJECT 3
Daily Nutrition: How nutritious is my diet?

Purpose/Hypothesis This project will help you determine if you are taking in the recommended nutrients and calories. A calorie is a unit of energy. The amount of energy and nutrients your body needs depends upon many factors, such as your age and if you are male or female. It also depends upon how much energy you "burn" every day through sports or simply moving around.

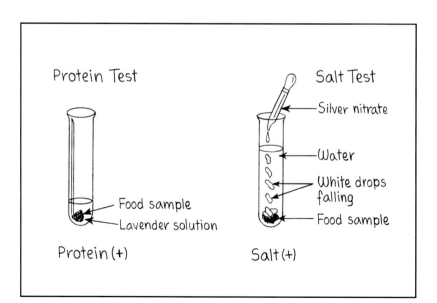

Steps 3 to 6: Testing food samples for either protein or salt content. GALE GROUP.

Although everyone is different, there are general guidelines for the amount of nutrients and total energy that people require. In this project, you can find out if you are taking in a healthy amount of energy and nutrients by determining your intake.

The Nutrition Facts Label on food packages provides the calories and amounts of nutrients in each serving of food. The labels state the amount of nutrients both as a number and percentage of the Daily Value. The government chose an average daily value: 2,000 calories a day. If the percent Daily Value of carbohydrates lists 10%, that means the food gives 10% of the carbohydrates generally needed for the day. The percent Daily Values are calculated based on fat as 30% of total calories and carbohydrates as 60% of calories (protein is the other 10%). Some youths (and adults) will need more than that, and some will need less.

In this project, you will measure the amount of energy, fats, and carbohydrates you consume. For some foods, you may have to estimate the amount you eat and nutrient information. If you eat lasagna, for example, you will need to look up the nutritional information for each serving for each ingredient and then add them together. You will also have to determine if you had one or more servings, as it is listed on the Nutrition Facts Label.

By measuring the nutrition information over the course of three to five days, you can calculate the average to find out your typical nutrient intake.

Level of Difficulty Moderate to Difficult, because of the time and precision involved.

Materials Needed

- paper and pencil
- Nutrition Facts Labels from foods eaten throughout days of project
- measuring cup and spoons
- Internet access (optional)
- calculator (optional)

Approximate Budget $0.

Timetable Approximately 30 minutes per day for three to five days.

Food	Servings	Fat	Carbohydrates	Calories
TOTAL DAY 1:				

Step 2: Make a chart listing the food items and its major nutrients. ILLUSTRATION BY TEMAH NELSON.

Step 3: Make sure you write down information from all the foods you are eating. ILLUSTRATION BY TEMAH NELSON.

Step-by-Step Instructions

1. If you have access to the Internet, visit the MyPyramid site listed below and write down how many calories and nutrients you should be consuming every day. If you do not have Internet access, you can ask a health professional or use the average of 2,000 calories.

2. Make a chart listing the food items and its major nutrients. See the illustration for an example.

3. For each food you eat, write in your chart the calories, fats, and carbohydrates listed on the Nutrition Facts Label. Make sure you look at the serving size and judge whether you are eating one serving. For many foods, such as breakfast cereals, it is easy to eat more than one serving size. You can use measuring cups to figure out how much is in your bowl or on your plate. If you eat two serving sizes, you will need to double the amount of calories and nutrients listed on the label. Also, make sure you write down information from all the foods you are eating, such as the milk and any fruit or sugar on your cereal. For fast food items, restaurants often provide nutritional information (you may have to ask).

4. At the end of the day, look at your chart and think about any foods you may have forgotten to list. If you did forget anything, such as snacks, add them to your chart.

5. Continue to measure your nutrient intake for three to five days.

6. When you have finished, add up the total calories and nutrients for each day. Calculate the average of the fats, carbohydrates, and calories. You can do this by adding up each item and dividing by the number of days. For example, if you ate 12,000 calories over five days, divide the calories by five. That means you

consumed about 2,400 calories a day on average.

7. Compare the calories and nutrients you ate on average to your recommended intake.

Summary of Results How does your recommended intake compare to what you actually consumed? Are they close? Look at your chart and see if you are eating a healthful variety of food groups. Are there are a lot of high sugar and fat food? Are you eating more or less than the five or more servings of fruits and vegetables recommended each day? You can also continue this project by measuring your consumption of proteins, specific vitamins, and minerals throughout the day.

Design Your Own Experiment

How to Select a Topic Relating to this Concept Diet is such a vital part of a healthy lifestyle that studying your eating habits is important. You might decide to research the major nutrients and learn more about how they can help improve your health.

Check the Further Readings section and talk with your science teacher or school or community media specialist to gather information on nutrition questions that interest you. As you consider possible experiments, be sure to discuss them with a knowledgeable adult before trying them.

Steps in the Scientific Method To do an original experiment, you need to plan carefully and think things through. Otherwise, you might not be sure what question you are answering, what your are or should be measuring, or what your findings prove or disprove.

Here are the steps in designing an experiment:

- State the purpose of—and the underlying question behind—the experiment you propose to do.
- Recognize the variables involved, and select one that will help you answer the question at hand.
- State a testable hypothesis, an educated guess about the answer to your question.

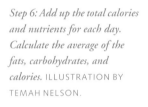

Step 6: Add up the total calories and nutrients for each day. Calculate the average of the fats, carbohydrates, and calories. ILLUSTRATION BY TEMAH NELSON.

Troubleshooter's Guide

Here is a problem that may arise during this project, a possible cause, and a way to remedy the problem.

Problem: It looks like I am not getting enough calories even though I am never hungry.

Possible cause: You may have forgotten to list several foods. It is extremely hard to remember every food we eat in a day. Try taking your chart with you as you go about your daily activities, and jotting down the food item as soon as you eat it. You can calculate the nutritional information at a later time, but that will help you remember to include it.

Problem: It looks like I am not getting enough nutrients even though I am never hungry.

Possible cause: You may have forgotten to list several foods (see above) or you may actually not be consuming enough nutrients. If most of the foods you are eating are highly processed and contain a lot of fats and oils, these foods may be low in nutrients.

- Decide how to change the variable you selected.
- Decide how to measure your results.

Recording Data and Summarizing the Results It's always important to write down data and ideas you gather during an experiment. Keep a journal or record book for this purpose. If you keep notes and draw conclusions from your experiments and projects, other scientists could use your findings in their own research.

Related Projects Nutrition-related projects or experiments can go in many different directions. For example, you might identify the types and quantity of nutrients you eat daily. You might decide to start regulating your intake of the less-healthful foods. As a start, all you need to do is read the nutritional facts found on all food packages.

For More Information

Eating for Health. Vol. 3. Chicago: World Book Inc., 1993. Part of the "Growing Up" series, this volume provides thorough, interesting information about carbohydrates, vitamins, and minerals as well as metabolism, eating disorders, and processing.

Food Standards Agency. "Vitamins and Minerals." *eatwell*. http://www.eatwell.gov.uk/healthydiet/nutritionessentials/vitaminsandminerals/ (accessed on February 19, 2008). Information about vitamins, minerals, and where they are found.

Kids Health. *Food and Nutrition*. http://www.kidshealth.org/kid/nutrition/index.html#All_About_Food (accessed on February 19, 2008). Series of easy-to-read articles on food and nutrients.

Levchuck, Caroline, and Michele Drohan. *Healthy Living*. Detroit: UXL, 2000. Contains chapters on nutrition, eating disorders, and other health issues.

United States Department of Agriculture. *MyPyramid Plan*. http://www.mypyramid.gov/mypyramid/index.aspx (accessed on February 19, 2008). Customized food guide.

United States Department of Agriculture. *MyPyramid for Kids*. http://www.fns.usda.gov/TN/kids-pyramid.html (accessed on February 19, 2008). Nutritional information, a food tracking worksheet, and games.

59

Oceans

If you were to look down at Earth from space you would see a planet that was covered in blue. That is because oceans cover almost three-quarters of the Earth's surface and contain about 97% of the planet's water supply. Life on Earth began in the ocean almost three-and-a-half billion years ago and life could not exist without a healthy ocean environment. Today, the oceans are home to an incredible variety of creatures, from the largest animal that ever lived, the blue whale, to microscopic organisms that can live in boiling waters.

People depend on the oceans in many ways. Oceans have an important effect on weather patterns. They are essential for transportation, for both economic and military purposes. Many people throughout the world rely on the ocean for food and their livelihood. People also use the oil and minerals that come from beneath the ocean floor.

The first voyage planned specifically to study the oceans was a British expedition that set out in 1872. In the twentieth century, interest in the oceans grew enormously. A new field evolved for oceanographers or people who study the ocean. Technological development allowed oceanographers to travel further and longer into the ocean depths. The discovery of previously unknown species and minerals in the ocean sparked further excitement and, today, the ocean is considered the last unexplored frontier.

A handful of seawater Earth's oceans are all connected to one another. Until the year 2000, there were four recognized oceans: the Pacific, Atlantic, Indian, and Arctic. In 2000 the International Hydrographic Organization, the organization responsible for setting the oceans' boundaries, recognized a new ocean, the Southern Ocean, encircling Antarctica.

The main chemicals in ocean water are sodium and chlorine combined as sodium chloride, better known as ordinary table salt. Ocean waters also contain smaller amounts of many other chemicals. Salt, along with the other substances, flows into oceans from smaller bodies of water.

Concentrations of seawater minerals

S A L T	Chlorine	55.04%
	Sodium	30.61%
	Sulfate	7.69%
	Magnesium	3.69%
	Calcium	1.16%
	Potassium	1.1%
	Remaining elements (these include manganese, lead, gold, silver, iron, and zinc)	.71%

The main chemicals in ocean water are sodium and chlorine combined as sodium chloride, better known as ordinary table salt. GALE GROUP.

Salt is a mineral that is found in soil and rocks. As river water flows, it picks up small amounts of salts from the rocks and soil. The rivers carry it into the ocean where it remains.

The salinity, or salt content, of ocean water varies across the oceans. Oceanographers report salinity in parts per thousand. On average, ocean salinity is thirty-five parts per thousand. That means there are 35 pounds of salt for every 1,000 pounds of water, or 3.5% salt.

Changing properties On average, the ocean extends about 2.3 miles (3.7 kilometers) downwards from the surface. Seawater has different properties depending on its depth, from the surface to the ocean floor. As the water deepens, its pressure increases. The water near the ocean's surface has very little water pressing down on it and so the water pressure is low. On the bottom of the ocean, the weight of all the water above presses down and the water pressure is high. At the deepest point in the ocean, the pressure is more than 8 tons per square inch (1.1 metric tons per square centimeter)—equal to one person trying to support 50 jumbo jets.

Sunlight gives the surface water warmth. On average, sunlight extends down to a depth of about 650 feet (250 meters). Water near the ocean floor gets no sunlight and is cold and dark. Both temperature and salinity affect the density of the water. Density is how much mass a certain volume of water contains. Molecules in warm water have more energy to move about. They spread farther apart, which results in less mass in a certain volume and therefore less density. Molecules in cold water have less energy and stay close together, resulting in a more mass in a certain volume and greater density. Water that is heavier or denser than the water around it sinks, while water that is less dense rises.

Differences in density cause seawater to form layers in a process called stratification. A liquid will float on a liquid less dense than itself, such as oil on water. The layers formed in ocean waters can be incredibly stable and last for thousands of years.

Rising and falling Currents are large streams of water flowing through the ocean. Currents occur in all bodies of salt water and can be caused by wind, salinity, heat content, the characteristics of the ocean's bottom, and Earth's rotation. Currents in the top layer of the ocean are called surface currents and these are mainly caused by steady winds. Surface currents flow clockwise north of the equator and counterclockwise (in the opposite direction) south of the equator. The Gulf Stream runs along the east coast of the United States and is one of the strongest and warmest currents known. In some places it may travel more than 60 miles (96.6 kilometers) in a day. The currents carry the Sun's heat from warmer regions to cooler areas, bringing mild weather to places that would otherwise be much cooler.

Currents also flow up and down within the water. These currents occur due to changes in seawater temperature and density and are called convection currents or density-driven currents. When warm surface water loses some of its heat to the air, the surface water becomes cooler and denser and starts to sink. This forces some of the water at lower levels to rise to form an up-and-down current. Deep ocean currents are important to marine life. Water at the ocean surface takes in oxygen from the air. Convection currents carry the oxygen down to the animals and plants that live in the bottom ocean regions. Minerals along the bottom of the floor are carried up to the sunlight layer, where animals use them. This process of lower-level, nutrient-rich waters rising upward to the ocean's surface is called upwelling.

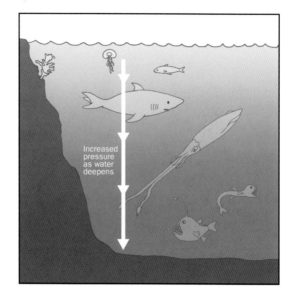

Seawater has different properties depending on its depth from the surface to the ocean floor. As the water deepens, its pressure increases. GALE GROUP.

The waters in the ocean are constantly in motion. When wind blows over the ocean's surface, it tries to pick up some of the water and creates waves. Waves are movements of water that rise and fall. The size of the wave depends on the wind's power. Gentle breezes form tiny ripples along the surface; strong winds can create large waves. Even though it looks like waves push the water forward, the water actually moves very little. When a wave arrives it lifts the water particles up and forward. As the wave passes, each particle falls and flows backwards underwater to return to its starting point. That is why a bottle, or anything else, floating in the ocean will remain in roughly the same place as the waves pass.

The highest point the waves reach is called the crest. The lowest point is called the trough. The distance from one crest to the next is the wavelength.

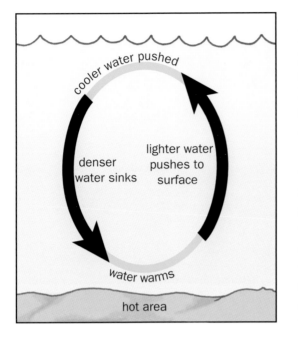

Convection currents are caused when waters of different temperatures and densities meet. GALE GROUP.

Tides are periodic rises and falls of large bodies of water. English mathematician and physicist Isaac Newton (1642–1727) was the first person to explain tides scientifically with his understanding of gravity. Gravity is a force of attraction between any two masses, such as the Sun and Earth.

Tides are caused primarily by the gravitational pull of the Moon on Earth, and by the rotation of Earth. The tug of gravity from the Sun also affects the tides, but it has about half of the Moon's force. The gravitational attraction causes the oceans to bulge out in the direction of the Moon. Another bulge occurs on the opposite side of the Earth due to the water being thrown outward by the planet's spin. These are high tides. The areas between the tidal bulges experience low tide. (For a more detailed explanation of tides see the Rotation and Orbits chapter.)

Sea life The oceans are filled with all types of amazing and bizarre-looking creatures. Although the Sun's light only reaches a small layer of the seawater, the majority of animals and plants live in the top sunlight regions. Microscopic organisms called plankton are the main food supply in the ocean. They live at or near the surface of the water and many produce oxygen, much of which escapes into the air for humans to breathe.

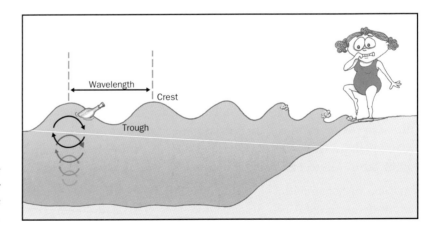

Even though it may appear as though waves move the water forward, water moves in a circular motion. GALE GROUP.

Tidal bulge
caused by the
gravitational pull
of the moon and
the sun

Tidal bulge
resulting from the force
of Earth's rotation

Tides are caused primarily by the gravitational pull of the Moon on Earth, and by the rotation of Earth. GALE GROUP.

In the lower ocean regions, deep-sea creatures have developed unique adaptations to survive in the dim, high-pressure, cold waters. Many deep-water fish are bioluminescent or they make their own light. The anglerfish uses a lighted "lure" on the top of its head to attract prey. The flashlight fish carries bioluminescent bacteria in pouches under its eyes that it can flash on and off at will to capture prey or find a mate. A shrimp heaves bioluminescent vomit onto an attacking fish, perhaps to blind the attacker and allow the shrimp to escape.

Other deep-sea fish have expandable stomachs that can hold a fish much larger than themselves—a useful talent with the lack of food on the ocean floor. Fanglike teeth, hinged skulls, and large mouths are all traits that help these fish catch food. Some creatures attach themselves to the ocean floor, such as giant tube worms that can grow more than 10 feet (3 meters) long. In the 1970s, researchers discovered these worms, along with bacteria and giant clams, living in bubbling hot water with temperatures up to 650°F (350°C) spurting out from beneath the ocean floor.

A giant squid netted from the waters near Melbourne, Australia, in February 2001. Measuring 12 feet (4 meters) long, it is estimated its feeding tentacles would likely bring the size to 36 feet (12 meters). AP/WIDE WORLD

EXPERIMENT 1

Stratification: How does the salinity in ocean water cause it to form layers?

Purpose/Hypothesis Layers of seawater with different densities can lead to stratification that can last for centuries. Anyone who has gone into

WORDS TO KNOW

Bioluminescence: The chemical phenomenon in which an organism can produce its own light.

Control experiment: A setup that is identical to the experiment, but is not affected by the variable that acts on the experimental group.

Convection current: Also called density-driven current, a cycle of warm water rising and cooler water sinking.

Crest: The highest point of a wave.

Currents: The horizontal and vertical circulation of ocean waters.

Density: The mass of a substance compared to its volume.

Gravity: Force of attraction between objects, the strength of which depends on the mass of each object and the distance between them.

Hypothesis: An idea in the form of a statement that can be tested by observation and/or experiment.

Oceanographer: A person who studies the chemistry of the oceans, as well as their currents, marine life, and the ocean floor.

Salinity: A measure of the amount of dissolved salt in seawater.

Stratification: Layers according to density; applies to fluids.

Tides: The cyclic rise and fall of seawater.

Trough: The lowest point of a wave. (Pronounced trawf.)

Upwelling: The process by which lower-level, nutrient-rich waters rise upward to the ocean's surface.

Variable: Something that can affect the results of an experiment.

Wave: The rise and fall of the ocean water.

Wavelength: The distance between one peak of a wave and the next corresponding peak.

---

the ocean and felt distinct layers of cold meeting the warm water has experienced the effect of stratification. Temperature and salinity are the two key factors determining density and, thus, ocean stratification. High salinity makes the water denser than low salinity, and cold water is denser than warm water. The denser the water relative to the water around it, the lower that water sinks.

In this experiment you will examine how salinity affects stratification. You will make two saltwater solutions of different salinity concentrations: a 40 percent salinity solution and a 20% salinity solution. To visually observe the different densities, you will dye the water blue and place an object in the saltwater that is denser than fresh water—a small potato. You will then carefully place fresh water above the salt water and observe what happens.

Before you begin, make an educated guess about the outcome of this experiment based on your knowledge of density and stratification. This educated guess, or prediction, is your hypothesis. A hypothesis should explain these things:

- the topic of the experiment
- the variable you will change
- the variable you will measure
- what you expect to happen

A hypothesis should be brief, specific, and measurable. It must be something you can test through further investigation. Your experiment will prove or disprove whether your hypothesis is correct. Here is one possible hypothesis for this experiment: "Water that is higher in salinity is denser than water of lower salinity; the greater the difference between the densities, the more defined the stratification."

In this case, the variable you will change is the percentage of salt in the water. The variable you will measure is the density of the water.

Conducting a control experiment will help you isolate each variable and measure the changes in the dependent variable. Only one variable will change between the control experiment and your experiment. For your control in this experiment you will use a jar of fresh water. At the end of the experiment you can compare the control and the experimental results.

Note: When making a solid/liquid solution, it is standard to use weight/weight (grams/grams) or weight/volume (grams/milliliters). With water, 1 gram of water equals 1 milliliter. In this experiment, teaspoons and tablespoons are used to measure the solid.

Level of Difficulty Easy to Moderate.

Materials Needed

- water
- 3 glass jars (mayonnaise jars work well)

What Are the Variables?

Variables are anything that might affect the results of an experiment. Here are the main variables in this experiment:

- the temperature of the water
- the type of salt
- the quantity of salt
- the item placed in the water

In other words, the variables in this experiment are everything that might affect the stratification of the water. If you change more than one variable at the same time, you will not be able to tell which variable had the most effect on stratification.

The tide is low along this Washington State beach.
PHOTOGRAPH BY CINDY CLENDENON.

How to Experiment Safely

Have an adult present when handling hot water.

- container to hold water
- salt
- 3 small red potatoes
- measuring cup
- measuring spoons
- baster
- blue or red food coloring
- marking pen
- masking tape

Approximate Budget $5.

Timetable 15 minutes for the initial setup; about two hours waiting time.

Step-by-Step Instructions

1. Use the masking tape to label each glass jar: "Control," "40% salinity," and "20% salinity."
2. Pour 3 cups (700 milliliters) of hot water in each jar.
3. In the jar labeled "40% salinity," add 8 tablespoons of salt. Stir vigorously.
4. In the jar labeled "20% salinity," add 4 tablespoons of salt. Stir vigorously.
5. Add several drops of food coloring to the solution in each jar and stir.
6. Using one of the measuring spoons, carefully place a potato in each jar.
7. Allow the water to cool to room temperature. The jars should be about half full. If necessary, pour out some of the water at this point.
8. Fill up a container with plain water. Use the baster to carefully add this water to each jar until the jar is almost full. Dribble the water along the inside of the jar so that it does not mix up the solution.
9. Set the jars aside for 15 minutes and observe.

Step 8: Dribble the water along the inside of the jar so that it does not mix up the solution.
GALE GROUP.

40% salt

Summary of Results Write down or draw the results of the experiment. Was your hypothesis correct? Was there a difference in the stratification between the higher salinity water and the water of lower salinity? How does each compare to the control experiment? What does this tell you about the seawater where stratification occurs that lasts for hundreds or thousands of years? Name some reasons why stratification might occur for a short period of time. In the ocean both salinity and temperature affect density. As you write up your conclusions, hypothesize how changing the temperature of the salt water would affect the results.

Change the Variables In this experiment you can change the variables in several ways. You can alter the temperature of the water, mimicking the ocean conditions by using water of the same salinity and making the bottom layer cold and the top layer warm. You could make the salt water on the bottom warm and the fresh water cold. You can also use objects of differing densities to observe the relative density of the water.

Modify the Experiment Bodies of water have varying levels of salinity. You can modify this experiment by measuring how different salinity levels affect ocean density. Collect several small, light objects, such as the potato you used, a rubber band, button, tiny pebble, plastic bottle cap, small paperclip, or toothpick. If possible, collect two of each object. Fill three jars with warm water. In one jar, make a supersaturated solution of salt water. Stir in salt by the spoonful until the salt no longer dissolves in the water.

Drop the items you have collected into the jar of plain water and stir. Wait a few moments and then collect only the items that sank to the bottom. If you have two of each item, leave them in the water jar. Now drop these items into the jar of salt water. Collect only the items that float.

Use your third jar to measure how varying salinity levels affects density and items in the sea. Rinse off the items that sank in fresh water and floated in the supersaturated salt water. You should have at least two different objects. (You may need to test several more small items around

Troubleshooter's Guide

Below is a problem that may arise during this experiment, some possible causes, and some ways to remedy the problem.

Problem: The water does not stratify and the potato sinks.

Possible cause: Your tap water could have minerals in it, which would make it less dense. Try conducting the experiment again with purified water.

Possible cause: You may not have thoroughly mixed the salt into the water. Try the experiment again, making sure to mix until the water is clear.

What Are the Variables?

Variables are anything that might affect the results of an experiment. Here are the main variables in this experiment:

- the temperature of the water
- the water contents
- the quantity of hot or cold water placed in each jar
- the quantity of the base water

In other words, the variables in this experiment are everything that might affect the movement of the water. If you change more than one variable at the same time, you will not be able to tell which variable had the most effect on water's density.

the house until you find ones that sink in water and float in the supersaturated salt water.) Place the items in the third jar and wait for them to sink. Mix into the water one tablespoon of salt at a time, stirring well after each addition. At what point does the salt water become denser than the items? Make a chart of the different objects and amount of salt you added until each item floats. If you know the amount of water, you can determine the percentage of salt. Is it more or less than the ocean?

EXPERIMENT 2
Currents: Water behavior in density-driven currents

Purpose/Hypothesis One way that seawater moves vertically is when a mass of water changes densities. These convection or density-driven currents occur at a slower rate than surface currents. Density-driven currents occur when water becomes less dense and begins to rise, or water becomes more dense and begins to sink. Either way, the moving water pushes the water below or above it to take its place.

Density in ocean water is caused by both its salinity and temperature. This experiment focuses on how temperature differences help form density-driven currents. You will add liquids of different temperatures to various temperatures of water, and observe the behavior of the water. Dyes will allow you to observe the different temperature waters.

Before you begin, make an educated guess about the outcome of this experiment based on your knowledge of density-driven currents. This educated guess, or prediction, is your hypothesis. A hypothesis should explain these things:

- the topic of the experiment
- the variable you will change
- the variable you will measure
- what you expect to happen

A hypothesis should be brief, specific, and measurable. It must be something you can test through further investigation. Your experiment will prove or disprove whether your hypothesis is correct. Here is one possible hypothesis for this experiment: "Colder water is denser than warmer water and will sink, while the relatively warmer water will rise."

In this case, the variable you will change is the temperature of the water. The variable you will measure is the movement of the water.

Conducting a control experiment will help you isolate each variable and measure the changes in the dependent variable. Only one variable will change between the control experiment and your experiment. For the control in this experiment, the temperature of the added liquid will be the same as the water already in the control jar.

How to Experiment Safely

Have an adult present when handling hot water. Either throw away the medicine or eyedropper or ask an adult to help you rinse out and sterilize the dropper before putting it away.

Level of Difficulty Easy.

Materials Needed

- water
- 3 glass jars
- red and blue food coloring
- 2 cups for mixing
- 3 pieces of white paper or cardstock
- tea strainer or tongs
- eyedropper or medicine dropper
- ice-cube tray or small plastic cup

Approximate Budget $4.

Timetable 15 minutes for the experiment; about one hour waiting time.

Step-by-Step Instructions

1. Use the masking tape to label each jar: "Control," "Hot," and "Cold."
2. Add several drops of blue dye to enough water to make two small, blue, ice cubes. Freeze.
3. When the blue water has frozen into ice, fill the "Cold" jar about two-thirds full with ice-cold water.
4. Fill the "Hot" jar about two-thirds full with hot water. Cover the jar to prevent the heat from escaping.
5. Fill the "Control" jar with room-temperature water.

Step 9: Use the tea strainer or tongs to hold one of the blue ice cubes and gently place it in the middle of the hot water in the "Hot" jar. GALE GROUP.

6. Fold the three pieces of paper or card-stock in half and place one in back of each jar. This will help you observe the experiment.

7. Let the water sit until completely still, about a minute.

8. While the water is sitting, add a small amount of red dye to about a quarter of a cup of hot water in a separate mixing cup.

9. Use the tea strainer or tongs to hold one of the blue ice cubes and gently place it in the middle of the "Hot" jar.

10. Use the eyedropper to release a small amount of the red-colored hot water in the middle of the cold water in the "Cold" jar.

11. Note the results.

12. In the "Control" jar, which has room-temperature water, gently place the second blue ice cube on the top of the water. Next, use the dropper to place a small amount of the hot, red-colored water deep in the water. Record the results.

13. For the control experiment, empty either the "Cold" jar or the "Hot" jar and refill with room-temperature water (allow the empty jar to return to room temperature before refilling). Use the dropper to place a small amount of room-temperature blue dye and room-temperature red dye in the water (rinse the dropper after placing the first color). Record the results.

Summary of Results Examine the results of your experiment and draw the movement of the water. Compare the results of the control to what you observed in the "Control" jar. How does what you observed relate to upwelling? In the ocean, both temperature and salinity affect the density of water; thus, both have an effect on density-driven currents. From what you have learned about seawater and density, write a paragraph on how adding salt to the dyed waters would affect the results.

Change the Variables To change the variables in this experiment you can alter the content of the water by adding salt or other substances found in the ocean. You can also alter where the dyed water is placed in the jars. If a larger container was used you can vary the temperature of part of the water by using a heat lamp or heating the water from underneath.

Design Your Own Experiment

How to Select a Topic Relating to this Concept The ocean is an immense subject with many possible projects that can branch from it. You could examine the properties of oceans and ocean life. You could also look at how oceans impact people's lives. With oceanographers using incredible technological tools in their work, the study of the oceans is another possible topic to explore.

Check the Further Readings section and talk with your science teacher to learn more about oceans. You can also gather ideas from following ocean explorers, who often show life footage or descriptions of their expeditions on the Internet. People who live near an ocean could consider taking a field trip to collect samples, look at sea life, or observe the ocean. If you do take a field trip, make sure to discuss your trip with an adult.

Troubleshooter's Guide

Below is a problem that may arise during this experiment, some possible causes, and some ways to remedy the problem.

Problem: The dyed water mixes into the jar's water so quickly it is difficult to observe its movements.

Possible cause: You may have dropped or placed too much of the cold and/or hot water in the jar. Try the experiment again, using a smaller blue ice cube and only one large drop of the red water.

Problem: The results from the room-temperature water jar were the same as that of the Cold jar or Hot jar.

Possible cause: The water in the jars may not have enough temperature variation between them. To make sure both the Control jar and the room-temperature jar have room-temperature water, allow lukewarm water to sit out for at least two to four hours. If you have a thermometer, it should be approximately 70–73° Fahrenheit (21–23° Celsius). Make sure the hot water is hot; 140–149° Fahrenheit (60–65° Celsius).

Steps in the Scientific Method To conduct an original experiment, you need to plan carefully and think things through. Otherwise, you might not be sure what question you are answering, what you are or should be measuring, or what your findings prove or disprove.

Here are the steps in designing an experiment:

- State the purpose of—and the underlying question behind—the experiment you propose to do.

- Recognize the variables involved and select one that will help you answer the question at hand.

- State your hypothesis, an educated guess about the answer to your question.
- Decide how to change the variable you selected.
- Decide how to measure your results.

Recording Data and Summarizing the Results Your data should include charts and drawings such as the one you did for these experiments. They should be clearly labeled and easy to read. You may also want to include photographs and drawings of your experimental setup and results, which will help other people visualize the steps in the experiment.

If you are preparing an exhibit, you may want to display your results, such as any experimental setup you designed. If you have completed a nonexperimental project, explain clearly what your research question was and illustrate your findings.

Related Projects Many of the findings about oceans are relatively recent and you can draw on this new information that oceanographers are discovering. The ocean is filled with life, from bacteria to fish to plants. You can explore the varied types of life and look at what lives in different parts of the ocean. Bioluminescence is one of the many adaptations that ocean creatures have developed. You can purchase bioluminescent organisms and observe their characteristics. Ocean plants differ from land plants in several ways. You can purchase an ocean plant and examine its characteristics. You could conduct a research project and study how the oceans support life suitable to that particular environment.

You could also examine the physical properties of oceans. Waves and tides are two basic properties of oceans. You can create a small body of water in your bathtub or large container to examine the movements of waves. Place an object on the wave to examine if waves carry an object. Tides are dependent on geographic location and time of year. You can gather data on the Internet or reference books to predict the high and low tides of oceans around the world. Researching how scientists take the salt out of the ocean is another possible project.

For More Information

Berger, Gilda, and Melvin Berger. *What Makes an Ocean Wave?* New York: Scholastic, 2001. Question-and-answer format about oceans and ocean life.

"Deep Ocean Creatures." *Extreme Science.* http://www.extremescience.com/ DeepestFish.htm (accessed on March 14, 2008.) Nice pictures and facts on deep ocean creatures.

Fleisher, Paul. *Our Oceans: Experiments and Activities in Marine Science.* Brookfield, CT: The Millbrook Press, 1995. Information on the physics and chemistry of the ocean with basic experiment ideas.

Oceana. http://www.oceana.org (accessed on March 14, 2008). The "Beneath the Surface" area has lots of ocean information, live pictures, and interactive maps.

"Ocean in Motion." *Office of Naval Research.* http://www.onr.navy.mil/focus/ ocean/motion/tides1.htm (accessed on March 14, 2008). Brief explanation and animation of the tides.

Pulley, Sayre, and April Pulley. *Ocean.* Brookfield, CT: The Millbrook Press, 1997. Description of the physical features, life, and use of the ocean.

"Sea Dwellers." *Secrets of the Ocean Realm.* http://www.pbs.org/oceanrealm/ seadwellers/index.html (accessed on March 14, 2008) Pictures of life in the ocean.

"Water on the Move: The Ebbs and Flows of the Sea." *Museum of Science.* http:// www.mos.org/oceans/motion/tides.html (accessed on March 13, 2008). From a museum ocean exhibit, includes real-time tide data.

Woods Hole Oceanographic Institute. *Dive and Discover: Expeditions to the Seafloor.* http://www.divediscover.whoi.edu (accessed on March 14, 2008). Follow ocean expeditions in this interactive web site.

60

Optics and Optical Illusions

D o you ever wonder how your eyes allow you to see? The science of light waves and how we see them is called optics. To understand optics, you must first understand a little about light itself.

What is light made of? Visible light is a series of electromagnetic waves. These waves make up a small part of the electromagnetic spectrum, which includes many kinds of energy waves. You may be familiar with some of these, such as radio waves, microwaves, and X rays. Visible light is made of waves that are about 0.000014 to 0.000027 inches (360 to 700 nanometers) long. A nanometer is one-billionth of a meter. In this range are all the colors we can see; each color has a slightly different wavelength.

Light does all kinds of interesting things. It can bounce off surfaces, particularly smooth surfaces. This is called reflection. It can also bend as it moves from one kind of material to another, such as from air to water. (That's why a pencil sticking out of a glass of water looks bent.) This is called refraction.

How do our eyes perceive light? The eye has a lens that focuses light onto a light-sensitive surface at the back of the eyeball, called the retina. The retina then sends nerve impulses to the brain, which the brain interprets as images.

The lens in your eye is made of membranes and fluid, while the artificial lenses used in telescopes and cameras are glass or plastic. A lens must be made of a transparent material so that it can transmit a beam of light, forming an image.

A prism separates the colors in sunlight so we can see them.
PHOTO RESEARCHERS INC.

What Are the Variables?

Variables are anything that might affect the results of an experiment. Here are the main variables in this experiment:

- the kind of lens being used
- the focal length of the lens
- the angle at which you hold the lens relative to the light source
- the distance from the object to lens

In other words, the variables in this experiment are everything that might affect the point at which the light focuses. If you change more than one variable, you will not be able to tell which variable had the most effect on the focal length.

The focal length of a lens indicates where the image will be focused and how powerful the lens is. GALE GROUP.

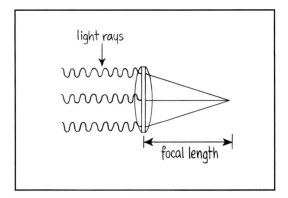

What questions do you have about light and how we see it? You will have an opportunity to explore optics in the experiments that follow.

EXPERIMENT 1

Optics: What is the focal length of a lens?

Purpose/Hypothesis In this experiment, you will identify the focal point of different lenses and measure their focal lengths. When light rays pass through a lens, they converge at a single point, the focal point of the lens. The distance from the middle of the lens to the focal point is called the focal length. Every lens has its own focal length.

The focal length of a lens indicates where the image will be focused and how powerful the lens is. In general, a lens has two rounded surfaces and its edges are fairly thin compared to its diameter. Focal length depends on the curvature of these surfaces. A convex lens has surfaces that curve outward, like a ball, while a concave lens has surfaces that curve inward, like the inside of a bowl.

Before you begin, make an educated guess about the outcome of this experiment based on your knowledge of optics. This educated guess, or prediction, is your hypothesis. A hypothesis should explain these things:

- the topic of the experiment
- the variable you will change
- the variable you will measure
- what you expect to happen

A hypothesis should be brief, specific, and measurable. It must be something you can test through observation. Your experiment will prove or disprove your hypothesis. Here is one possible hypothesis for this experiment: "The more convex the lens, the shorter the focal length."

WORDS TO KNOW

Concave: Hollowed or rounded inward, like the inside of a bowl.

Convex: Curved or rounded outward, like the outside of a ball.

Electromagnetic spectrum: The complete array of electromagnetic radiation, including radio waves (at the longest-wavelength end), microwaves, infrared radiation, visible light, ultraviolet radiation, X rays, and gamma rays (at the shortest-wavelength end).

Electromagnetic waves: Waves of energy that are part of the electromagnetic spectrum.

Focal length: The distance of a focus from the center of a lens or concave mirror.

Focal point: The point at which rays of light converge or from which they diverge.

Hypothesis: An idea in the form of a statement that can be tested by observation and/or experiment.

Lens: A piece of transparent material with two curved surfaces that bend rays of light passing through it.

Nanometer: A unit of length; this measurement is equal to one-billionth of a meter.

Optics: The study of the nature of light and its properties.

Prism: A piece of transparent material with a triangular cross-section. When light passes through it, it causes different colors to bend different amounts, thus separating them into a rainbow of colors.

Reflection: The bouncing of light rays in a regular pattern off the surface of an object.

Refraction: The bending of light rays as they pass at an angle from one transparent or clear medium into a second one of different density.

Retina: The light-sensitive part of the eyeball that receives images and transmits visual impulses through the optic nerve to the brain.

Variable: Something that can affect the results of an experiment.

In this case, the variable you will change will be the kind of lens, and the variable you will measure will be the focal length. You expect that lenses which are more convex will produce shorter focal lengths.

Level of Difficulty Moderate, because of the materials needed.

Materials Needed

- 3 or 4 different lenses, labeled for convexity and concavity (You might borrow them from school or buy them at a science museum shop.)
- ruler or tape measure
- large, white piece of paper or tagboard
- small lamp

How to Experiment Safely

Do not drop the lenses, and try not to touch the lens surfaces with your fingers. Hands naturally have a lot of oils on them, which will affect how the lenses work.

Troubleshooter's Guide

Experiments do not always work out as planned. Even so, figuring out what went wrong can definitely be a learning experience. Here are some problems that may arise during this experiment, some possible causes, and ways to remedy the problems.

Problem: You cannot see an image at all.

Possible cause: Your room is not dark enough or your object is not bright enough. Try darkening the room more or choosing a brighter light source.

Problem: The focal length measurements are all alike.

Possible causes:

1. Your lenses are too similar. Check the lens labels and make sure you have lenses with different characteristics. Someone at the store where you purchased them should be able to help.

2. You are not looking closely enough at the image to see where it is in focus. Sometimes the focus can be subtle. Look more closely at your cards.

Approximate Budget $20 to purchase lenses.

Timetable 2 hours.

Step-by-Step Instructions

1. Choose a room where you can dim the lights and set up the experiment. Place your lamp at least 3 feet (1 meter) away from your first lens.

2. In the dim light, hold the white card on the other side of the lens and look for the image of your object (the lamp). If you cannot see it, move the card closer to or farther from the lens until you can find it. Keep adjusting the distance of the card until your image is focused.

3. Set up a data chart, and describe what you see. How does the image look in comparison to the actual object? Write down any differences you observe.

4. Measure and record the distance between the lens and the card on which the focused image appears. Be sure to note which lens you were using.

5. Repeat the above steps with your other lenses. Record your findings on your chart.

Summary of Results Study the results on your chart. Which kind of lenses produced short focal lengths? Which produced longer ones? Was your hypothesis correct? Summarize what you have found.

Change the Variables You can vary this experiment in several ways. For example, try varying where you place the object on the other side of the lens. Measure and record what you find. You can also try placing two or more lenses next to each other and observe the effect on the image. Do the lenses add their effects together or do they cancel each other out? Does the image change size or direction? Record what you find.

EXPERIMENT 2

Optical Illusions: Can the eye be fooled?

Purpose/Hypothesis After the lenses in your eyes focus light, your brain must make sense of the images formed. This is not always easy. Optical illusions occur when the brain is tricked into thinking things are not as they are. These illusions use the way your brain processes optical information to fool you into seeing things that are not there.

Examining how people react to optical illusions will help you understand how the eyes and brain work. In this set of experiments, you will explore how people perceive images. For each of the images illustrated, write a hypothesis about what people will see. For example, for the second picture, you will ask ten people this question: "Which figure is larger?" How do you think people will answer?

Before you begin, make an educated guess about the outcome of this experiment based on your knowledge of how your brain perceives images. This educated guess, or prediction, is your hypothesis. A hypothesis should explain these things:

- the topic of the experiment
- the variable you will change
- the variable you will measure
- what you expect to happen

A hypothesis should be brief, specific, and measurable. It must be something you can test through observation. Your experiment will prove or disprove your hypothesis. Here is one possible hypothesis for the first image in this experiment:

What Are the Variables?

Variables are anything that might affect the results of an experiment. Here are the main variables in this experiment:

- the image you are testing
- the people you use as test subjects
- the different ways the image can be seen
- the lighting on the image
- what you tell the test subject about the image before he or she views

In other words, the variables in this experiment are everything that might affect how a person perceives the image. If you change more than one variable, you will not be able to tell which variable had the most effect on the test subject's perception.

Optical illusion #1.
GALE GROUP.

What do you see?

Which figure is larger?

Optical illusion #2. GALE GROUP.

Optical illusion #3. GALE GROUP.

Which inner circle is larger?

"Eight out of ten people will see non-parallel lines." Write a hypothesis for the other images.

In this case, the variable you will change will be the person viewing the image, and the variable you will measure will be how that person perceives the image. For the first image, you expect that most, but not all, of the people will perceive that the lines are not parallel.

Remember, the more people you test, the more accurate your results will be. After you complete these experiments, you will draw some conclusions about how the mind perceives visual images.

Level of Difficulty Difficult, because of the need to gather test subjects.

Materials Needed

- images provided throughout Experiment 2
- at least 10 people as test subjects
- paper and pencil
- a well-lighted room

Approximate Budget $0.

Timetable Depends on the subjects' availability.

Step-by-Step Instructions

1. Find at least 10 people who are willing to participate in your project. Explain the task to them.

2. Photocopy the images illustrated throughout Experiment 2, enlarging them if possible. Make sure the copies are clear.

3. Prepare a question for each of the images.

4. List the images on a data sheet, number them, and record the question you will ask for each one. Make a column where you

will write each subject's answer. Make a copy of the data sheet for each subject.

5. Conduct your interviews with one subject at a time. Carefully record their answers on a data sheet.

Summary of Results Study your findings carefully. Did people have similar reactions to the images, or were they varied? What conclusions, if any, can you draw about the way the eyes and the brain work together on perception? Were any or all of your hypotheses correct?

Change the Variables You can vary this experiment in several ways. For example, locate other optical illusions and test people's reactions. How does this add to what you learned about perception in the first set of experiments? Does it change your ideas, or confirm them? Or you can try testing a different set of people. Ask young children, older people, or another group. Do their responses change? Can you draw any conclusions about the way people perceive things as they get older?

Modify the Experiment You can make this experiment more difficult by testing what reasons could influence people seeing illusions. In order to do this, you will need to focus on only one of the images provided.

Think about some reasons why the brain may cause people to see an illusion, and then form a hypothesis. For example, familiarity of a picture may lead people to draw conclusions about an image that looks like the familiar image. A person may need more time to process certain images. If a test person were warned beforehand that there is something odd about an image, does the person still perceive the illusion? If the test person were given 60 seconds to study the image, instead of 10 seconds, what is the result? What if a contrasting color were placed behind the image?

After you come up with a series of possible factors that may influence the perception of a test person, write them down in a chart. Select

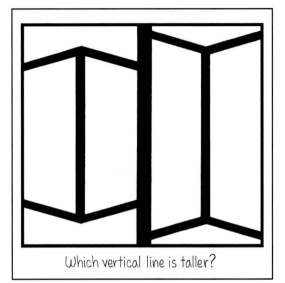

Which vertical line is taller?

Optical illusion #4. GALE GROUP.

Optical illusion #5. GALE GROUP.

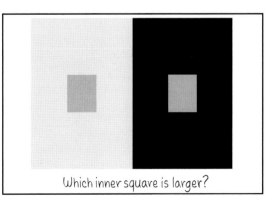

Which inner square is larger?

How to Experiment Safely

There are no hazards associated with this experiment.

Troubleshooter's Guide

Experiments using people can be difficult. Here are some problems that may arise during this experiment, some possible causes, and ways to remedy the problems.

Problem: Subjects look at images for a long time and say they can see it in many ways.

Possible cause: Explain clearly that you are trying to explore the way perception works and so you want their first reaction. Tell them not to spend too much time analyzing what they see.

Problem: It is difficult to draw conclusions from the many different answers subjects gave.

Possible cause: Everyone perceives things a little differently. Study how your subjects responded, think about what you see, and try to think of reasons why people may see things differently. Do you think it has to do with their eyes? Their brains? Their past experience? You may decide that you cannot draw any conclusions from the data you collected. That often happens in the field of science.

the one you hypothesize will play the largest role in perception and start testing people. You will need a lot of test subjects, because you will only be able to test one hypothesis for each group of ten people. For example, if you are testing how looking at an image for a longer amount of time will affect subjects' perception, you will need to show the image to ten subjects for a relatively long amount of time. Compare those results with the results from Experiment 1. Then, you will need another set of ten subjects to test out another hypothesis.

Design Your Own Experiment

How to Select a Topic Relating to this Concept If you are interested in optics, you could further investigate kinds of lenses. You could examine reflection and refraction with mirrors or prisms, which bend light and separate out the different wavelengths so you can see different colors. You could study the effects of polarizers, which line up different wavelengths of light, creating interesting effects, like the polarizing filters used on cameras.

If you are interested in optical instruments, you can build your own camera or investigate telescopes, microscopes, and magnifying lenses. You can explore illusions involving color, movement, and three-dimensional objects. Or you could explore the work of M.C. Escher, who drew pictures that confuse the mind.

Check the Further Readings section and talk with your science teacher or school or community media specialist to start gathering information on optics questions that interest you.

Steps in the Scientific Method To do an original experiment, you need to plan carefully and think things through. Otherwise you might not be sure what question you are answering, what you are or should be measuring, or what your findings prove or disprove.

Here are the steps in designing an experiment:

- State the purpose of—and the underlying question behind—the experiment you propose to do.
- Recognize the variables involved, and select one that will help you answer the question at hand.
- State a testable hypothesis, an educated guess about the answer to your question.
- Decide how to change the variable you selected.
- Decide how to measure your results.

Recording Data and Summarizing the Results
Your data should include charts, such as the ones you did in these experiments, that are clearly labeled and easy to read. You may also want to include photos, graphs, or drawings of your experimental set-up and results.

If you are preparing an exhibit for a science fair, display any optical instruments you built or copies of the illusions you worked with. If you have done a nonexperimental project, explain clearly what your research question was and illustrate your findings.

The lens in a camera focuses light from a subject you are photographing onto the camera film. U.S. GEOLOGICAL SURVEY.

Related Projects There are also other ways you can explore the topic of optics, such as building models of optical instruments or studying their history.

If you are interested in perception, you could explore the connections between perception and art and research artists who have studied how the mind perceives images. All of these ideas would lead to fascinating projects.

For More Information

Ardley, Neil. *Science Book of Light.* Burlington, MA: Harcourt Brace, 1991.
Simple experiments demonstrating principles of light.

Armstrong, Tim. *Make Moving Patterns: How to Make Optical Illusions of Your Own.* Jersey City, NJ: Parkwest Publications, 1993. Ideas for creating your own series of optical illusions.

Davidson, Michael W., and The Florida State University. *Science, Optics & You.* http://micro.magnet.fsu.edu/optics/index.html (accessed on January 14, 2008).

Levine, Shar, Leslie Johnstone, and Jason Coons. *The Optics Book: Fun Experiments with Light, Vision & Color.* New York: Sterling Publications, 1998. Informative book on light, vision, and optical instruments, with experiments, explanations, and drawings.

Seckel, Al. *Optical Illusions: The Science of Visual Perception.* Buffalo, NY: Firefly Books, 2006. Collection of optical illusions, with information on the science of visual perception.

61

Osmosis and Diffusion

G as and liquid molecules are always in motion. They move randomly in all directions and bounce around and into each other. As they move, molecules have a tendency to spread out, moving from areas with many molecules to areas with fewer molecules. This process of spreading out is called diffusion.

You have probably noticed diffusion in your home. If you opened a bottle of vanilla in your kitchen, for example, you probably could soon smell the vanilla in all parts of the room. The vanilla spread through the air from an area of high concentration of vanilla molecules to areas of less concentration. They diffused throughout the room—and perhaps throughout the house.

Osmosis (pronounced oz-MO-sis) is a kind of diffusion. Osmosis occurs when a substance diffuses across a semipermeable membrane from an area of high concentration to an area of low concentration. A semipermeable membrane lets some substances through but not others.

What are some examples of diffusion? Diffusion takes place constantly in our bodies and is vital to cell functioning. Cell walls are selectively permeable, meaning that certain substances can pass through them, but others cannot. Diffusion allows certain materials to move into and out of cell walls, from a higher concentration to a lower concentration.

For example, oxygen diffuses from the air sacs in your lungs into your blood capillaries because the concentration of oxygen is higher in the air sacs and lower in the capillary blood.

The smell of vanilla quickly diffuses in all directions. KELLY A. QUIN.

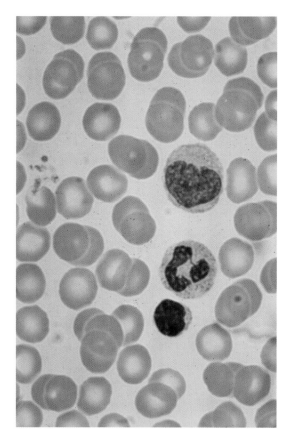

Oxygen enters blood cells by diffusing from areas of high concentration to areas of low concentration. PHOTO RESEARCHERS INC.

Different kinds of membranes allow differing amounts of diffusion to occur. Think about a helium balloon. It starts out full of helium and floats upwards, but over a period of a day or two it loses helium until it is no longer lighter than air and cannot float any more. Why does this happen? The balloon allows the helium atoms to pass through it into the atmosphere. Helium atoms slowly diffuse from an area of high concentration (inside the balloon) to an area of lesser concentration (the great outdoors).

How does osmosis work? When materials move into and out of a cell at equal rates, the cell is said to be balanced, or in dynamic equilibrium. An isotonic solution has a concentration of materials the same as that inside a cell. If a cell is placed in an isotonic solution, molecules will still move into and out of the cell, but the cell will be in dynamic equilibrium. If a substance is in lower concentration outside a cell than inside the cell, the substance will leave the cell through osmosis. Likewise, the substance will move into the cell if the situation is reversed.

A hypotonic solution, where the concentration of substances is lower than that in the cell, draws substances out of the cell. What do you think will happen if the cell is in a hypertonic solution, where the concentration of materials in the solution is higher than that inside the cell?

We see examples of osmosis and diffusion all around us. When you add water to a wilted plant, for example, it soon stands up straight. You have just seen osmosis in action! Do you have questions of your own about osmosis? You will have an opportunity to explore osmosis and diffusion in the following experiments.

EXPERIMENT 1

Measuring Membranes: Is a plastic bag a semipermeable membrane?

Purpose/Hypothesis In this experiment, you will find out how a thin plastic bag functions as a membrane. If it is semipermeable, it will allow

WORDS TO KNOW

Concentration: The amount of a substance present in a given volume, such as the number of molecules in a liter.

Control experiment: A set-up that is identical to the experiment but is not affected by the variable that will be changed during the experiment.

Diffusion: Random movement of molecules that leads to a net movement of molecules from a region of high concentration to a region of low concentration.

Dynamic equilibrium: A situation in which substances are moving into and out of cell walls at an equal rate.

Hypertonic solution: A solution with a higher concentration of materials than a cell immersed in the solution.

Hypothesis: An idea in the form of a statement that can be tested by observation and/or experiment.

Hypotonic solution: A solution with a lower concentration of materials than a cell immersed in the solution.

Isotonic solutions: Two solutions that have the same concentration of solute particles and therefore the same osmotic pressure.

Molecule: The smallest particle of a substance that retains all the properties of the substance and is composed of one or more atoms.

Osmosis: The movement of fluids and substances dissolved in liquids across a semipermeable membrane from an area of its greater concentration to an area of its lesser concentration until all substances involved reach a balance.

Semipermeable membrane: A thin barrier between two solutions that permits only certain components of the solutions, usually the solvent, to pass through.

Variable: Something that can affect the results of an experiment.

some kinds of molecules to pass through but not others. For example, the plastic might allow small molecules to pass through, but not larger ones. You will test two solutions—iodine and starch, each with a different size molecule—to see what happens. Before you begin, make an educated guess about the outcome of this experiment based on your knowledge of osmosis. This educated guess, or prediction, is your hypothesis. A hypothesis should explain these things:

- the topic of the experiment
- the variable you will change
- the variable you will measure
- what you expect to happen

A helium balloon is a semipermeable membrane.
PHOTO RESEARCHERS INC.

What Are the Variables?

Variables are anything that might affect the results of an experiment. Here are the main variables in this experiment:

- the kind of solution
- the kind of membrane
- the thickness of the membrane
- the temperature of the solutions
- the color of the solutions
- the volume of the solution inside the bag and in the measuring cup

In other words, the variables in this experiment are everything that might affect whether a solution passes through a membrane. If you change more than one variable, you will not be able to tell which variable had the most effect on the passage of the solution through the membrane.

Step 3: Water baggie in the measuring cup. GALE GROUP.

A hypothesis should be brief, specific, and measurable. It must be something you can test through observation. Your experiment will prove or disprove your hypothesis. Here is one possible hypothesis for this experiment: "Iodine will cross through the plastic membrane, while starch will not."

In this case, the variable you will change will be the solutions. The variable you will measure will be changes in the solutions in the bag and in the measuring cup that holds the bag. You expect the iodine solution to pass through the plastic baggie, while the starch solution will not.

Setting up a control experiment will help you isolate one variable. Only one variable will change between the control and the experimental set-up, and that is the solution in the plastic bag. For the control, you will use a bag of water. For your experiment, you will use a bag of starch solution. You will put both bags into iodine solutions in measuring cups.

After you allow the solutions time to diffuse through the bag, you will observe the color and the volume of water in both the plastic bags and the measuring cups. A color change may occur because when iodine comes into contact with starch, the starch solution turns bluish-black. If the starch solution in the bag turns bluish-black, you will know that iodine solution in the measuring cup has crossed through the plastic membrane and entered the bag. If the blue iodine solution in the measuring cup turns black, you will know that starch has crossed through the membrane into the cup. If the solution in the bag turns black, but the cup solution does not, you know your hypothesis is correct: iodine crossed through the plastic membrane, but the starch did not.

Level of Difficulty Moderate.

Materials Needed

- 2 quart-size (1-liter size) measuring cups
- a smaller measuring cup or graduated cylinder
- small sealable plastic bags
- cornstarch
- water
- iodine with dropper
- masking tape
- measuring spoons and cups
- goggles

How to Experiment Safely

Wash your hands before, during, and after the experiment, so you do not transfer the starch or iodine on your hands. Wear goggles so you do not get the iodine in your eyes. Be careful with all glassware.

Approximate Budget Less than $10. (Most of these materials should be available in the average household.)

Timetable 2 days, leaving experiments overnight.

Step-by-Step Instructions

1. Prepare your solutions. Add 1 tablespoon (15 milliliters) of cornstarch for each cup of water to make the starch solution. Add 10 drops of iodine for each cup of water to make the iodine solution. You will probably need a total of 10 to 12 cups of each solution.
2. For your control, fill one baggie with water. Seal it tightly to prevent leakage. Place 2 to 3 cups iodine solution in one large measuring cup. Record the exact amount of solution in the cup, using the measuring lines on the side of the cup.

Steps 7 and 8: "Control" and "Experiment" measuring cups.
GALE GROUP.

Troubleshooter's Guide

Experiments do not always work out as planned. Even so, figuring out what went wrong can be a learning experience. Here are some problems that may arise during this experiment, some possible causes, and ways to remedy the problems.

Problem: The iodine solution changed color right away.

Possible cause: Starch solution leaked out or was on the outside of the bag. Seal your bag tighter and wash the outside carefully.

Problem: There was no change in color.

Possible cause: Those plastic baggies are not permeable to either solution. Try a thinner baggie or a different brand.

Problem: There is no change in volume.

Possible cause: The solutions are not strong enough. Try adding more cornstarch or iodine to your solutions.

3. Fill another measuring cup with 2 cups (500 milliliters) of plain water. Place the water baggie in this cup and record how much the water level rises. The difference in the water level is the volume of the water in your baggie.

4. Place the water baggie in the cup of iodine solution you prepared. Label the cup "control" with masking tape and set it aside.

5. Fill another baggie with starch solution and seal it. Measure and record its volume, as in Step 3. Carefully rinse the outside of the bag with water to wash off any starch solution.

6. Place 2 cups (500 milliliters) of iodine solution in another large measuring cup. Record the exact volume.

7. Lower the bag of starch solution into the iodine solution. Label this cup "experiment."

8. Let the control and experimental cups sit overnight.

9. The next day, check the solutions in the bags and in the cups. What colors are they? Measure and record the volume of water in the cups and the bags.

Data Chart		
	Control (iodine/water)	Experiment (iodine/starch)
Start Volume		
End Volume		
Start color in Bag		
End color in Bag		

Step 9: Data chart for Experiment 1. GALE GROUP.

Summary of Results Study the results on your chart. Did the color of the solutions change? Remember that if the starch solution in the bag turned black, iodine entered through the plastic membrane. If the iodine solution in the cup turned black, starch must have leaked out of the bag. If the volume of solution in the bag increased, you know that molecules were entering the bag, but few were leaving. Was your hypothesis correct? What have you discovered? What happened in the control cup?

Change the Variables You can change the variables and repeat this experiment. For example, try adding more iodine and cornstarch to create stronger solutions. See how that affects the change in volume and/or the rate of osmosis. (Or try using weaker solutions.) You can also try using different varieties of plastic bags or different materials altogether. See which ones allow certain solutions through and how quickly.

EXPERIMENT 2

Changing Concentrations: Will a bag of salt water draw in fresh water?

Purpose/Hypothesis In this experiment, you will see osmosis in action. You will place a balloon filled with salt water into a bucket of fresh water and watch what happens. Before you begin, make an educated guess about the outcome of this experiment based on your knowledge of osmosis. This educated guess, or prediction, is your hypothesis. A hypothesis should explain these things:

- the topic of the experiment
- the variable you will change
- the variable you will measure
- what you expect to happen

What Are the Variables?

Variables are anything that might affect the results of an experiment. Here are the main variables in this experiment:

- type of solution in balloon
- thickness of balloon
- the temperature of the water
- amount of water in the bucket and the balloon

In other words, the variables in this experiment are everything that might affect the movement of water across the membrane. If you change more than one variable, you will not be able to tell which variable had the most effect on the movement across the membrane.

Step 2: Funneling fresh water into a balloon. GALE GROUP.

How to Experiment Safely

There are no safety hazards in this experiment.

A hypothesis should be brief, specific, and measurable. It must be something you can test through observation. Your experiment will prove or disprove your hypothesis. Here is one possible hypothesis for this experiment: "A balloon filled with salt water will expand when placed in fresh water."

In this case, the variable you will change will be the kind of water you put in the balloon and the variable you will measure will be how much water enters the balloon as reflected by changes in the volume of the balloon. You expect the balloon filled with salt water will absorb fresh water and expand.

Only one variable will change between the control experiment and the experimental balloon, and that is the kind of solution inside the balloon. For the control, you will use fresh water. For your experimental balloons, you will use two different concentrations of salt water. You will measure how much water is in the balloons after they soak in fresh water. If the experimental balloons gain water when they have salt water in them, and the control balloon does not, then your hypothesis will be supported.

Level of Difficulty Easy.

Materials Needed

- salt
- at least three thin balloons or sealable baggies
- 3 buckets or other large containers

Steps 2 to 5: Balloons in labeled buckets. GALE GROUP.

- funnel
- measuring cup
- measuring spoons
- 2 bowls
- stirrer

Approximate Budget $3 for balloons.

Timetable 1 hour to set up the experiment; 1 day to view the results.

Step-by-Step Instructions

1. Measure 12 cups (6 pints or 2.8 liters) of water into each bucket.
2. Use the funnel to pour 1 cup (.5 liter) of fresh water into a balloon. Tie the balloon tightly and place it in a bucket labeled "control."
3. Use the bowls to prepare two salt solutions with different concentrations. For Solution 1, add 3 teaspoons of salt to 2 cups of water. For Solution 2, add 9 teaspoons of salt to another 2 cups of water. Stir both solutions until the salt dissolves.
4. Use the funnel to pour one cup of Solution 1 into one balloon and tie it tightly. Rinse the funnel. Then use the funnel to pour one cup of Solution 2 into another balloon and tie it tightly.
5. Place each balloon into its own bucket, labeled "Solution 1" and "Solution 2."
6. Leave all three buckets overnight.

Data Chart

	Control Balloon	Solution 1 Balloon	Solution 2 Balloon
Start Volume			
End Volume			

Step 7: Data chart for Experiment 2. GALE GROUP.

Troubleshooter's Guide

Here are some problems that may arise during this experiment, some possible causes, and ways to remedy the problems.

Problem: No volume change occurred at all.

Possible causes:

1. You have used a very thick balloon that is not permeable. Try a different kind of balloon or baggie.
2. Your solutions were not well mixed. Try adding more salt and stirring longer.

Problem: One or more of the balloons exploded.

Possible cause: The balloon membrane is very thin and too much water entered. Try using weaker salt solutions or not leaving the balloon in the water for as long.

7. The next day, examine all three balloons. Measure the change in volume by placing each one in a large (1000-milliliter) measuring cup filled with 2 cups (500 milliliters) of water. Record how high the water rises. The difference is the volume in the balloon.

Summary of Results Study the results on your chart. Compare the change in volume for each balloon to any change in your control. The more volume the balloons gained, the greater amount of osmosis occurred. What did you find? Was your hypothesis correct? Write a paragraph summarizing and explaining your findings.

Change the Variables There are several ways you can vary this experiment. For example, try other salt concentrations. Add more salt or less. Or try sugar or starch solutions and see what effect those have on amount of osmosis that occurs. You can also experiment with different membranes, such as thicker or thinner balloons or baggies or balloons made of Mylar. See what kind of effect these have on osmosis. Finally, you can see how long osmosis takes under the different conditions you are testing.

EXPERIMENT 3

Changing Sizes: What effect does molecule size have on osmosis

Purpose/Hypothesis In this experiment, you will see how molecules of certain sizes can move through a membrane through osmosis. A semi-permeable membrane allows smaller molecules, such as water, to move through the membrane. Larger molecules, such as sugar, that are too large to move through the membrane cannot pass. The membrane you will use will be the membrane of an egg. The solutions you will use will be water and corn syrup, which contains sugar.

You will first need to dissolve the shell to expose the membrane. The acid in vinegar will dissolve the eggshell. Vinegar contains about 5 percent acid. In order to speed up the experiment, you can strengthen the concentration of the acid by boiling off some of the water. Then you will observe osmosis with the egg membrane in distilled water and another egg membrane in corn syrup.

Before you begin, make an educated guess about the outcome of this experiment based on your knowledge of osmosis. This educated guess, or prediction, is your hypothesis. A hypothesis should explain these things:

- the topic of the experiment
- the variable you will change
- the variable you will measure
- what you expect to happen

A hypothesis should be brief, specific, and measurable. It must be something you can test through observation. Your experiment will prove or disprove your hypothesis. Here is one possible hypothesis for this experiment: "The smaller the molecular size the more readily the solution will move through the membrane and the more the egg will weigh."

In this case, the variable you will change will be the size of the molecules that surround the egg membrane. The variable you will measure will be the weight of the egg, both before and after the egg is immersed in the water and corn syrup.

Level of Difficulty Moderate.

Materials Needed

- corn syrup
- white vinegar
- 2 glass containers, just large enough to fit an egg
- 2 large slotted spoons
- 2 eggs
- distilled water
- pot
- stove or hot plate

What Are the Variables?

Variables are anything that might affect the results of an experiment. Here are the main variables in this experiment:

- the type of solution
- the temperature of the solution
- the type of egg

In other words, the variables in this experiment are everything that might affect the movement of the solution through the egg membrane. If you change more than one variable, you will not be able to tell which variable had the most effect on the movement of the solution across the membrane. In this experiment, you will compare the two eggs against one another.

How to Experiment Safely

Have an adult help you simmer the vinegar, and be careful when handling any hot solutions. Wash your hands after handling the egg or vinegar.

Step 2: Pour the concentrated vinegar over the egg. ILLUSTRATION BY TEMAH NELSON.

Steps 4 and 9: Weigh the eggs on a gram scale and note their weight. ILLUSTRATION BY TEMAH NELSON.

- measuring cup
- gram scale

Approximate Budget $10.

Timetable 30 minutes to set up the experiment; three to five days to complete.

Step-by-Step Instructions

1. Simmer 4 cups of vinegar on a hot pot or stove until the vinegar boils down to 1 cup. Cool completely.

2. Place each egg in a small glass jar. Pour enough of the concentrated vinegar over each egg until the egg is completely covered. Set aside.

3. After two days, the shell should be dissolved completely. If it's not, set aside for another day. Using a slotted spoon, carefully scoop out the egg. Rinse each egg under running water until it is clean.

4. Weigh the egg on a gram scale and note its weight.

5. Rinse and wipe dry the two glass jars. Label one jar "Distilled Water." Label the second jar "Corn Syrup."

6. Place one shelled egg in each of the glass jars.

7. In the jar labeled "Distilled Water," immerse the egg with distilled water. In the jar labeled "Corn Syrup," immerse the egg with corn syrup. Set aside.

8. After one day, look at the eggs and note the description.

9. Using a slotted spoon, carefully scoop out each egg and weigh. Note the weight of each egg.

Summary of Results Compare the appearance and weight of the eggs. Did both the corn syrup and distilled water move through the membrane? How did the size of the molecules in the water and corn syrup play a role in osmosis? Was your hypothesis correct? Write a paragraph summarizing and explaining your findings.

Change the Variables There are several ways you can vary this experiment. For example, try other sugary liquids, such as different types of maple syrup or sugar water. You can also try various types of eggs, to test if the membranes are different. You can change the temperature also, repeating the experiment in a cold or warn water bath.

Design Your Own Experiment

How to Select a Topic Relating to this Concept
If you are interested in osmosis and diffusion, you might study their effects on living organisms or the effects of different solutions on plants or on simple one-celled organisms, such as a paramecium.

Are you interested in rates of diffusion? Try timing how long different solutions take to diffuse throughout water. Or create solutions using different-size molecules and higher and lower concentrations. You might separate solutions and then watch what diffuses through membranes.

Check the Further Readings section and talk with your science teacher or school or community media specialist to start gathering information on osmosis questions that interest you.

Steps in the Scientific Method To do an original experiment, you need to plan carefully and think things through. Otherwise you might not be sure what question you are answering, what you are or should be measuring, or what your findings prove or disprove.

Here are the steps in designing an experiment:

- State the purpose of—and the underlying question behind—the experiment you propose to do.

Troubleshooter's Guide

Here are some problems that may arise during this experiment, some possible causes, and ways to remedy the problems.

Problem: The egg shell is not dissolving.

Possible causes: There may not be enough acid in the vinegar or you did not wait long enough for the eggshell to dissolve. Try immersing the egg in vinegar again and waiting slightly longer.

Problem: The solution did not move into or out of the membrane.

Possible cause: The membrane was too dirty with the shell remains. Repeat the experiment, rinsing off the egg thoroughly with warm water until the egg is completely smooth to the touch.

Step 7: In the jar labeled "Distilled Water," immerse the egg with distilled water. In the jar labeled "Corn Syrup," immerse the egg with corn syrup. ILLUSTRATION BY TEMAH NELSON.

- Recognize the variables involved, and select one that will help you answer the question at hand.
- State a testable hypothesis, an educated guess about the answer to your question.
- Decide how to change the variable you selected.
- Decide how to measure your results.

Recording Data and Summarizing the Results Your data should include charts, such as the ones you did in these experiments. All charts should be clearly labeled and easy to read. You may also want to include photos, graphs, or drawings of your experimental set-up and results.

If you are preparing an exhibit for a science fair, display your results, such as any experimental set-ups you built. If you have done a nonexperimental project, explain clearly what your research question was and illustrate your findings.

Related Projects You can design projects that are similar to these experiments, involving trials and charts of data to summarize your results. You could also prepare a model that demonstrates a point you are interested in with regard to osmosis or diffusion. Or you could investigate the effects of osmosis in a certain environment. There are many options.

For More Information

Gardner, Robert. *Experimenting with Water.* New York: Franklin Watts, 1993. Fascinating experiments that explore the strange properties of water.

Vancleave, Janice Pratt. *Janice Vancleave's Biology for Every Kid: One Hundred One Easy Experiments That Really Work.* New York: John Wiley & Sons, 1989. Basic principles of biology of plants and animals through informative text and experiments.

62

Oxidation-Reduction

Do you know what rusting metal, photographic processes, battery operation, and clothes bleaching have in common? They are all examples of an important and common kind of chemical reaction called an oxidation-reduction reaction. This kind of reaction involves the transfer of electrons, which are tiny particles in atoms. During oxidation, a substance's atoms lose electrons. During reduction, a substance's atoms gain electrons.

What actually happens during oxidation? To understand oxidation, it is important to understand how atoms work. All atoms have three kinds of tiny particles—electrons, protons, and neutrons. Electrons have negative electrical charges, while protons have positive charges. Neutrons are neutral—neither positive nor negative. The sum of the electrical charges in each atom are balanced, so atoms is electrically neutral.

The oxidation state of an atom is the sum of its positive and negative charges, and the oxidation state of any atom is zero. Oxidation reactions involve a change in the oxidation state of the atoms involved, caused by a loss or gain of electrons.

During oxidation, an atom loses electrons and becomes a positively charged ion. (An ion is an atom or a group of atoms that carries an electrical charge, either positive or negative.) Metal atoms tend to undergo oxidation easily. In an oxidation reaction, the metal loses one, two, or three electrons and becomes positively charged. The other substance, a nonmetal, gains electrons, becoming a negatively charged ion. The nonmetal is thus reduced. Remember that oxidation cannot occur without a corresponding reduction reaction.

Rust destroys millions of dollars in property every year. PHOTO RESEARCHERS INC.

WORDS TO KNOW

Atom: The smallest unit of an element, made up of protons and neutrons in a central nucleus surrounded by moving electrons.

Control Experiment: A set-up that is identical to the experiment but is not affected by the variable that affects the experimental group. Results from the control experiment are compared to results from the actual experiment.

Corrosion: An oxidation-reduction reaction in which a metal is oxidized (reacted with oxygen) and oxygen is reduced, usually in the presence of moisture.

Electron: A subatomic particle with a mass of about one atomic mass unit and a single negative electrical charge that orbits the nucleus of an atom.

Hypothesis: An idea in the form of a statement that can be tested by observation and/or experiment

Ion: An atom or groups of atoms that carries an electrical charge—either positive or negative—as a result of losing or gaining one or more electrons.

Neutron: A subatomic particle with a mass of about one atomic mass unit and no electrical charge that is found in the nucleus of an atom.

Oxidation: A chemical reaction in which oxygen reacts with some other substance and in which ions, atoms, or molecules lose electrons.

Oxidation-reduction reaction: A chemical reaction in which one substance loses one or more electrons and the other substance gains one or more electrons.

Oxidation state: The sum of an atom's positive and negative charges.

Oxidizing agent: A chemical substance that gives up oxygen or takes on electrons from another substance.

Proton: A subatomic particle with a mass of about one atomic mass unit and a single positive electrical charge that is found in the nucleus of an atom.

Reduction: A process in which a chemical substance gives off oxygen or takes on electrons.

Variable: Something that may affect the results of an experiment.

What are some examples of oxidation? One common example of an oxidation reaction is the one that occurs between sodium, a soft metal, and chlorine, a gas. When these elements exchange one electron, a violent reaction occurs, and a new substance, sodium chloride, is formed. We know it as the hard, white substance often found on the kitchen table: salt.

Here is what happens: both sodium (Na) and chlorine gas (Cl_2) are electrically neutral. When they combine, sodium undergoes oxidation, loses an electron, and becomes positively charged. Chlorine undergoes reduction and becomes negatively charged. Because atoms do not "like" to be charged, the sodium and the chlorine are attracted to their opposite charges and combine to create salt.

Oxidation reactions play an important role in many processes of modern life; the results are all around us. One of the most common places you see the results of oxidation is in the process of corrosion, particularly involving iron and steel. Iron oxide flakes off in what we call rust.

An oxidizing agent is anything that causes another substance to lose electrons. Bleaches are one example. Bleaches remove electrons that are activated by light to produce colors.

What kind of questions do you have about oxidation-reduction? You'll have an opportunity to explore oxidation in the following experiments and think about designing your own experiments on this important and far-reaching topic.

EXPERIMENT 1

Reduction: How will acid affect dirty pennies?

Purpose/Hypothesis In this experiment, you will find out how an acid leads to a reducing reaction, and you will explore the movement of atoms during the reaction. Acids are important reducing agents, involved in many common chemical reactions in our daily lives.

Pennies are coated with copper oxide (CuO), which forms when copper combines with oxygen from the air. Pennies look dirty when they are coated copper oxide. In this experiment, you will immerse pennies into a mixture of vinegar or lemon juice and salt—which dissolves copper oxide. (Vinegar and lemon juice are weak acids; the salt helps the reaction.) When you put the dirty pennies into the solution, the copper oxide and copper will dissolve into the water. Some of the copper atoms will leave their electrons behind and float in the water as positively charged copper ions, missing two electrons. They have been reduced.

When you put steel nails into the same solution, the salt and vinegar dissolve some of the iron from the nails. When the iron atoms leave, they also leave electrons behind just as the copper did. Now you will have positively charged iron ions floating around in the solution with the positively charged copper ions. Since the nails will now have extra electrons left on them from the iron atoms that dissolved into the

What Are the Variables?

Variables are anything that might affect the results of an experiment. Here are the main variables in this experiment:

- the kind of solution being used
- the cleanliness of the pennies prior to the experiment
- the time allowed for the pennies and nails to soak in the solution
- the color of the pennies and the nails after they have soaked in the solution

In order to test your hypothesis, you can change only one variable at a time. If you change more than one, you will not be able to tell which factor caused a change in the outcome of your experiment.

How to Experiment Safely

Wash your hands before and after handling the dirty pennies and other materials. Wear goggles and rubber gloves to avoid eye and skin contact with the acid solutions. Be careful in handling the nails to avoid cuts or punctures.

solution, the nails are negatively charged. What happens when there are positive and negative charges near each other? They attract! What do you think will happen to the copper ions as they get near the negatively charged nails?

Do you have an educated guess about what will happen to the pennies and the nails in the acidic solution? That educated guess, or prediction, is your hypothesis. A hypothesis should explain these things:

- the topic of the experiment
- the variable you will change
- the variable you will measure
- what you expect to happen

A hypothesis should be brief, specific, and measurable. It must be something you can test through observation. Your experiment will prove or disprove your hypothesis. Here is one possible hypothesis for this experiment: "An acidic solution will cause the pennies to become clean and copper to coat the nails."

Variables are anything that can be changed in an experiment. In this case, the variable you will change will be the acid in your solution, and the variable you will measure will be the color (a measure of cleanliness) of the pennies and the color of the nails after they have soaked in the solution.

Setting up a control experiment will help you isolate one variable. Only one variable will change between the control and the experimental bowls, and that variable is the kind of solution you use to immerse the pennies and nails. For the control, you will use plain water. For your experimental bowls, you will use lemon juice and vinegar.

Steps 1 to 5: Bowl set-up with pennies. GALE GROUP.

Water   Lemon juice   Vinegar

Solution	Penny color before	Penny color after	Nail color after 10 minutes	Nail color after one hour

Step 3: Data sheet for Experiment 1. GALE GROUP.

You will record the color of the pennies and the nails both before and after you immerse them in the solutions. If the pennies become cleaner and brighter, and the nails become copper-colored, your hypothesis is supported.

Level of difficulty Moderate.

Materials Needed

- 45 equally dirty pennies
- ¼ cup lemon juice
- ¼ cup white vinegar
- ¼ cup water
- 2 teaspoons salt
- 3 glass or ceramic bowls
- 6 clean steel nails (not galvanized nails)
- paper towels
- goggles
- rubber gloves

Approximate Budget Up to $5. (Try to borrow the goggles from your school.)

Timetable 2 hours.

Step-by-Step Instructions

1. Put water in one bowl, lemon juice in another, and vinegar in a third. Label

Step 9: Place a nail in each bowl. Lean a second nail against the side of the bowl so only about half of it is in the solution. GALE GROUP.

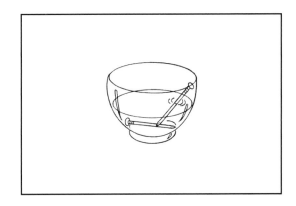

Troubleshooter's Guide

Below are some problems that may occur during the experiment, possible causes, and ways to remedy the problems.

Problem: The pennies did not change color in any of the solutions.

Possible causes:

1. Your pennies were not dirty enough. Find dirtier pennies and repeat the experiment.

2. Your solutions are not acidic enough. Check the expiration dates on your bottles of vinegar and lemon juice, and replace them, if necessary.

Problem: The nails did not pick up any copper at all.

Possible causes:

1. Make sure your nails are steel and clean. Impurities can affect the oxidation reaction.

2. You may not have left them in solution long enough, or if the pennies did not have much copper oxide on them, little copper will be in solution. Run the experiment again with dirtier pennies and leave the nails for a longer time.

each bowl if you need help telling them apart.

2. Add 1 teaspoon salt to the vinegar solution and to the lemon juice, and stir until it dissolves.

3. Examine the color of the pennies carefully. Describe the color on your data sheet, illustrated.

4. Place one penny in each bowl. Describe what happens on your data sheet.

5. Place 14 more pennies in each bowl. Watch what happens to them.

6. After five minutes, remove the pennies from one bowl. Rinse them thoroughly under running water and place them on a paper towel to dry. Write the kind of solution they were soaking in on the paper towel.

7. Repeat Step 6 with the pennies from the other two bowls.

8. Examine the nails carefully and describe their color on your data sheet.

9. Place a nail in each bowl. Lean a second nail against the side of the bowl so only about half of it is in the solution.

10. After 10 minutes, examine the nails. Record the colors on your data sheet.

11. Leave the nails for an hour and then examine them again.

Summary of Results Study the results on your chart. What have you discovered? What color changes took place? Why? Was your hypothesis correct? Write a paragraph to summarize and explain your findings.

Change the Variables You can vary this experiment. Here are some possibilities:

- Try different solutions to see how they affect the oxidation/reduction reaction, such as baking soda, bleach, or tomato juice. Or try diluting the solutions with water to vary the ratio of water to acid. Be sure to record how much of each you use. Again, be careful in handling these liquids. Wear goggles and gloves and work in a ventilated area, especially when using bleach.

• Vary the time you leave the pennies and nails in the solution. What happens?

EXPERIMENT 2

Oxidation and Rust: How is rust produced?

Purpose/Hypothesis One of the most common oxidation reactions is the production of rust, otherwise known as corrosion. Iron readily combines with water and oxygen to form rust.

In this experiment, you will explore the process of iron oxidation, which produces rust. You will see the result of the depletion of oxygen as this element is removed from the air to combine with iron.

Do you have an educated guess about how water will affect a piece of steel wool? What might happen to a candle burning in the same container as the steel wool? That educated guess, or prediction, is your hypothesis. A hypothesis should explain these things:

• the topic of the experiment
• the variable you will change
• the variable you will measure
• what you expect to happen

A hypothesis should be brief, specific, and measurable. It must be something you can test through observation. Your experiment will prove or disprove your hypothesis. Here is one possible hypothesis for this experiment: "Wet steel wool will oxidize to form rust when left for several days. This process removes oxygen from the air, so a candle placed in the same space will burn for a shorter amount of time."

What Are the Variables?

Variables are anything that could affect the results of an experiment. Here are the variables in this experiment:

• the amount of water in jars
• the amount of air in each jar
• the material used in water
• the type of steel wool
• the type of candles
• the time the candles burn after the steel wool is removed

In order to test your hypothesis, you can change only one variable at a time. If you change more than one, you will not be able to tell which factor caused a change in the outcome of your experiment.

How to Experiment Safely

Be careful handling glass jars to avoid breakage. As with all fire, be extremely careful handling matches. You are strongly urged to have an adult help you light the candles. Have water or a fire extinguisher close by in case of an accident.

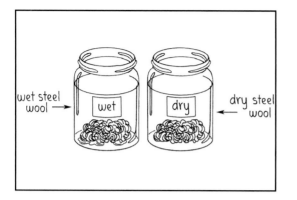

Step 1: Set-up of "wet" and "dry" jars. GALE GROUP.

Steps 3 and 4: Dropping lit candle into experimental jar. GALE GROUP.

In this case, the variable you will change will be whether the steel wool is exposed to water. The variable you will measure will be the amount of rust on the steel wool and the length of time the candle burns.

Setting up a control experiment will help you isolate one variable. Only one variable will change between the control and the experimental jar, and that is whether the steel wool is exposed to moisture. For the control, you will use dry steel wool. For your experimental jar, you will use damp steel wool.

You will measure how much oxidation or rust occurs and how long the candles burn. If the control shows no rust while your experimental jar shows some, AND the candle burns for a shorter amount of time in the experimental jar, your hypothesis is supported.

Level of Difficulty Easy/moderate; ask an adult to help you light the candles.

Materials Needed

- 2 equal-sized pieces of steel wool (Do not use scouring pads that contain soap.)
- 2 identical glass jars with metal lids
- water
- 2 small birthday candles
- matches
- a small amount of modeling clay
- stopwatch

	Rust?	Candle burning time
Dry steel wool		
Wet steel wool		

Data chart for Experiment 2. GALE GROUP.

Approximate Budget $5 to $7 if you need to purchase steel wool, modeling clay and/or candles.

Timetable 3 days.

Step-by-Step Instructions

1. Wet one piece of steel wool and place it in one of the jars. In the other jar, place a dry piece of steel wool. Label each jar carefully.
2. Close both lids tightly and place the jars in a cool, dark place for three days.
3. Have an adult light one of the candles.
4. Open the experimental jar and have the adult drop in the candle. Quickly close the jar again.
5. Use the stopwatch to time how long the candle burns. Record the time on a chart like the one illustrated.
6. Repeat Steps 3 to 5, having your adult helper drop the other lighted candle in the control jar.
7. After both candles have burned, remove the steel wool from both jars and record what you find.

Troubleshooter's Guide

Below are some problems that may occur during this experiment, possible causes, and ways to remedy the problems.

Problem: No rust showed on the either piece of steel wool.

Possible causes:

1. You did not put enough water on the experimental steel wool. Try wetting it more, or putting a small amount of water in the base of the jar before leaving it.
2. You did not leave the jars long enough. Try leaving both jars for several more days.

Problem: The candles burned the same length of time.

Possible cause: You let in too much outside air when you opened the jars. Open and close the jars as quickly as possible so little outside air will have an opportunity to mix with the air in the jars.

Summary of Results Study your results, comparing the amounts of rust on each piece of steel wool and the times the two candles burned. The more rust you observe, the more oxidation occurred. The shorter time the candles burned, the less oxygen was present in the jars, showing that more oxidation occurred. What did you discover? Was your hypothesis supported? Write a paragraph summarizing and explaining your results.

Change the Variables You can vary this experiment. Here are some possibilities:

- Try using other kinds of metal, such as screws and nails, tinfoil, painted steel wool, or even different brands of steel wool, to see what oxidizes more readily. See if you can isolate factors that cause more rust than others, such as the amount of exposed surface area or the shape, size, or color of the metal.

What Are the Variables?

Variables are anything that might affect the results of an experiment. Here are the main variables in this experiment:

- the type of acid being used
- the cleanliness of the copper
- exposure to the atmosphere
- the concentration of acid being used

In order to test your hypothesis, you can change only one variable at a time. If you change more than one, you will not be able to tell which factor caused a change in the outcome of your experiment.

- See what happens when you leave the experimental set-up for several more days. How much more rust do you find? Can you make any additional predictions about the effect of oxidation on other objects?

EXPERIMENT 3

Oxidation Reaction: Can acid change the color of copper?

Purpose/Hypothesis In this experiment, you will examine how an acid can form a blue-green solid in an oxidation/reduction reaction with copper. The acid you will use is vinegar, which is about 5% acetic acid.

When acetic acid is added to copper (Cu), the copper loses two electrons. The acetic acid gains two electrons. The metal copper gets oxidized and the acetic acid gets reduced. The result is copper acetate, which is a blue-green solid. Copper acetate dissolves in acid but not in water.

You will use a sheet or coil of copper and add acetic acid. In order to speed up the reaction, you will need to make the acid stronger than 5%. The more acetic the vinegar, the faster the reaction occurs. You will use two different concentrations of vinegar so that you can compare the reaction speed. You can do this by carefully heating the vinegar and boiling off some of the water. (The water boiling point is lower than

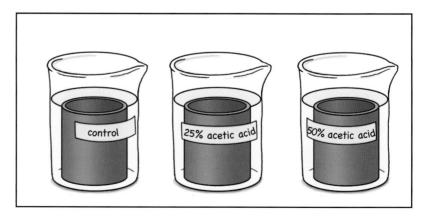

Steps 1–8: Label the three jars appropriately, placing the copper item in the jar and filling with liquid.
ILLUSTRATION BY TEMAH NELSON.

the acetic acid boiling point, and so water will boil of first.) The reaction also needs air and time.

Make an educated guess about what will happen to the copper when it is bathed in acidic acid? That educated guess, or prediction, is your hypothesis. A hypothesis should explain these things:

- the topic of the experiment
- the variable you will change
- the variable you will measure
- what you expect to happen

A hypothesis should be brief, specific, and measurable. It must be something you can test through observation. Your experiment will prove or disprove your hypothesis. Here is one possible hypothesis for this experiment: "Acetic acid will cause the copper to turn blue-green".

Variables are anything that can be changed in an experiment. In this case, the variable you will change will be the acid in your reaction, and the variable you will measure will be the color (a measure of cleanliness) of the copper and the solid that is formed from the reaction.

Setting up a control experiment will help you isolate one variable. Only one variable will change between the control and the experimental copper reaction. The variable you will change is the acid used to immerse the copper. For the control, you will use distilled water.

You will record the color of the copper before the experiment and the solid that forms on top of the copper.

Level of Difficulty Moderate.

Materials Needed

- 3 copper items that are the same, such as wires or thin sheets (available at hardware or craft stores)
- white vinegar
- hot pot or stove
- 3 wide mouth small jars, such as baby jars
- potholder

How to Experiment Safely

Be extremely careful when heating the vinegar and ask for an adult to help. Do not touch the vinegar.

Step 11: After approximately a week, the surface of the copper item will have changed.
ILLUSTRATION BY TEMAH NELSON.

Troubleshooter's Guide

Here are some problems that may arise during this experiment, some possible causes, and ways to remedy the problems.

Problem: The copper did not change.

Possible causes:

You did not allow enough time for the change to occur, or the copper was not exposed to enough air. Try placing the copper in a wider-mouth jar and letting it sit for more time.

Problem: The copper only darkened.

Possible cause:

You may not have been using pure copper. Purchase more copper and ask if it is 100% copper before trying the experiment again.

- measuring cups
- bowl
- distilled water
- plastic knife
- wax paper or paper plate
- magnifying glass (optional)

Approximate Budget $5.

Timetable 2 hours to set up the experiment; 2 days to a week to see results.

Step-by-Step Instructions

1. Label the three jars: "control." "25% acetic acid." "50% acetic acid.".
2. Place the copper item in each jar.
3. Pour 1 cup of vinegar into the pot and simmer until the vinegar boils down to ¼ cup. You will probably have to pour it into the measuring cup and back into the pot until it is at ¼ cup. Remember to use a potholder.
4. Using a potholder, pour the acetic acid into a bowl to cool.
5. Pour another 1 cup of vinegar into the pot and simmer.
6. When the vinegar boils to ½ cup, allow it to cool.
7. Pour enough of the ¼ cup of vinegar into the jar labeled "25% acetic acid." until the solution just covers the copper. Pour the ½ cup acetic acid solution into the jar labeled "50% acetic acid." until it just covers the copper.
8. In the control jar, cover the copper with distilled water.
9. Set the jars aside. Do not cover. The vinegar will evaporate over time.
10. After two days, examine all three jars. Note any changes to the surface of the copper.
11. Every day continue to examine all three jars. After approximately a week, if the surface of the copper has changed, carefully pour the acetic acid of each jar down the sink. Wait

Step 12: Using a plastic knife, gently scrape the blue-green solid off the copper onto wax paper or a paper plate. ILLUSTRATION BY TEMAH NELSON.

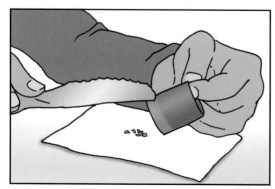

another day until the solution has all evaporated.

12. Using a plastic knife, gently scrape the blue-green solid off the copper onto wax paper or a paper plate. If you have a magnifying glass you can take a closer look at the newly-formed solid.

Summary of Results Describe the blue-green copper acetate that has formed. Study the results on your chart. Compare the change in the copper immersed in distilled water to the copper items in the acetic acid. Did one reaction occur faster than the other two? Did the copper turn blue-green or did the copper change into another solid? Was your hypothesis correct? Write a paragraph summarizing and explaining your findings.

Change the Variables There are several ways that you can vary this experiment. For example, you can try other acetic acid concentrations. You can test lower and higher concentrations (carefully and with adult help). You can also experiment with different metals or copper alloys. A copper alloy is copper blended with other metals, such as bronze, zinc or lead.

You can see rust on metal fences all over the world. PETER ARNOLD INC.

Design Your Own Experiment

How to Select a Topic Relating to this Concept Oxidation-reduction reactions take place all around you every day. Are you interested in corrosion of metals? Try experimenting with different kinds of metals to see which ones corrode faster and what happens to them when they corrode. Or investigate bleaching action, involving electrons activated by light. Another reaction involving light is that of photo-chromic glass, which causes eyeglasses to darken in direct sunlight because of photo-oxidation.

Perhaps you are interested in how batteries work. Most of them involve oxidation-reduction reactions with various compounds such as ammonium chloride, silver oxide, mercury, or nickel/cadmium. If

Batteries work by an oxidation/reduction reaction. PHOTO RESEARCHERS INC.

you experiment with batteries, use extreme caution because they contain potentially toxic compounds.

Oxidation-reduction reactions are involved in photosynthesis, metabolism, nitrogen fixation, fuel combustion, and many other things. The possibilities for investigation are endless. Think about your interests and check the Further Readings section. Talk with your teachers or librarians about how you can get further information on the topics that interest you.

Steps in the Scientific Method To do an original experiment, you need to plan carefully and think things through before you do it. Otherwise you might not be sure what question you are answering, what you are or should be measuring, or what your findings prove or disprove.

Here are the steps in designing an experiment:

- State the purpose of—and the underlying question behind—the experiment you propose to do.
- Recognize the variables involved, and select one that will help you answer the question at hand.
- State a testable hypothesis, an educated guess about the answer to your question.
- Decide how to change the variable you selected.
- Decide how to measure your results.

Recording Data and Summarizing the Results Your data should include charts, such as the one you did for these experiments. They should be clearly labeled and easy to read. You may also want to include photos, graphs, or drawings of your experimental setup and results.

If you are preparing an exhibit, you may want to display your results, such as rusted metals or bleached fabrics clearly labeled as to what you did with them. These materials will make your exhibit more interesting for viewers. If you have done a nonexperimental project, explain clearly what your research question was and illustrate your findings.

Related Projects You can design projects that are similar to these experiments, involving trials and charts of data to summarize results. You could also prepare a model that demonstrates the point that interest you with regard to oxidation-reduction and its effects in everyday life. Or you could do a research project investigating how oxidation-reduction is involved in acid rain or other environmental problems. You could explore the history of scientists who have studied oxidation-reduction and the kinds of experiments that led them to discoveries. The possibilities are numerous.

For More Information

Burns, George, and Nancy Woodman. *Exploring the World of Chemistry.* Danbury, CT: Franklin Watts, 1995. Outlines several experiments in oxidation.

Fitzgerald, Karen. *The Story of Oxygen.* Danbury, CT: Franklin Watts, 1996. Explores the history, chemistry, and uses of oxygen.

Gutnik, Martin. *Experiments that Explore Acid Rain.* Millbrook Press, 1992. Investigates how oxidation reactions affect acid rain, among other experiments.

Mebane, Robert, Thomas Rybolt, and Ronald Perkins. *Adventures with Molecules: Chemistry Experiments for Young People.* Enslow Publishers, 1987. Outlines more ways to explore oxidation-reduction reactions.

63

Periodic Table

Considered one of the most important chemistry reference tools, the periodic table is a familiar sight around the world. The periodic table is an arrangement of the elements by their properties. An element is a substance in pure form, meaning that it cannot be broken down into any other substance. The smallest particle of an element is an atom.

With one glance, the periodic table can provide a great deal of information on both individual elements and groups of them. A person familiar with the table can extract an element's relative mass, basic properties, and how it compares with its neighbors without knowing any facts about the element itself.

Elemental developments All matter on Earth is made up of elements. There are only a finite number of natural elements, although others are synthesized or manufactured by people. (As of 2008, there were 118 officially named elements.) The periodic table leaves spaces for unknown elements still to be discovered.

The desire to categorize elements goes back to the fifth century B.C.E. when ancient Greeks theorized that all matter falls under four elements: Earth, air, fire, and water. In 1789 French chemist Antoine Lavoisier (1743–1794) published the definition and first set of thirty-three chemical elements. Lavoisier grouped them into four categories on the basis of their chemical properties: gases, nonmetals, metals, and earths.

As more elements were discovered, many scientists worked on classifying them. The turning point came when Russian chemist Dmitri Mendeleev (1834–1907) made up cards of each of the elements and worked on arranging them in patterns. At that time there were sixty-three known elements. He found that there were repeating or periodic relationships between the properties of the elements and their atomic weights. By arranging the elements in order of increasing atomic weight, the

Russian chemist Dmitri Mendeleev created the basic structure of the periodic table.
THE LIBRARY OF CONGRESS.

properties of the elements were repeated periodically. The arrangement of elements in this manner was called the periodic table.

In 1869 Mendeleev published the first periodic table. In his table, rows (across) and columns (down) each shared certain properties. Mendeleev's table even left placeholders for elements that had yet to be identified. Over the next two decades, more elements were discovered, including gallium, scandium, and germanium. When these elements fit into the predicted spaces, the table gained acceptance. Over the next century the periodic table changed in several ways, yet its basic structure set down by Mendeleev remained.

Blocks of data Each block in the periodic table contains the name and properties of that element. The letters are the abbreviation or atomic symbol of the chemical element. Each element has a one- or two-letter abbreviation as its symbol, often taken from the Latin word for a description, place, or name. For example, the atomic symbol for gold, Au, comes from the first two letters of the Latin word *aurum,* meaning shining dawn. Mercury's symbol, Hg, comes from the Latin *hydragyrum,* meaning liquid silver, and lead's symbol, Pb, comes from the Latin *plumbum,* meaning heavy.

Above the symbol is the atomic number of the element. The atomic number represents the number of protons, or positively charged particles, in an atom of that element. The number of protons in an atom equals the number of electrons, negatively charged particles, which move around the center of the atom. The number and arrangement of protons and electrons in an atom determines the chemical behavior of the element.

The number below the symbol is the atomic mass, the average mass of an element. Also known as atomic weight, atomic mass is given in atomic mass units (amu). An atom's atomic mass is the weight of its protons and neutrons. A neutron is a particle that has no charge and is located in the center of the atom.

Across and down Each row of elements across the table is called a period. Rows in the periodic table are read left to right. All of the elements in a period have the same number of shells. A shell is the number of areas an atom needs to hold its electrons. The first shell holds two electrons, the second shell holds up to eight, and the third shell can hold up to eighteen electrons. The maximum number of shells found around any atom is seven. Thus, there are seven periods.

For example, carbon (C) atoms have six electrons: two electrons in the first shell and the remaining four are in the second shell. Hydrogen (H), which has one electron, needs only one shell. Helium (He), which has two electrons, is the only other element with one shell and the two elements share a row by themselves. Calcium (Ca) and Magnesium (Mg) each have two shells and, thus, are in the second row.

Each column of elements down the periodic table is called a group or family. Elements in a group have the same number of electrons in their outer shell. The group at the left edge of the periodic table has one electron in its outer shell. Every element in the second column has two electrons in its outer shell, and so on. Groups are numbered from left to right. There are two sets of groups: the A and B groups. The A groups run along the high columns of the table and have similar properties. The B groups in the middle section of the table are called transition elements. Transition elements have common properties; they are hard, strong metals that conduct heat and electricity well. These elements also have their electrons arranged in a complex arrangement, which is lacking in the A group.

Periodic patterns Both periods and groups supply information on the element's characteristics and behavior.

In a period, as the atomic mass increases from left to right the atomic size decreases. (The more electrons there are, the more they are pulled towards the center and the atom tightens.) Metals are on the left and middle sections of the periods with the most active metal in the lower left corner. Nonmetals are located on the right side. With the exception of hydrogen, the first element in a period is a solid, and the last element in a period is always a gas that does not react with other elements.

Elements that share the same number of electrons in their outer shell, the groups, share many of the same behaviors. Examples of shared

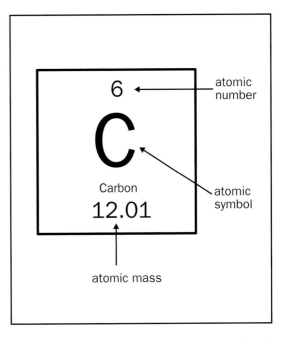

Each block in the periodic table provides information on a particular element. GALE GROUP.

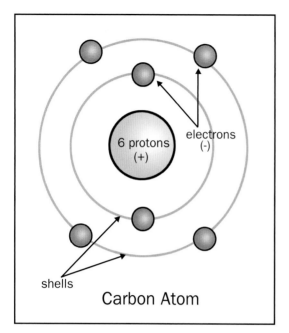

Carbon Atom

characteristics include their stability, boiling point, and conductivity. For example, the elements on the far right of the table is called the noble gases. Noble gases are colorless gases that are all nonreactive because their outermost shell is full. When the outermost shell is full the atom is completely stable and does not react. The groups on the far left also share many properties with each other. With few electrons in their outer shells, these metals are highly reactive and react strongly with nonmetals.

Although the properties in groups are similar, they change as you move up or down the column. For example, chemical activity generally increases as you go down a metal group and decreases as you move down a nonmetal group.

EXPERIMENT 1

Metals versus Nonmetals: Which areas of the periodic table have elements that conduct electricity?

Purpose/Hypothesis Conductivity is one of the properties that relates to the position of the element in the periodic table. Conductivity relates to the electron configuration in the element's atoms. Atoms are constantly working to get a full count of atoms in their outer shell. They can do this by losing or gaining electrons. A full count gives the atom stability and, thus, it does not need to react with other atoms. Elements in the low-number groups have atoms with one or few electrons in their outer shell. This causes these atoms to lose electrons easily. Their electrons move among all the atoms in the substance. Atoms in the highest groups have a full or almost-full outer shell and usually gain electrons. Their electrons do not move about freely.

The periodic table is composed of two main groups: metals and nonmetals. Metals are on the left and middle of the table; nonmetals make up parts of groups IIIA to VIIIA. Almost all metals are solids (mercury, a liquid, is the exception). Nonmetals can be solids, liquids, or gases.

In this experiment you will determine what areas of the periodic table have elements that are electrical conductors. A conductor provides a path that allows electricity to flow from a battery's positive terminal to its

Main-Group Elements

Main-Group Elements

Transition Metals

Inner-Transition Metals

Period

Atomic number 86 (222) **Atomic weight**
Symbol Rn
Name radon

	1 IA	2 IIA	3 IIIB	4 IVB	5 VB	6 VIB	7 VIIB	8	9 VIIIB	10	11 IB	12 IIB	13 IIIA	14 IVA	15 VA	16 VIA	17 VIIA	18 VIIIA
1	1 1.00794 H hydrogen																	2 4.002602 He helium
2	3 6.941 Li lithium	4 9.012182 Be beryllium											5 10.811 B boron	6 12.011 C carbon	7 14.00674 N nitrogen	8 15.9994 O oxygen	9 18.9984032 F fluorine	10 20.1797 Ne neon
3	11 22.989768 Na sodium	12 24.3050 Mg magnesium											13 26.981539 Al aluminum	14 28.0855 Si silicon	15 30.973762 P phosphorus	16 32.066 S sulfur	17 35.4527 Cl chlorine	18 39.948 Ar argon
4	19 39.0983 K potassium	20 40.078 Ca calcium	21 44.955910 Sc scandium	22 47.88 Ti titanium	23 50.9415 V vanadium	24 51.9961 Cr chromium	25 54.9305 Mn manganese	26 55.847 Fe iron	27 58.93320 Co cobalt	28 58.69 Ni nickel	29 63.546 Cu copper	30 65.39 Zn zinc	31 69.723 Ga gallium	32 72.61 Ge germanium	33 74.92159 As arsenic	34 78.96 Se selenium	35 79.904 Br bromine	36 83.80 Kr krypton
5	37 85.4678 Rb rubidium	38 87.62 Sr strontium	39 88.905585 Y yttrium	40 91.224 Zr zirconium	41 92.90638 Nb niobium	42 95.94 Mo molybdenum	43 (98) Tc technetium	44 101.07 Ru ruthenium	45 102.90550 Rh rhodium	46 106.42 Pd palladium	47 107.8682 Ag silver	48 112.411 Cd cadmium	49 114.82 In indium	50 118.710 Sn tin	51 121.75 Sb antimony	52 127.60 Te tellurium	53 126.90447 I iodine	54 131.29 Xe xenon
6	55 132.90543 Cs cesium	56 137.327 Ba barium	57-70 *	72 178.49 Hf hafnium	73 180.9479 Ta tantalum	74 183.85 W tungsten	75 186.207 Re rhenium	76 190.2 Os osmium	77 192.22 Ir iridium	78 195.08 Pt platinum	79 196.96654 Au gold	80 200.59 Hg mercury	81 204.3833 Tl thallium	82 207.2 Pb lead	83 208.98037 Bi bismuth	84 (209) Po polonium	85 (210) At astatine	86 (222) Rn radon
7	87 (223) Fr francium	88 (226) Ra radium	89-102 †	104 (261) Rf rutherfordium	105 (262) Db dubnium	106 (263) Sg seaborgium	107 (264) Bh bohrium	108 (265) Hs hassium	109 (268) Mt meitnerium	110 (269) Uun ununnilium	111 (272) Uuu unununium	112 (277) Uub ununbium	114 (289) Uuq ununquadium		116 (289) Uuh ununhexium		118 (293) Uuo ununoctium

71 174.967 *Lu lutetium
103 (262) Lr lawrencium

*Lanthanides

| 57 138.9055 La lanthanum | 58 140.115 Ce cerium | 59 140.90765 Pr praseodymium | 60 144.24 Nd neodymium | 61 (145) Pm promethium | 62 150.36 Sm samarium | 63 151.965 Eu europium | 64 157.25 Gd gadolinium | 65 158.92534 Tb terbium | 66 162.50 Dy dysprosium | 67 164.93032 Ho holmium | 68 167.26 Er erbium | 69 168.93421 Tm thulium | 70 173.04 Yb ytterbium |

†Actinides

| 89 (227) Ac actinium | 90 232.0381 Th thorium | 91 (231) Pa protactinium | 92 238.0289 U uranium | 93 (237) Np neptunium | 94 (244) Pu plutonium | 95 (243) Am americium | 96 (247) Cm curium | 97 (247) Bk berkelium | 98 (251) Cf californium | 99 (252) Es einsteinium | 100 (257) Fm fermium | 101 (258) Md mendelevium | 102 (259) No nobelium |

In the periodic table, groups and periods share certain properties. GALE GROUP.

WORDS TO KNOW

Alkali metals: The first group of elements in the periodic table, these metals have a single electron in the outermost shell.

Atom: The smallest unit of an element, made up of protons and neutrons in its center, surrounded by moving electrons.

Atomic mass: Also known as atomic weight, the average mass of the atoms in an element; the number that appears under the element symbol in the periodic table.

Atomic number: The number of protons (or electrons) in an atom; the number that appears over the element symbol in the periodic table.

Atomic symbol: The one- or two-letter abbreviation for a chemical element.

Control experiment: A setup that is identical to the experiment, but is not affected by the variables that affects the experimental group.

Electron: A subatomic particle with a mass of about one atomic mass unit and a single electrical charge that orbits the center of an atom.

Element: A pure substance composed of just one type of atom that cannot be broken down into anything simpler by ordinary chemical means.

Family: A group of elements in the same column of the periodic table or in closely related columns of

the table. A family of chemical compounds share similar structures and properties.

Group: A vertical column of the periodic table that contains elements possessing similar chemical characteristics.

Hypothesis: An idea in the form of a statement that can be tested by observation and/or experiment.

Neutron: A particle that has no electrical charge and is found in the center of an atom.

Noble gases: Also known as inert or rare gases; the elements argon, helium, krypton, neon, radon, and xenon, which are nonreactive gases and form few compounds with other elements.

Period: A horizontal row in the periodic table.

Periodic table: A chart organizing elements by atomic number and chemical properties into groups and periods.

Proton: A positively charged particle in the center of an atom.

Shell: A region of space around the center of the atom in which electrons are located.

Variable: Something that can affect the results of an experiment.

---

negative terminal. You will test the electrical conductivity of several elements by placing each one in the path of the electricity, and connecting the path to a small light. If the light comes on, the flow of electricity is passing through the element; if the light remains off, then the element did not pass the flow of electricity. There are many elements you can test. Options are provided in the materials section.

To begin this experiment make an educated guess, or prediction, of what you think will occur based on your knowledge of the periodic table. This educated guess, or prediction, is your hypothesis. A hypothesis should explain these things:

- the topic of the experiment
- the variable you will change
- the variable you will measure
- what you expect to happen

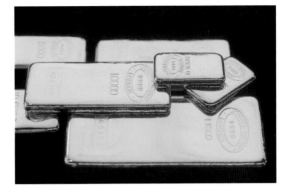

Gold is a transition metal. Will it conduct electricity?
© CHARLES O'REAR/CORBIS.

A hypothesis should be brief, specific, and measurable. It must be something you can test through further investigation. Your experiment will prove or disprove whether your hypothesis is correct. Here is one possible hypothesis for this experiment: "Elements in the middle and left of the periodic table will conduct electricity, and the light will come on; elements on the right side of the table will not be good conductors, and the light will not come on."

In this experiment the variable you will change will be the element; the variable you measure will be whether electricity is conducted to the light.

Conducting a control experiment will help you isolate each variable and measure the changes in the dependent variable. Only one variable will change between the control and the experimental trials. The control experiment will test for a complete circuit. The positive and negative wires will carry the electric current directly to the light bulb.

Level of Difficulty Moderate.

Materials Needed

- periodic table
- wire strippers (such as a knife)
- pliers
- scissors or wire cutters
- 2 1.5-volt batteries
- battery holder, (wires should be attached to holder)
- 6 insulated alligator clips
- insulated copper wire (about 2 feet or 61 centimeters)
- small light bulb and light bulb socket, less than 3 volts
- Elements: aluminum (foil, wire); silver (jewelry, silverware, wire); gold (jewelry); zinc (penny made after 1982, which is made of 97.5% zinc, the remaining 2.5% is copper); copper (wire; penny

What Are the Variables?

Variables are anything that might affect the results of an experiment. Here are the main variables in this experiment:

- the element
- the battery voltage

In other words, the variables in this experiment are everything that might affect whether electricity is conducted to the light. If you change more than one variable at the same time, you will not be able to tell which variable had the most effect on conducting the electricity.

How to Experiment Safely

Make sure there is no water nearby as water will carry the electricity. Be careful when cutting wire. If the wire gets hot to the touch at any point, immediately disconnect the wire from the battery. Make sure the wire is fully insulated.

dated 1962 to 1982, which is 95% copper and 5% zinc); carbon (lead in pencil, diamond on piece of jewelry); silicon (glass)

Approximate Budget $12–$20.

Timetable 1 hour

Step-by-Step Instructions

1. Insert the two batteries in the battery holder so the positive and negative ends are opposite to one another.
2. Cut three pieces of wire, each 6 to 12 inches (15 to 30 centimeters) long.
3. Strip about 0.5 inch (1.3 centimeters) of the insulation off both ends of each piece of wire.
4. Insert each end of the wire through the hole in the alligator clip and twist. There should now be three pieces of wire with clips on each end.
5. Twist or press the light bulb into the base.
6. Assemble the control experiment. With one wire, attach one clip to the exposed end of the battery wire and the clip on the other side to the light socket. Repeat with a second wire on the other side of the light socket. Note the results.
7. Remove one clip from the socket, and attach the third wire's clip in place of that clip.
8. Attach the clip of the free end of the third wire to one of the test elements. Attach the free end of the second wire to the other end of the element. When the path is complete, note whether the light glows.
9. Repeat Step 8, replacing the element with each test element one at a time. Note the results for each.

Summary of Results Create a chart of your results, writing down whether each element was a conductor or nonconductor. Examine the results. What elements conducted electricity and where are they located in the periodic table? Air is made up of gases, mostly oxygen and nitrogen. Look at the periodic table and examine why gases do not conduct electricity. Examine the number of electrons in the elements you used. Look up how many electrons are in their outer shell. Write a brief summary of the experiment, explaining why some elements would make better conductors than others.

Change the Variables To change the variable in this experiment, you can use a different voltage battery. You can also use a light with a different voltage.

EXPERIMENT 2

Soluble Families: How does the solubility of an element relate to where it is located on the periodic table?

Purpose/Hypothesis Groups are columns running down the periodic table. In this experiment you are determining an element's solubility. Solubility is the ability of a substance to dissolve in a liquid. For example, sugar dissolves in water and is therefore called soluble in water. Chocolate chips mixed with water do not dissolve and are called insoluble in water. Solubility is one of the properties that relates to the location of the element in the periodic table.

In this experiment you will determine what areas of the periodic table have the property of being soluble in water. You will use substances made from elements in the first two families of the periodic table. The first group on the left, Group 1A, is the Alkali Metals. Group 2A is called Alkali Earth Metals. These elements will form salts when a metal combines with a non-metal. For example, sodium and chloride combine to make table salt. By mixing these salts

Troubleshooter's Guide

Below are some problems that may arise during this experiment, some possible causes, and some ways to remedy the problem.

Problem: The light bulb does not light as expected.

Possible cause: The wire to the alligator clip may not be securely fastened to the element, or the alligator clip may not be touching the exposed wire. Repeat the experiment, scraping off enough plastic and checking that the exposed wires connect with each other.

Problem: The control light does not light for any element.

Possible cause: See "possible cause" above. Also, the battery may be dead and have no charge. Repeat the experiment with a fresh battery.

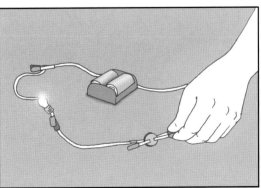

Step 8: Attach the clips to the test element and note if the current flows to the light. GALE GROUP.

What Are the Variables?

Variables are anything that might affect the results of an experiment. Here are the main variables in this experiment:

- the type of salt
- the temperature of water
- the quantity of salt
- the size of the salt particles

In other words, the variables in this experiment are everything that might affect whether the salts are soluble in water. If you change more than one variable at the same time, you will not be able to tell which variable had the most effect on solubility.

in water, you can then determine if either is soluble.

To begin this experiment make an educated guess, or prediction, of what you think will occur based on your knowledge of the periodic table, solubility, and groups. This educated guess, or prediction, is your hypothesis. A hypothesis should explain these things:

- the topic of the experiment
- the variable you will change
- the variable you will measure
- what you expect to happen

A hypothesis should be brief, specific, and measurable. It must be something you can test through further investigation. Your experiment will prove or disprove whether your hypothesis is correct. Here is one possible hypothesis for this experiment: "Salts made from elements in the Alkali Metals will dissolve in water more readily than salts in the Alkali Earth Metals."

In this experiment the variable you will change will be the type of salt; the variable you measure will be the solubility of the salt.

Note: When making a solid-liquid solution (solid/liquid), it is standard to use weight/weight (grams/grams) or weight/volume (grams/milliliters). With water, 1 gram of water equals 1 milliliter. In this experiment, teaspoons and tablespoons are used to measure the solid.

Level of Difficulty Easy to Moderate.

Materials Needed

- washing soda (sodium carbonate: available at many supermarkets in the detergent section)
- potassium carbonate (available at chemical supply houses: an adult must order this)
- chalk (calcium carbonate; active ingredient in many antacids)
- water
- measuring spoons
- metal spoon

- measuring cup
- plastic gloves
- three glasses
- masking tape
- marking pen

Approximate Budget $15.

Timetable 30 minutes.

How to Experiment Safely

Be careful when working with potassium carbonate. Wear plastic gloves during this experiment. Do not ingest it or get it near your eyes. Wash your hands thoroughly after the experiment.

Step-by-Step Instructions

1. Pour 1 cup (about 0.25 liters or 250 milliliters) of room-temperature water into each glass. Label each glass with the name of one of the salts.
2. Crush the calcium carbonate into a powder by wrapping a small piece of chalk or tablet in plastic wrap and pressing down on it with a spoon.
3. Measure out 1 teaspoon of the crushed calcium carbonate and stir it thoroughly in the water in the glass labeled "calcium carbonate" for at least one minute. You may need to stir for up to two minutes.
4. Examine the bottom of the glass for any powder residue and note the solubility.
5. Repeat Steps 4 and 5 for the other two salts using the other two glasses of water.

Summary of Results Was your hypothesis correct? Why are the salts of Alkali Metals more soluble than Alkali Earth Metals? Determine the electron configuration of the three salts. Write up a brief description of the experiment, analyzing your conclusion.

Change the Variables It is difficult to find pure elements as most are naturally found mixed with other elements. To change the variable in this experiment, you can try to change the water temperature. You can hypothesize what the combination of other salts would be

Step 3: Stir each of the salts in the water to determine its solubility. GALE GROUP.

Troubleshooter's Guide

Below are some problems that may arise during this experiment, some possible causes, and some ways to remedy the problems.

Problem: The powder did not dissolve as expected.

Possible cause: The salt particles may be too large to dissolve. The particles should be a fine powder. Try repeating the experiment, crushing the chalk or tablets completely and stirring thoroughly.

Problem: The salt does not completely dissolve where it theoretically should dissolve.

Possible cause: See "possible cause" above. The metallic element you used may not be pure. Make sure you are not using colored chalk. You can also try purchasing real chalk or use another antacid tablet.

and then conduct research to verify your hypothesis.

EXPERIMENT 3

Active Metals: What metals give off electrons more readily than others?

Purpose/Hypothesis Some metals are more active than others, meaning they let go of their electrons more easily than other metals. In general, the activity of different elements relates to its position in the periodic table. Elements that are larger are generally more likely to lose their outer electrons than the smaller elements).

In this experiment you will determine which of two metals is more active: zinc or copper. In order to help the metals give off electrons, you will boil each in a salt and vinegar solution. Vinegar is a weak acid that helps loosen the electrons, and salt acts like a bridge for the electrons to move. The metal that loses electrons more readily will get plated, meaning a thin layer of metal will deposit on it. When the electrons move from one metal onto the more active metal, it will cause a visual change. By trying this experiment with both metals, you will be able to determine which metal is more active.

To begin this experiment make an educated guess, or prediction, of what you think will occur based on your knowledge of the periodic table, metals, and groups. This educated guess, or prediction, is your hypothesis. A hypothesis should explain these things:

- the topic of the experiment
- the variable you will change
- the variable you will measure
- what you expect to happen

A hypothesis should be brief, specific, and measurable. It must be something you can test through further investigation. Your experiment will prove or disprove whether your hypothesis is correct. Here is one possible hypothesis for this experiment: "Zinc is more active than copper and therefore will lose its electrons when placed in an acidic solution."

In this experiment the variable you will change will be the type of metal. The variable you measure will be the visual changes to the metals.

Level of Difficulty Moderate.

Materials Needed

- white vinegar
- table salt
- 2 small glass bowls
- small pan
- measuring cup
- measuring spoon
- copper wire, small gage, approximately 20 feet (6 meters), tightly wound into ball (copper wire for jewelry works well, found at craft stores)
- 4 zinc washers (found at hardware stores)
- steel wool
- tongs or fork

Approximate Budget $10.

Timetable Approximately 2 hours

Step-by-Step Instructions

1. Pour 1 cup of white vinegar and one tablespoon of table salt into a small pan.
2. Place the copper wire into the pan.
3. Boil the wire in the vinegar solution for 15 minutes.
4. While the vinegar solution is coming to a boil, clean the zinc washer with steel wool until scratching is visible.
5. Place the zinc washer in a glass bowl.
6. Once the vinegar solution has boiled for 15 minutes, pour only the solution into the glass bowl. Use a pair of tongs or fork to remove the copper wire. Make sure the solution covers the washer.
7. Observe and record changes to the zinc washer at 15 minute intervals for 45 minutes.

What Are the Variables?

Variables are anything that might affect the results of an experiment. Here are the main variables in this experiment:

- the type of metal
- the length of time the metal is boiled
- the length of time the metal is placed in acid solution
- the purity of the metal tested
- the amount of salt in the solution

In other words, the variables in this experiment are everything that might affect the activity of metals in the solution. If you change more than one variable at the same time, you will not be able to tell which variable had the most effect on the metal's activity.

How to Experiment Safely

Be careful when boiling the vinegar and salt solution. Have an adult helper assist you with this part of the experiment. Allow the metals to cool before you touch them after they are taken out of the boiling solution.

8. Repeat all the steps above, switching the two metals. Replace the copper wire with three zinc washers. Make sure to make a new vinegar and salt solution. After boiling the zinc washers for 15 minutes, pour only the solution into a glass bowl that holds copper wire.

9. Observe and record changes to the copper wire at 15 minute intervals.

Summary of Results Compare the appearance of the zinc washers and copper wire that were in the glass bowls. Was your hypothesis correct? Did the zinc accept more electrons and change color? How do the results relate to their placement in the periodic table? Write a summary of the experiment, explaining which of the metals was more active. You might want to include pictures and notes from your observations.

Step 1: Gather your materials (salt, vinegar, copper wire, and zinc washer). ILLUSTRATION BY TEMAH NELSON.

Change the Variables To change the variable in this experiment, you can use alkali earth metals such as magnesium and calcium found in common antacid medications. You can experiment with different metals and changing the temperature of the vinegar and salt solution.

Design Your Own Experiment

How to Select a Topic Relating to this Concept There are many ways to categorize and group the elements in the periodic table. All matter is made up of elements, yet it is difficult to find elements in their pure form. When experimenting with the properties of elements, look for the active ingredient on major products.

Check the Further Readings section and talk with your science teacher to learn more about the periodic table and the elements.

Steps in the Scientific Method To conduct an original experiment, you need to plan carefully and think things through. Otherwise, you might not be sure what question you are answering, what you are or should be measuring, or what your findings prove or disprove.

Here are the steps in designing an experiment:

- State the purpose of—and the underlying question behind—the experiment you propose to do.
- Recognize the variables involved and select one that will help you answer the question at hand.
- State your hypothesis, an educated guess about the answer to your question.
- Decide how to change the variable you selected.
- Decide how to measure your results.

Step 3: Boil the wire in the vinegar solution for 15 minutes. ILLUSTRATION BY TEMAH NELSON.

Recording Data and Summarizing the Results Your data should include charts and graphs such as the one you did for these experiments. They should be clearly labeled and easy to read. You may also want to include photographs and drawings of your experimental setup and results, which will help other people visualize the steps in the experiment.

If you are preparing an exhibit, you may want to display your results, such as any experimental setup you designed. If you have completed a nonexperimental project, explain clearly what your research question was and illustrate your findings.

Step 6: Once the vinegar solution has boiled for 15 minutes, pour only the solution into the glass bowl with the zinc washer. ILLUSTRATION BY TEMAH NELSON.

Related Projects For projects related on the periodic table, you can compare a variety of metals with one another to determine their differences and similarities. Some properties you can look at are the metal's relative softness, conductivity, and how it is affected by oxygen. Because elements are difficult to come across in their pure form, you can theorize on the properties of other metals and then conduct research. Certain groups of elements also react with bases, such as baking soda. If you order elements from a lab supply house, make sure you follow all the

Troubleshooter's Guide

Below are some problems that may arise during this experiment, some possible causes, and some ways to remedy the problems.

Problem: The metals did not change.

Possible cause: The wire may not have a high enough copper content. Make sure you are using real copper wire. You can also use a piece of copper. Repeat the experiment.

Possible cause: The copper wire may not have lost enough electrons. Make sure the vinegar solution is brought to a rolling boil for at least 15 minutes. You may want to boil the copper wire for 20 minutes.

Possible cause: The copper's electrons were not able to move onto the zinc washer. There may not have been enough salt in the vinegar solution. Make sure you add 1 tablespoon of salt and stir well.

necessary safety precautions. Scientists are continuing to discover elements in the laboratory. For a research project you could look at the history of the periodic table and the story of the discoveries.

For More Information

Andrew Rader Studios. "Elements." *Rader's Chem4Kids.com.* http://www. chem4kids.com/files/elem_intro.html (accessed on February 18, 2008). Detailed information about the periodic table, elements, metals, and other subjects for intermediate and advanced students.

Baum, Rudy. "The Periodic Table of the Elements." *Chemical & Engineering News.* http://pubs.acs.org/cen/80th/elements.html (accessed on February 18, 2008).

BBC. "Mixtures." Chemical Symbols: The Periodic Table. *Schools. Science: Chemistry.* http://www. bbc.co.uk/schools/ks3bitesize/science/chemistry/elements_com_mix_2.shtml (accessed on February 18, 2008). Basic information on the chemistry of mixtures.

Emsley, John. "The Development of the Periodic Table." *Chem.Soc: the ASC's Chemical Science Network.* http://www.chemsoc.org/viselements/pages/history.html (accessed on February 18, 2008). The history of the development of the periodic table.

Heiserman, David L. *Exploring Chemical Elements and their Compounds.* Blue Ridge Summit, PA: Tab Books, 1992. A basic introduction to chemical elements.

PeriodicTable.com http://periodictable.com/ (accessed on February 18, 2008). Information about the periodic table suited to different audiences.

"The Periodic Table of Comic Books." *Department of Chemistry, University of Kentucky.* http://www.uky.edu/Projects/Chemcomics (accessed on February 18, 2008). An informative and amusing collection of information about various chemical elements and their properties as found in the pages of comic books.

Sacks, Oliver. *Uncle Tungsten: Memories of a Chemical Boyhood.* New York: Vintage Books, 2002. Autobiography of Sacks tells of early chemistry experiments and learning about the elements.

64

Pesticides

A pesticide is any substance that prevents, repels, or kills pests. The definition of a pest is a relative one. A pest is an organism that is unwanted by humans at a specific time or in a specific place. Pests can range from cockroaches and mice, to fungi and plants. In modern day, pesticides are an integral part of food production and household use.

The use of pesticides has a long history. There is evidence that ancient Romans and Chinese, for example, used various minerals and plant extracts as pesticides. Manufactured chemical pesticides began in the 1930s and dramatically increased after World War II (1939–45). The widespread use of chemical pesticides led to an increased concern for how pesticides were affecting the environment, animals, and people. Over the years, pesticides have undergone much advancement, including the development of natural substances and improvements on the traditional.

Pest control Pesticides are categorized according to what type of pests they affect. Some common types of pesticides include insecticides for insects, herbicides for weeds, fungicides for fungi, and rodenticides for rodents.

A pesticide can be a natural or a chemically synthesized substance. Chemical pesticides are toxic, meaning they contain poisons. Natural pesticides do not use poisons to affect pests. Both types of pesticides have positives and negatives. These pesticides control pests by physically, chemically, or biologically disrupting a pest's life cycle or behavior.

There are hundreds of different synthetic chemicals used in pesticides. How each pesticide works depends on its active ingredient(s). Some pesticides have similar properties based on their chemical structure. There are several groups of synthetic chemical pesticides that interrupt a pest's nerves from communicating with each other and from activating certain muscles. Organophosphates, for example, are a group of long-lasting pesticides that affect the central nervous system (brain) and peripheral

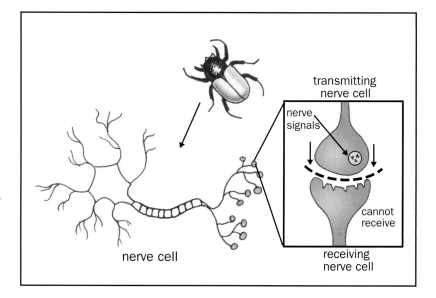

Organophosphates, one type of synthetic pesticide, prevent the nerves from signaling to the muscles that control the pest's breathing, resulting in suffocation and death. GALE GROUP.

nervous system (nerves found outside of the brain or spinal cord). In one pesticide, for example, the organophosphates prevent the nerves from signaling to the muscles that control the pest's breathing, resulting in suffocation and death.

The possible health effects for humans associated with an excess of chemical pesticide exposure include headaches, dizziness, muscle twitching, nausea, and damage to the central nervous system and kidneys.

Biopesticides are pesticides produced from substances found in nature; these do not use poison to affect pests. There are three main categories of biopesticides. One category includes those in which the active ingredient occurs in nature. For example, pheromones are chemical scents animals use to communicate, attract mates, and mark territory. If a pheromone-based pesticide is released into the air at a time when insects are looking for each other to mate, the insects will become confused. Less mating and far fewer offspring will result. Other types of this biopesticide include garlic, mint, and red peppers.

The active ingredient in another type of biopesticide is microorganisms or microbes, such as bacteria and fungi. Microbes produce substances that destroy a range of other microbes. For example, there are fungi that control weeds, and other fungi that kill specific insects. The most widely used microbial insecticide is the soil-dwelling bacterium *Bacillus*

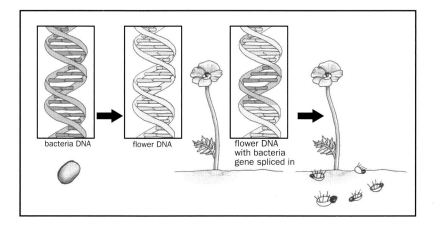

bacteria DNA

flower DNA

flower DNA
with bacteria
gene spliced in

By splicing bacteria DNA into the plant's DNA, scientists can create a genetically engineered plant that destroys specific pests. GALE GROUP.

thuringiensis, also known as Bt. When certain insects ingest the bacteria during the larvae stage, the bacteria interfere with the insect's digestion and cause the insect to starve.

One of the fastest-growing categories of biopesticides includes pesticide products that are genetically engineered or modified. Developed in the 1970s, genetic engineering is based on the understanding that genes are responsible for a species' characteristics. Genes are segments of deoxyribonucleic acid (DNA), a molecule in every organism's cell that carries genetic information for its development. Many organisms have genes that are responsible for producing substances that kill or prevent the growth of other organisms. This technique inserts the gene of one species into the DNA of the same or another species. The genetically modified organism then produces a desired trait. For example, scientists have taken the pest-fighting gene out of the Bt bacteria and inserted it into a corn plant's genetic material. The Bt corn then manufactures the substance that destroys the corn borer or another hungry insect.

The good, the bad, and the pesty Pesticides both directly and indirectly hold many benefits for people. They increase agricultural yields by eliminating pests and weeds, providing more food and income for people around the world. They protect crops from disease that can devastate food supplies. In the mid-1800s, for example, a fungus spread quickly through Ireland's potato crops, resulting in the starvation of more than a million people and causing mass emigration. Shielding plants from disease also lessens disease in plant-eating livestock and, ultimately, in humans who would eat that plant or livestock. For the nonfarmer, the use of pesticides has become commonplace. Insect repellents, flea and tick pet

A cotton farmer in India points to genetically modified Bt cotton infected with bollworms, January 2003. Bt cotton has failed to prevent bollworm attacks, for which it was designed. AP/WIDE WORLD

collars, weed killers, and mildew cleaners are just a few of the household products that contain pesticides.

Yet because pesticides are designed to control living organisms, some affect organisms they are not targeted to control, called nontarget organisms. The result can harm humans, animals, and the environment. The pesticide dichlorodiphenyltrichloroethane (DDT) is the classic example of how pesticides can cause unintended effects. DDT was discovered to be an effective insecticide in 1939 and within a few years it became one of the most widely used pesticidal chemicals in the United States. Farmers used it on their crops, and the government used it to protect people against disease-carrying insects, such as mosquitoes that carried malaria.

For years scientists warned about the possible harmful effects of DDT; then in 1962 Rachel Carson's book *Silent Spring* was published. Her book mapped out how DDT was harming wildlife, the environment, and people. In one scenario, DDT sprayed on plants was eaten by small animals, which were then consumed by birds. The pesticide harmed both the adult birds and their eggs. The eggs' shells were so thin they were often crushed when the mother sat on them during their incubation period. Eggs that were not crushed often did not hatch. The book stimulated widespread public concern, and in 1973 the chemical was banned in the United States (it is still used in other countries).

A balancing act The danger of pesticides to humans and the environment depends upon the pesticide and its mechanism for pest control. Some factors that determine a pesticide's potential harm are its toxicity, specificity in its targets, and how long it remains in the environment before it breaks down or degrades.

Pesticides can enter nontarget plants, insects, and other organisms in several ways. Pesticides do not always stay where they are put down. Wind

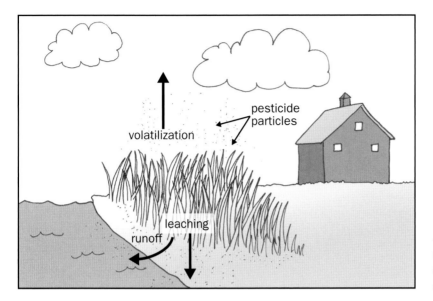

Pesticides can spread through the environment through volatilization, runoff, and leaching. GALE GROUP.

or rain can carry the pesticide into bodies of water. There, it can affect sea life and contaminate water. It can move through or leach into the soil. Leaching is the movement of dissolved chemicals with water downward through the soil. Water not absorbed into the soil also causes pesticides to travel. When this water moves over a sloping surface it is called runoff; the runoff picks up and carries the pesticides. Leaching and runoff cause pesticides to travel into unintended locations, sometimes winding up in groundwater, lakes, oceans, or neighboring areas. In a process called volatilization, some pesticides convert into a gas and move in the air. These pesticides can travel long distances before they settle down into waters or on land.

One of the most important factors that affects the risk of pesticide leaching is the amount of time it takes for the pesticide to degrade. Pesticides degrade into substances that are usually less toxic. Pesticides can attach to soil particles and remain in effect long after the manufacturers intended. The longer a pesticide lasts, the greater the chance it will accumulate in an unintended area or nontarget organism. DDT was an example of a long-lasting pesticide.

The advantage of biopesticides is that they have a low danger level (toxicity) to organisms they are not targeted for and to humans. Low toxicity means less risk to water supplies and life. Many of these biopesticides also degrade relatively rapidly.

The drawback to biopesticides is that they are not as powerful as conventional chemical pesticides. Because these pesticides degrade

A swarm of locusts surrounds a Filipino farmer. A locust infestation of rice and sugar farms in Tarlac, Philippines, in 1994 caused major crop and financial losses for farmers. © REUTERS NEWMEDIA/CORBIS.

quickly, they have only a short time period where they can be used. In addition, certain microbial pesticides can become inactive if exposed to extreme environmental conditions, such as too much heat or dryness. Some environmental and citizens groups are also concerned about genetically modified organisms. They say that these plants may produce unintended consequences to people, the environment, and animals.

The U.S. federal government evaluates and regulates pesticide use. Regulations on pesticides applied to foods have especially strict safety standards. Pesticides are labeled as to their level of toxicity. Washing and cooking foods are ways that people can reduce pesticide residue.

EXPERIMENT 1

Natural versus Synthetic: How do different types of pesticides compare against a pest?

Purpose/Hypothesis Many plants produce substances that prevent or harm pests. Some of these substances kill their insect predators and others repel them. For example, a plant can emit an odor that prevents pests from approaching. Yet while biopesticides are generally safer to the environment and carry fewer risks to people, chemicals remain the

WORDS TO KNOW

Biopesticide: Pesticide produced from substances found in nature.

Control experiment: A setup that is identical to the experiment, but is not affected by the variables that affects the experimental group.

Degrade: Break down.

Deoxyribonucleic acid (DNA): Large, complex molecules in cells that carries genetic information for an organism's development.

Hypothesis: An idea in the form of a statement that can be tested by observation and/or experiment.

Leaching: The movement of dissolved chemicals with water that is percolating, or oozing, downward through the soil.

Pest: Any living thing that is unwanted by humans or causes injury and disease to crops and other growth.

Pesticide: Substance used to reduce the abundance of pests.

Runoff: Water not absorbed by the soil; moves downward and picks up particles along the way.

Synthesized: Prepared by humans in a laboratory; not a naturally occurring process.

Synthetic: A substance that is synthesized, or manufactured, in a laboratory; not naturally occurring.

Toxic: Poisonous.

Variable: Something that can affect the results of an experiment.

Volatilization: The process by which a liquid changes (volatilizes) to a gas.

---

pesticide of choice for the vast majority of professionals. Because pesticides are so important to society, people are continuously searching for the most effective substance that will cause the least harm.

In this experiment you will examine how biopesticides compare to a synthetic pesticide. The two natural pesticides are a spray made from chili peppers and one made from garlic. These are commonly used among gardeners as repellents. With chili, it is the hot chilies that make the most effective repellent. Garlic's strong odor can also act as a repellent. With the synthetic insecticides, look for one that works against general pests, such as aphids, caterpillars, beetles. Evidence of these pests can be seen in the holes they bore or bits of leaves that they have munched. Aphids will leave a sticky residue on the leaves.

Once you have made a spray of the natural substances, you can apply all the pesticides to the same type of plant and set outside. To measure the effectiveness of each pesticide you can examine the plant's general health, count holes in the leaves and pests on the plant, and feel the leaves.

What Are the Variables?

Variables are anything that might affect the results of an experiment. Here are the main variables in this experiment:

- the type of plant
- the pests in the environment
- the type of pesticide
- the climate

In other words, the variables in this experiment are everything that might affect the amount of pests that are attracted to the plant. If you change more than one variable at the same time, you will not be able to tell which variable had the most effect on the pesticide's effectiveness.

Before you begin, make an educated guess about the outcome of this experiment based on your knowledge of synthetic pesticides and biopesticides. This educated guess, or prediction, is your hypothesis. A hypothesis should explain these things:

- the topic of the experiment
- the variable you will change
- the variable you will measure
- what you expect to happen

A hypothesis should be brief, specific, and measurable. It must be something you can test through further investigation. Your experiment will prove or disprove whether your hypothesis is correct. Here is one possible hypothesis for this experiment: "The synthetic pesticide product will better prevent pests from harming the plants than the biopesticides."

In this case, the variable you will change is the type of pesticide sprayed on the plant. The variable you will measure is the amount of damage to the plant caused by pests.

Conducting a control experiment will help you isolate each variable and measure the changes in the dependent variable. Only one variable will change between the control and your experiment. For your control in this experiment you will not apply any pesticide to a plant. At the end of the experiment you can compare the control plant to the experimental plants.

Level of Difficulty Moderate.

Materials Needed

- 4 small plants of the same type, preferably broad leafed (coleus works well)
- 1 hot chili pepper (habañeros work well)
- 1 garlic bulb (five cloves) or crushed garlic
- spray bottle
- chemical pesticide (available from hardware store, drugstore, or greenhouse)

- outside area
- water
- 2 bowls
- marking pen
- chopping knife
- cheesecloth
- funnel
- rubber gloves
- several nice days

Approximate Budget $15.

Timetable 45 minutes setup; overnight waiting; 10 minutes every three days for about two weeks.

Step-by-Step Instructions

1. Label the plant containers: "Pepper," "Garlic," "Chemical," and "Control."
2. Prepare the chili pepper spray: Chop one chili and place the pieces in a bowl. Boil 1 cup (about 240 milliliters) of water and pour over the chopped peppers. Set aside overnight.
3. The next day, prepare the garlic spray: Finely chop about five cloves of garlic and add 1 cup (about 240 milliliters) of hot water. Set aside for two hours until cool.
4. When the solutions are ready, use the cheesecloth to strain out the garlic and the peppers. Use the funnel to pour one of the solutions into the spray bottle.
5. In an open area outside, spray the first solution on the plant labeled for that pesticide. After each application, set the plant in a distant area to keep each pesticide isolated from the other plants. Make sure to wash out the spray bottle thoroughly between the pepper and garlic spray (save each solution in a covered and labeled container). Repeat with the other two solutions. Do not spray anything on the control.

Materials needed to compare different pesticides in Experiment 1. GALE GROUP.

Troubleshooter's Guide

Below are some problems that may arise during this experiment, some possible causes, and some ways to remedy the problems.

Problem: The natural sprays did not stick to the plant leaves.

Possible cause: The mixtures adhere to the leaves of some plants more than others. Try adding a drop of nondetergent dishwashing soap and mixing well, then reapply.

Problem: None of the plants had much evidence of pests.

Possible cause: This experiment works best when there are many insects around, often during the spring and summer months. Try to set your plants down in a wooded area or one that has a large quantity of plants and then continue your observations.

6. Set the four plants outside in the same general area, leaving enough room between the plants so they do not touch one another.

7. Every three days for the next 15 days observe the plants and note any pests or effects of pests. Reapply the sprays if it rains. If you reapply, again make sure to isolate each plant when you spray.

Summary of Results Was your hypothesis correct? Look at your data and determine how the pesticides compared to one another. Was there one type of pest that was on one plant more than another? Some types of insects, such as aphids, gather on the underside of leaves. Note the relative amount of any different type of pests on each plant. How did the control plant compare to the experimental plants?

Change the Variables In this experiment you can change the variables in several ways:

- change the type of plant
- use the same pesticide and set the plants down in different environments, such as near lush plant growth or in an open space
- apply different types of synthetic pesticides
- make up and apply different natural pesticides, such as pesticides made from onions, soaps, neem oil, and molasses.
- use the same pesticide and see how close you need to apply it to the plant for it to be effective.

EXPERIMENT 2

Moving through Water: How can pesticides affect nontarget plant life?

Purpose/Hypothesis Leaching and runoff can cause pesticides to move away from their target location. When pesticides mix with rain or irrigation water, they can seep into the soil and travel to another area where they can affect the plant, animals, and environment. In this experiment, you will examine the effects of pesticides on new growth. You will plant a lettuce seed and nurture it with water that has insecticide in it. Planting three sets of seeds, you will add two varying amounts of insecticide to the water and compare them to lettuce grown in unaltered water.

Before you begin, make an educated guess about the outcome of this experiment based on your knowledge of leaching, runoff, and pesticides. This educated guess, or prediction, is your hypothesis. A hypothesis should explain these things:

- the topic of the experiment
- the variable you will change
- the variable you will measure
- what you expect to happen

A hypothesis should be brief, specific, and measurable. It must be something you can test through further investigation. Your experiment will prove or disprove whether your hypothesis is correct. Here is one possible hypothesis for this experiment: "Water with the greatest amount of pesticide will result in stunted or no plant growth."

In this case, the variable you will change is the amount of insecticide in the water. The variable you will measure is the plant health.

Conducting a control experiment will help you isolate each variable and measure the changes in the dependent variable. Only one variable will change between the control and your experiment. For the control in this experiment you will give the lettuce plant plain water. At the end of the experiment, you can compare the results from the control experiment with the experimental plants.

Level of Difficulty Easy to Moderate.

Materials Needed

- 15 lettuce seeds
- peat pots, with moist to dry soil (available at garden stores)
- water
- liquid synthetic insecticide

What Are the Variables?

Variables are anything that might affect the results of an experiment. Here are the main variables in this experiment:

- the type of plant
- the environment
- the amount of pesticide
- the type of pesticide

In other words, the variables in this experiment are anything that might affect the growth of the plant. If you change more than one variable at the same time, you will not be able to tell which variable had the most effect on the plant's health.

How to Experiment Safely

Have an adult present for this experiment. Be careful when working with the pesticide. Measure the pesticide outside or in a sink. Follow the warnings carefully and wash your hands afterwards. Make sure you throw away the disposable cups and spoons that come into contact with the pesticide. Keep younger children away from the cups containing the pesticide mixtures.

- marking pen
- masking tape
- ruler
- area with light
- paper towels
- plastic wrap
- two rubber bands
- plastic teaspoon
- measuring cup
- three disposable plastic cups

Approximate Budget $7.

Timetable 20 minutes setup; about 5five minutes daily for eight to 12 days (longer if desired).

Step-by-Step Instructions

1. Label the disposable cups: "Low Pesticide," "High Pesticide," and "Control." Label each peat pot "Low," "High," and "Control." The dirt should be dry to moist.
2. In the Low Pesticide cup, use the plastic spoon to place 2 teaspoons (about 10 milliliters) of the pesticide in the cup.
3. In the High Pesticide cup, use the plastic spoon to place 5 teaspoons (about 25 milliliters) of the pesticide in the cup.
4. Measure and pour 0.5 cup (about 125 milliliters) of water into each of the cups. The Control cup should have plain water. Use plastic spoons to stir the High and Low cups, making sure to throw the spoons away when you have finished.
5. In each peat pot, plant five lettuce seeds per the instructions on the package.
6. Working over a sink or paper towels, pour the High pesticide water into the peat pot labeled High. Pour enough water to saturate the lettuce seeds. Water will start to drip out the bottom when you have poured enough.
7. Repeat with the Low water, and the Control water. Set the plants on a plastic

Step 9: Note the number of sprouts in each pot and measure the height of the plants. GALE GROUP.

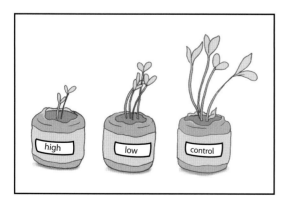

container or holder to catch the water dripping out the bottom.

8. To seal in the water, tightly cover the disposable cups (not the peat pots) with plastic wrap and wrap a rubber band around the plastic. Place the water cups aside near the plants and make sure labeling is clearly visible.

9. After the seeds sprout (about five days), start daily observations of the plants. Count how many sprouts there are in each pot and measure the height. Make your measurements at the same time every day.

10. When the seeds need more water, use the water from its designated cup until the water is gone. (You may need to restir.)

Summary of Results Examine the height and number of sprouts from each peat pot. Average the heights of each group and graph the results. Is there a difference between the experimental trials and the control? Are there any other physical characteristics that are different among the groups of lettuce sprouts? Write up a brief summary of the experiment.

Change the Variables You can change the variables in this experiment in several ways:

- Change the brand of insecticide; try to find one with different main ingredients than the one you used
- Alter the type of pesticide, to a herbicide or fungicide
- Compare different types of plants, such as peas, tomatoes, and a flower

Design Your Own Experiment

How to Select a Topic Relating to this Concept Pesticides are a continuously evolving groups of products, which have a significant impact on society. Organic food products are not treated with chemical-based

---

Troubleshooter's Guide

Below are some problems that may arise during this experiment, some possible causes, and some ways to remedy the problem.

Problem: None of the plants grew.

Possible cause: Make sure you are following instructions as to the amount of light and warmth the seeds need. You may also have bought defective seeds. Try the experiment again with a new packet, making sure to follow the instructions.

Problem: There was not much difference between the two groups of seeds watered with the pesticides.

Possible cause: All the pesticide water may not have soaked into the plants. Make sure you stir the water thoroughly before applying it to the seeds, and repeat the experiment.

pesticides. You can compare organic fruits and vegetables to chemically treated foods. You can also look at the impact pesticides have had on food production throughout the world.

When experimenting with pesticides, always make sure to work in an open area and take proper safety precautions. Check the Further Readings section and talk with your science teacher to learn more about pesticides. You could also speak with a professional at a local greenhouse or nursery, or any knowledgeable gardener.

Steps in the Scientific Method To conduct an original experiment, you need to plan carefully and think things through. Otherwise, you might not be sure what question you are answering, what you are or should be measuring, or what your findings prove or disprove.

Here are the steps in designing an experiment:

- State the purpose of—and the underlying question behind—the experiment you propose to do.
- Recognize the variables involved and select one that will help you answer the question at hand.
- State your hypothesis, an educated guess about the answer to your question.
- Decide how to change the variable you selected.
- Decide how to measure your results.

Recording Data and Summarizing the Results Your data should include charts and graphs such as the one you did for these experiments. They should be clearly labeled and easy to read. You may also want to include photographs and drawings of your experimental setup and results, which will help other people visualize the steps in the experiment.

If you are preparing an exhibit, you may want to display your results, such as any experimental setup you designed. If you have completed a nonexperimental project, explain clearly what your research question was and illustrate your findings.

Related Projects With so many pesticide options, there are many possible project ideas. You can explore the biology of how pesticides work on insects. Choose one or two groups of chemical pesticides, then compare the effect of these to the substances that plants produce to ward off insects. How do herbicides affect plants? The amount of time pesticides remain in the soil and on plants is another area of study. An experiment can look at how often a pesticide needs to be reapplied for effectiveness.

You can also conduct a project that looks at how different pesticides move through the soil. Determining if a pesticide is on soil or in water is usually determined through chemical analysis. One home technique to find out where pesticides are would be to compare the test samples against a standard. Measure the standard by setting a pesticide-sprayed plant outside for a certain length of time and noting the results. You can then spray the water with possible pesticide in it and compare the results to the standard.

For a research project, you can explore the use of pesticides on food products, how pesticides have changed over the years, and the precautions that are taken on the foods. How do organic products compare in size and yield? Compare the United States to other countries' use of pesticides.

For More Information

"About Pesticides." *U.S. Environmental Protection Agency.* http://www.epa.gov/pesticides/about (accessed on February 3, 2008). Provides answers to frequently asked questions about pesticides.

"50 Ways Farmers Can Protect Their Groundwater: 24. Determine the Soil–Pesticide Interaction Rating." *University of Illinois Extension: College of Agricultural, Consumer, and Environmental Sciences.* http://www.thisland.uiuc.edu/50ways/50ways_24.html (accessed on February 3, 2008). This site is intended primarily for farmers, but offers good explanations of how pesticides get into soil and their effects.

Nancarrow, Loren, and Janet Hogan Taylor. *Dead Snails Leave No Trails.* Berkeley, CA: Ten Speed Press, 1996. Natural pest control information and recipes.

"Pesticides As Water Pollutants." *Food and Agriculture Organization.* http://www.fao.org/docrep/W2598E/w2598e07.htm#historical%20development%20of%20pesticides (accessed on February 3, 2008). Information on how pesticides can pollute groundwater.

pH

The numerical measurement of acids and bases in a solution is called pH (the abbreviation for potential hydrogen). Acids and bases are groups of chemicals. When dissolved in water, all acids release hydrogen atoms with a positive electric charge (H+). These atoms are known as hydrogen ions. The term pH means the strength of the hydrogen ions. The p is derived from the Danish word *potenz* meaning strength; H is the symbol for hydrogen. When dissolved in water, bases produce negatively charged hydroxide ions (OH–). When mixed together in the right proportions, acids and bases neutralize each other and form a water and a salt.

In 1909, Danish scientist Soren Peter Lauritz Sorensen, whose wife Margarethe Hoyrup Sorensen assisted him in much of his work, developed the concept of pH for determining hydrogen ion concentration.

Scaling it down The pH scale ranges from 0 to 14. Very acidic substances are at the lower end of the scale, with 0.0 being the most acidic, and very basic substances are at the upper end of the scale, with 14.0 being the most basic. A pH of 7.0 indicates a substance that is neutral—neither acidic nor basic.

They're everywhere Acids and bases are present in our daily lives more than we realize. We could not digest food without the diluted hydrochloric acid in our stomachs. Eight special amino acids in the protein foods we eat are necessary for good health. Acetic acid is found in vinegar. Sulfuric acid is used in dyes, drugs, explosives, car batteries, and fertilizer. Among the most commonly known bases are ammonia and sodium hydroxide, which is used to make soap.

Are you blue? No, I'm acid Measuring pH is important to chemists, biologists, bacteriologists,

Blue litmus paper turns pink in the presence of the acid in this lemon. PHOTO RESEARCHERS INC.

A digital pH meter measures pH. PHOTO RESEARCHERS INC.

and agriculture experts as well as others in science, medicine, and industry. Your life depends on the right pH of your body fluids, including your blood and digestive juices. Determining soil pH can help a farmer grow better crops because some plants thrive in acidic soils, while others grow better in alkaline (basic) soils. Lime is spread on fields to neutralize soil that is too acidic. The hydrangea plant actually communicates the type of soil it grows in by the color of its flowers. If the soil is alkaline, this plant blooms red. If the soil is acid, it blooms blue.

Quick! Get the litmus paper But what if you are not a hydrangea plant? How do you determine the pH of a solution? By using an indicator. Indicators are pigments that change color when they come into contact with acidic or basic solutions. Litmus paper is an indicator. By dipping litmus paper into liquids and watching the change in color, chemists can tell whether a liquid is an acid or a base.

To determine the pH of a solution, scientists also use a machine called a digital pH meter, which has an electric probe connected to it. The probe is dipped into a solution and measures its pH. A large dial on the meter shows the pH reading. To calculate the total amount of acid or base in a solution, the chemist uses a process called titration. Titration is a method of analyzing the makeup of a solution by adding known amounts of a standard solution until a reaction occurs, such as a color change.

It all falls down Remember the lime the farmer spread on the acidic field? Sometimes lime is added to a lake or stream that has become too acidic because of acid rain. Acid rain, an environmental problem that became much worse beginning in the 1950s, is rain, snow, or sleet made unnaturally acidic by sulfur dioxide and nitrogen oxide emissions. The emissions, which mix with air masses, come from the smokestacks of electric power plants that burn coal or from companies that burn high sulfur oil for fuel. Rainfall with a pH of 4, which occurs in the worst acid rain areas, is about one-tenth as acidic as vinegar. Acid rain damages trees and crops and even corrodes stone buildings and statues. Fish are not able to reproduce when their habitat becomes too acidic. Some larger aquatic plants cannot tolerate the acid and die.

Strong acids can damage metals and human skin. Some weaker acids are used as drugs, including aspirin. Strong bases, such as lye, can blind a person. Baking soda, which is used in baking, toothpaste, and as a cleaner, is a weak base. Measuring a substance's pH can give you valuable information about its structure and makeup.

EXPERIMENT 1

Kitchen Chemistry: What is the pH of household chemicals?

Purpose/Hypothesis The pH scale is used by chemists to determine the ratio of acids to bases present in a solution. The scale ranges from 0 to 14 and indicates whether the solution is more acidic or more basic.

In this experiment you will use an universal indicator to determine the pH of several common household chemicals, including vinegar, baking soda, lemon juice, water, and ammonia. Universal indicators, which change color in the presence of acids and bases over a broad range of the pH scale, exist in nature and are found in a few plants. Red

A scientist tests rain samples for acidity. PETER ARNOLD INC.

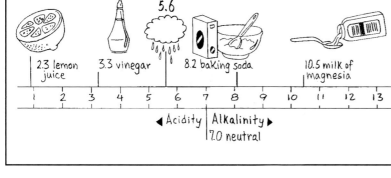

The pH scale ranges from 0 to 14 and indicates whether the solution is more acidic or more basic (alkaline). GALE GROUP.

WORDS TO KNOW

Acid: A substance that when dissolved in water is capable of reacting with a base to form salts and release hydrogen ions.

Acid rain: A form of precipitation that is significantly more acidic than neutral water, often as the result of industrial processes and pollution.

Base: A substance that when dissolved in water is capable of reacting with an acid to form salts and release hydrogen ions.

Hypothesis: An idea in the form of a statement that can be tested by observation and/or experiment.

Indicator: Pigments that change color when they come into contact with acidic or basic solutions.

Ion: An atom or group of atoms that carry an electrical charge—either positive or negative—as a result of losing or gaining one or more electrons.

Neutralization: A chemical reaction in which the mixing of an acidic solution with a basic (alkaline) solution results in a solution that has the properties of neither an acid nor a base.

pH: (The abbreviation for potential hydrogen.) A measure of acidity or alkalinity of a solution referring to the concentration of hydrogen ions present in a liter of a given fluid.

Titration: A procedure in which an acid and a base are slowly mixed to achieve a neutral substance.

Variable: Something that can affect the results of an experiment.

cabbage, grape juice, radish skin, and violet flowers all contain a pigment or coloring that changes in the presence of different chemicals.

The red cabbage "juice" used in this experiment is extracted during the boiling process. This solution is chemically neutral (pH 7), but when added to another substance, the color changes to indicate whether the substance contains a high concentration of an acid or a base. If the substance is an acid, the red cabbage solution will turn pink. If the substance is neutral, the solution will remain purple. If the substance is basic, the solution will become blue, green, or yellow. Yellow indicates a strong base, which may burn your skin on contact.

Before you begin, make an educated guess about the outcome of this experiment based on your knowledge of pH. This educated guess, or prediction, is your hypothesis. A hypothesis should explain these things:

- the topic of the experiment
- the variable you will change
- the variable you will measure
- what you expect to happen

A hypothesis should be brief, specific, and measurable. It must be something you can test through observation. Your experiment will prove or disprove whether your hypothesis is correct. Here is one possible hypothesis for this experiment: "Vinegar and lemon juice are acids, baking soda and ammonia are bases, and water is neutral."

In this case, the variable you will change is the substance being tested, and the variable you will measure is the color of the indicator solution. You expect the indicator solution to show that vinegar and lemon juice are acids, baking soda and ammonia are bases, and water is neutral.

Level of Difficulty Difficult, because of the care required in using a heat source and in handling ammonia and other chemicals.

Materials Needed

- red cabbage indicator solution (boil six to eight cabbage leaves in 1 cup of water for five minutes, retain only the colored solution and allow to cool)

What Are the Variables?

Variables are anything that might affect the results of an experiment. Here are the main variables in this experiment:

- the substance being tested
- the age or freshness of the substance
- the concentration of the acidic or basic components of the substance
- the presence and amount of any contaminants in the substance
- the age or freshness of the pH indicator
- the experimenter's ability to distinguish colors

In other words, the variables in this experiment are everything that might affect the pH of the substance and the resulting color of the indicator solution. If you change more than one variable, you will not be able to tell which variable had the most effect on the pH or color.

Materials for Experiment 1.
GALE GROUP.

How to Experiment Safely

Adult supervision is necessary for this experiment. Treat each chemical as if it were dangerous, and do not inhale the odors, especially from the ammonia. Do not eat or drink while conducting this experiment. Wear goggles to prevent eye injury. Wash your hands immediately if they come in contact with any of the chemicals. Consult your science teacher before you substitute any chemicals for the ones listed in this experiment.

Troubleshooter's Guide

Experiments do not always work out as planned. Even so, figuring out what went wrong can definitely be a learning experience.

Be aware of contamination. Always make sure the utensils and cups are clean. Use only fresh chemicals that have not spoiled. If you are not getting the desired results, place a scoop of baking soda (sodium bicarbonate) into a cup that has been washed, rinsed, and dried. Make sure you use a clean spoon. Pour in some indicator solution and stir. The resulting color should be blue, indicating a base.

- household chemicals: vinegar, baking soda, lemon juice, water, ammonia, white or clear detergent, etc.
- cups (3.5-ounce clear plastic) or test tubes (glass or plastic)
- measuring spoons
- goggles
- paper towels (for cleanup)

Approximate Budget $2 for the red cabbage, which is necessary for this experiment.

Timetable 1 hour.

Step-by-Step Instructions

1. Place a small amount (approximately ½ teaspoon) of one chemical into the cup. Wash the measuring spoon.
2. Place an equal amount of indicator solution (red cabbage water) in the same cup. Again, wash the measuring spoon.
3. Record the resulting color change of the indicator solution.
4. Determine the chemical property of the substance—acid, base, or neutral.
5. In clean cups, repeat this procedure for each of the other chemicals.

Summary of Results Record your results in a journal or notebook. Go back to your hypothesis and determine whether your original guesses were correct. Write a paragraph summarizing your findings.

Here is a general rule of thumb for acids and bases:

- Acids are corrosive but lose their acidity when combined with bases.
- Bases feel slippery when they come in contact with the skin; they lose their alkalinity when mixed with acids. (But do not test bases by touching them; they can burn your skin.)
- Salts are formed when acids and bases react.

Change the Variables You can vary this experiment in several ways. Try comparing different brand-name items or testing items that have spoiled. For instance, milk when fresh is base but when spoiled is an acid.

Modify the Experiment One reason this experiment is difficult is that you need to boil cabbage to make a universal indicator. You can simplify this experiment by purchasing a pH indicator. Also called litmus paper, pH indicator strips are commonly sold at drug stores and places that sell science supplies. Litmus papers are available in different sensitivity. Commonly available litmus papers will turn either blue or red, depending up if the solution is a base or acid.

If you want to explore pH more, you can compare the results of the litmus paper to your universal indicator. How close are the two indicators?

EXPERIMENT 2

Chemical Titration: What is required to change a substance from an acid or a base into a neutral solution?

Purpose/Hypothesis After you understand how to use indicators, you can begin testing and manipulating chemicals. Here is a general description of how acids and bases mix and the results. Acids produce a H+ particle called a hydrogen ion. Bases produce an OH–particle called a hydroxide ion. These H+ and OH–ions can join to form H2O or water, a neutral substance. The leftover substance is a salt.

What Are the Variables?

Variables are anything that might affect the results of an experiment. Here are the variables for this experiment:

- the acid or base being tested
- the age or freshness of the acid and base
- the concentration of the acidic or basic components (many acids are diluted in water)
- the presence and amount of any contaminants in the acid and base
- the amount of acid added to the base, and vice versa
- the age or freshness of the pH indicator
- the experimenter's ability to distinguish colors

In other words, the variables in this experiment are everything that might affect the pH of the substance and the resulting color of the indicator solution. If you change more than one variable, you will not be able to tell which variable had the most effect on the pH or color.

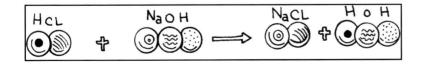

The chemical formula for a typical acid-base reaction between hydrochloric acid and sodium hydroxide. GALE GROUP.

How to Experiment Safely

Adult supervision is necessary for this experiment. Treat each chemical as if it were dangerous. Do not eat or drink while conducting this experiment. Wear goggles to prevent eye injury. Wash your hands immediately if they come in contact with any of the chemicals. Consult your science teacher before you substitute any chemicals for the ones listed in this experiment.

When acids and bases react to form a salt, the reaction can be violent. Gases, flames, heat, and other forms of energy can be released. In other words, use caution!

The chemical formula for a typical acid-base reaction between hydrochloric acid and sodium hydroxide is illustrated. The resulting products of this reaction are neutral sodium chloride (salt) and water.

When an acid and a base combine to form a neutral solution, the procedure is called a titration reaction.

Before you begin, make an educated guess about the outcome of this experiment based on your knowledge of pH. This educated guess, or prediction, is your hypothesis. A hypothesis should explain these things:

- the topic of the experiment
- the variable you will change
- the variable you will measure
- what you expect to happen

A hypothesis should be brief, specific, and measurable. It must be something you can test through observation. Your experiment will prove or disprove whether your hypothesis is correct. Here is one possible hypothesis for this experiment: "A basic substance can be neutralized by the addition of an acid, and vice versa."

Materials for Experiment 2.
GALE GROUP.

In this case, the variable you will change is the amount of acid being added to the base (or base to acid), and the variable you will measure is the color of the indicator solution. You expect the indicator solution to show a color indicating the basic pH changes to a neutral pH with the addition of an acid, and vice versa.

Level of Difficulty Difficult, because of the care required in using a heat source and in handling chemicals.

Materials Needed

- red cabbage indicator solution (refer to Experiment 1 for instructions)
- vinegar
- baking soda
- stomach antacids (such as Tums)
- baking powder
- clear plastic cups
- measuring spoons
- goggles

Approximate Budget $2 to $10.

Timetable 1 hour.

Step-by-Step Instructions

1. In a cup place 1 teaspoon of baking soda.
2. In the same cup place an equal amount of indicator solution, and then stir.
3. Note the color of the solution.
4. In the same cup slowly pour some vinegar. Watch the violent acid-base reaction, and stop when the solution turns purple.
5. If you add too much vinegar, the solution may turn pink. Slowly sprinkle more baking soda into the cup until the purple color reappears.

Step 4: Slowly pour vinegar into the cup and watch the violent acid-base reaction.
GALE GROUP.

Summary of Results When the baking soda (a base) was added to the indicator, the color changed from purple to blue indicating the presence of OH–ions (a base) with a pH of greater than 7. When the vinegar (an acid) was added, the H+ ions reacted with the OH–ions and produced water (a purple neutral solution, with a pH of 7). The gas CO_2 was produced during the reaction. When an acid and a base are joined equally, the resulting solution is neutral. You have caused a titration reaction. Summarize the results of your experiment in writing.

Change the Variables You can vary this experiment in several ways. Try adding substances such as antacids to vinegar and indicator solutions. Test the pH of baking powder, which is an acid and a base in a powdered mixture.

Design Your Own Experiment

How to Select a Topic Relating to this Concept Here is your chance to create a fun experiment about a topic that interests you. Chemistry is a great topic to experiment in because it is part of your everyday life. Everything from the detergent that washes your clothes to the vinegar in salad dressing is made up of chemicals, and so are you! Find an area of chemistry that interests you and start to investigate it. Cleaners, cosmetics, medicine, and food are some areas that you may want to examine.

Check the Further Readings section and talk with your science teacher or school or community media specialist to start gathering information on pH questions that interest you. As you consider possible experiments, be sure to discuss them with your science teacher or another knowledgeable adult before trying them. Some chemicals can be dangerous.

Steps in the Scientific Method To do an original experiment, you need to plan carefully and think things through. Otherwise, you might not be sure of what question you are answering, what you are or should be measuring, or what your findings may prove or disprove.

Here are the steps in designing an experiment:

- State the purpose of—and the underlying question behind—the experiment you propose to do.
- Recognize the variables involved, and select one that will help you answer the question at hand.

- State a testable hypothesis, an educated guess about the answer to your question.
- Decide how to change the variable you selected.
- Decide how to measure your results.

Recording Data and Summarizing the Results Keep a journal and record your notes and measurements in it. Your experiment can then be utilized by others to answer their questions about your topic.

Related Projects After you have chosen a topic to examine, develop an experiment to go with it. For example, you might want to investigate the power of detergents or cleaners. Since grass stains on jeans are common, your experiment could be to determine what detergent works best to remove them.

For More Information

Adams, Richard, and Robert Gardner. *Ideas for Science Projects.* New York: Franklin Watts, 1996. Well-organized science projects for middle-grade students.

Andrew Rader Studios. "Acids and Bases are Everywhere." *Rader's Chem4kids.com.* http://www.chem4kids.com/files/react_acidbase.html (accessed on March 13, 2008). Information on the chemistry of mixtures.

Newmark, Ann. *Eyewitness Science: Chemistry.* London: Dorling Kindersley, 1993. Great visual examples and interesting facts that include pH.

U.S. Environmental Protection Agency. "What is pH?" *Acid Rain.* http://www.epa.gov/acidrain/measure/ph.html (accessed on March 13, 2008). Brief explanation of the pH scale.

66

Photosynthesis

To get our food, we go to the supermarket, pick vegetables or fruit from our gardens, or cast a rod in our favorite fishing hole. A plant, however, makes its own food using sunlight as its major energy source in a process called photosynthesis. In fact, the term photosynthesis means "putting together by light."

Jan Ingenhousz discovered that sunlight stimulates photosynthesis in plants.
CORBIS-BETTMANN.

J.INGENHOUSZ.C.ET ARCHIAT.CÆS.
OB CÆSAREAM PROLEM
INSITIONE VARIOLARUM SERVATAM

Shining the light on vegetables In the eighteenth century, Jan Ingenhousz, a Dutch physician and plant physiologist, proved that sunlight was essential to the life activities of green plants. In 1779, he published experiments showing that plants have two respiratory cycles. At night, plants absorb oxygen and exhale carbon dioxide, just as animals do, but during the day the cycle is reversed. Another eighteenth-century scientist, Englishman Joseph Priestley, made similar discoveries about plant respiration; but it was Ingenhousz who proved through his vegetable experiments that it was *only* in the presence of light that plants absorbed carbon dioxide and gave off oxygen. This was a major discovery because until then most people thought the soil was the only source of a plant's nutrients.

How it works Think of a plant's leaf as a solar panel. Just like the flat glass panels you see on rooftops, a leaf's flat surface makes it an efficient sunlight absorber. Within each leaf cell are up to a hundred disc-shaped chloroplasts. Chloroplasts have a green pigment called chlorophyll, which traps light.

This underwater plant forms oxygen bubbles on the surfaces of its leaves as a result of photosynthesis. PHOTO RESEARCHERS INC.

We know that sunlight is actually a spectrum of many colors that have different wavelengths. The pigments in plants absorb different wavelengths of the sunlight spectrum. Chlorophyll is not the only pigment in plants, but it is the most plentiful pigment. It reflects the green part of the spectrum, which makes plants look green to the human eye, but absorbs other parts of the spectrum. Other pigments, such as carotene and xanthophyll reflect yellow-orange and yellow spectrum colors. These pigments act as a support team to chlorophyll.

Sunlight supplies the energy. Chlorophyll turns the switch that powers a plant's chemical reactions. Those reactions include taking carbon dioxide from the atmosphere, plus water and inorganic chemicals from the soil, and converting them into oxygen and glucose. Glucose is needed in every part of the plant. Cellulose, the tough, fibrous part of the plant, is formed from glucose. Starch, another glucose by-product, is stored within the roots, leaves, or stems of plants. Pores on the underside of the leaf let gases in and out. Tubes called xylem carry water throughout the plant; tubes called phloem distribute the food.

Light intensity, temperature, and water supply are some of the key factors that affect the rate of photosynthesis. In rain forests, plants grow in abundance,because the weather there is rainy and warm, and the Sun's rays are more intense.

Need oxygen? Get a plant The carbon dioxide given off by animals is consumed by plants. Plants on land and in the sea replace the oxygen taken in by animals. That is why there is so much concern for preserving forests, green spaces, and oceans. Besides being animal habitats, they are oxygen producers. Without plants, we would all die.

Interestingly, most of Earth's photosynthesis does not take place on land. Over 75% of photosynthesis processes on Earth actually takes place in our oceans. Chlorophyll is the vital link in photosynthesis in marine plants as well. But these underwater organisms have larger concentrations of other pigments than their plant "cousins" on land. Because little light penetrates below a depth of 330 feet (100 meters), photosynthesis takes place in the upper part of the ocean called the euphotic zone. Plants that live in this zone are called phytoplankton.

During photosynthesis, plants consume carbon dioxide produced by animals and replace oxygen consumed by animals. Unlocking the keys of this balanced activity through experiments will help you appreciate the hidden benefits of our national parks, nature preserves, and oceans. Plants are not green things that just sit there, but vital, living organisms that help us stay healthy.

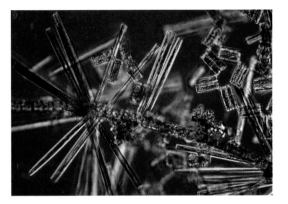

Phytoplankton are underwater plants that utilize photosynthesis to produce oxygen. PETER ARNOLD INC.

EXPERIMENT 1

Photosynthesis: How does light affect plant growth?

Purpose/Hypothesis This experiment deals with the concept of photosynthesis and how different wavelengths of light affect plant growth. Plants contain different pigments, including chlorophyll, carotene, and xanthophyll, so they can respond to different wavelengths. In this experiment, three different colors of light will be used to grow plants. The three colors will represent different wavelengths of light: red—long; yellow—medium; and violet or blue—short. A fourth plant will be grown under a white light, which contains all wavelengths. The amount of growth for each plant will demonstrate which color light promotes the most plant growth.

To begin your experiment, use what you know about photosynthesis to make an educated guess about light color and plant growth. This educated guess, or prediction, is your hypothesis. A hypothesis should explain these things:

- the topic of the experiment
- the variable you will change
- the variable you will measure
- what you expect to happen

A hypothesis should be brief, specific, and measurable. It must be something you can test through observation. Your experiment will prove or disprove whether your hypothesis is correct. Here is one

WORDS TO KNOW

Carotene: Yellow-orange pigment in plants.

Chlorophyll: A green pigment found in plants that absorbs sunlight, providing the energy used in photosynthesis for the conversion of carbon dioxide and water to complex carbohydrates.

Chloroplasts: Small structures in plant cells that contain chlorophyll and in which the process of photosynthesis takes place.

Euphotic zone: The upper part of the ocean where sunlight penetrates, supporting plant life, such as phytoplankton.

Glucose: A simple sugar broken down in cells to produce energy.

Hypothesis: An idea phrased in the form of a statement that can be tested by observation and/ or experiment.

Phloem: Plant tissue consisting of elongated cells that transport carbohydrates and other nutrients.

Photosynthesis: Chemical process by which plants containing chlorophyll use sunlight to manufacture their own food by converting carbon dioxide

and water to carbohydrates, releasing oxygen as a by-product.

Physiologist: A scientist who studies the functions and processes of living organisms.

Phytoplankton: Microscopic aquatic plants that live suspended in the water.

Pigment: A substance that displays a color because of the wavelengths of light it reflects.

Respiration: The physical process that supplies oxygen to an animal's body. It also describes a series of chemical reactions that take place inside cells. In plants, at night or in the dark, the process is the same as in animals. In light, plants absorb carbon dioxide to use in photosynthesis, and give off oxygen.

Xanthophyll: Yellow pigment in plants.

Xylem: Plant tissue of elongated, thick-walled cells that transport water and mineral nutrients.

Variable: Something that can affect the results of an experiment.

---

possible hypothesis for this experiment: "Plants grown under white light will grow the most because white light contains all the wavelengths that plants can use in photosynthesis and most closely duplicates natural sunlight."

In this case, the variable you will change is the color, or wavelength, of light, and the variable you will measure is the amount of plant growth over a period of several weeks. If the plants under the white light grow more than those under the colored lights, you will know your hypothesis is correct.

Level of Difficulty Moderate, since the plants in this experiment may require daily attention for a few weeks.

Materials Needed

- scissors
- 4 lamps (desk lamps with reflectors are best)
- 4 cardboard boxes, 18 inches (46 centimeters) square
- 4 light bulbs (25-watt), in white, red, yellow, and violet or blue
- 4 pots filled with soil
- 40–80 bean or corn seeds (These seeds sprout and grow rapidly, so results can be seen in two weeks. Use the same type of seeds in all pots.)

Approximate Budget $3 or each light bulb and $3 for bean and corn seeds.

Timetable Approximately 4 weeks, during which 15 minutes of daily attention is required, plus 1 hour to set things up.

Step-By-Step Instructions

1. Plant 10 to 20 seedlings in each pot. Water generously and allow the water to drain.

What Are the Variables?

Variables are anything that might affect the results of the experiment. Here are the main variables in this experiment:

- the types of plants chosen
- the color of light
- the intensity of light
- the amount of water provided to each plant
- the type of soil
- the surrounding air temperature

In other words, the variables in this experiment are everything that might affect the growth of the plants. If you change more than one variable, you will not be able to tell which variable had the most effect on plant growth.

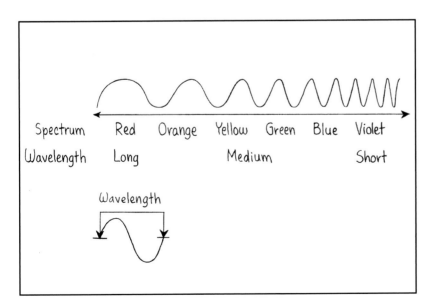

The spectrum and wavelength of different colors. GALE GROUP.

How to Experiment Safely

Use caution when handling hot lamps. Be sure the lamps and light bulbs are not touching the boxes or plants. Turn off the lights and move the lamps aside before watering the plants to avoid a possible electrical shock.

Materials for Experiment 1.
GALE GROUP.

2. Cut a hole into the top of your boxes. The hole should be 2 inches (5 centimeters) smaller in diameter than the diameter of the lamp. Try to place the hole in the center of the box top. Cut a door in the side of each box so that the door can be closed during the day to block outside light.

3. Locate the boxes side-by-side on a table away from windows in a warm, but not hot, room. Place a lamp with a different color light bulb over each box. Label each box as illustrated.

4. Place a plant inside each box under the light.

5. Plug in the lamps and turn them on.

6. After the seeds sprout, open each door every day and record the height of each plant on your results chart.

7. Leave the lights on each day for approximately eight to 12 hours. Turn them on in the morning, and shut them off at night. Remember to keep the doors in the boxes closed.

8. Sprinkle water over the soil every other day. Never allow the soil to completely dry out. Remember to turn the lights off and move the lamps aside before watering the plants to avoid a possible electrical shock. Replace the lamps when you are finished.

Steps 3 and 4: Place a lamp with a different color light bulb over each box. Label each box as illustrated. Place a plant inside each box under the light. GALE GROUP.

9. After two to four weeks, study your charted results and summarize them.

Summary of Results After the experiment is finished, collect the final data and organize it into usable statistics and charts. Graph the plant heights for a visual comparison of plant growth. Determine which wavelength/color affects growth the most. Reflect on your hypothesis. Which color/wavelength of light was most beneficial for plant growth?

Change the Variables Different plant species contain varying amounts of pigments. Instead of varying the color of light, you could vary the plant being tested—either by growing different seeds or by using different small house plants.

You could also test the effect of varying the intensity of light, which is what you can do in Experiment #2.

Troubleshooter's Guide

Here is a problem you may encounter, some possible causes, and ways to fix the problem.

Problem: All the plants are starting to wilt, turn yellow, or fall over.

Possible causes:

1. The plants may be in shock from being removed from their normal environment. Grow the plants outside the box, indoors, for one week before starting the experiment again.

2. The lamps are too close to the plants, causing them to wilt from the heat. Raise the lamp a few inches and try again.

EXPERIMENT 2

Light Intensity: How does the intensity of light affect plant growth?

Purpose/Hypothesis This experiment deals with the amount of light required for photosynthesis and growth. In this experiment, three wattages of light bulbs—40 watt, 25 watt, and 5 watt—will be used to determine how the different amounts of light intensity affect plant growth. A fourth plant will have no light bulb. In general, the more light present, the better a plant responds in its growth and vigor. However, light can also scorch or burn a plant if it is too intense.

To begin the experiment, use what you know about photosynthesis to make an educated guess about how light intensity will affect plant growth. This educated guess, or prediction, is your hypothesis. A hypothesis should explain these things:

- the topic of the experiment
- the variable you will change
- the variable you will measure
- what you expect to happen

What Are the Variables?

Variables are anything that might affect the results of an experiment. Here are the main variables in this experiment:

- the types of plants chosen
- the intensity of light
- the amount of water provided to each plant
- the type of soil
- the surrounding air temperature

In other words, the variables in this experiment are everything that might affect the growth of the plants. If you change more than one variable, you will not be able to tell which variable had the most effect on plant growth.

Plants can be categorized into those having a low, medium, or high preference for light. For this experiment, an ivy was chosen because it has a medium light preference.

A hypothesis should be brief, specific, and measurable. It must be something you can test through observation. Your experiment will prove or disprove whether your hypothesis is correct. Here is one possible hypothesis for this experiment: "A 25-watt light bulb will promote the most plant growth because its intensity is neither too dim nor too bright."

In this case, the variable you will change is the intensity of the light, and the variable you will measure is the amount of plant growth over a period of several weeks. If the plant under the 25-watt light bulb grows the most, you will know your hypothesis is correct.

Level of Difficulty Moderate because of the duration of the experiment. (It takes approximately four weeks to cause a noticeable result.)

Materials Needed

- scissors
- 3 lamps (desk lamps with reflectors are best)
- 4 cardboard boxes, 18 inches (46 centimeters) square
- 3 light bulbs: one 40-watt, one 25-watt, one 5-watt
- 4 potted ivy plants

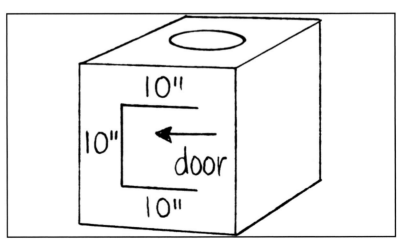

Step 2: Cut a door into each box. Door should be 10 inches wide on all sides; only three sides are cut with the fourth side acting as a hinge. GALE GROUP.

Approximate Budget $20 for light bulbs and plants.

Timetable 4 weeks, including 5 minutes a day for watering and recording growth, plus one hour for set up.

Step-By-Step Instructions

1. Cut a hole into the top of three boxes. The hole should be 2 inches (5 centimeters) smaller in diameter than the diameter of the lamp. Try to place the hole in the center of the box top. Do not cut a hole in the top of the fourth box.

2. Cut a door into each box, following the diagram illustrated.

3. Place a lamp with a light bulb over each box with a hole in it. Label each box.

4. Place a potted plant inside each of the four boxes.

5. Record the health of each plant. Measure its approximate size.

6. Plug in lamps and turn them on.

7. Keep the lights on for eight to 12 hours daily. Keep the doors closed to block outside light.

8. Water the plants every other day. Remember to turn off the lights and move the lamps aside before watering the plants to avoid a possible electrical shock.

9. Check on the plants daily. Record any changes in health, such as loss of leaves, plants turning brown, or plants growing toward light. Mark the headings Week 1, 2, 3, and 4, and record the changes in each plant.

10. After 4 weeks, the plant with no light will probably be dead and the experiment will be concluded.

Steps 3 and 4: Place a lamp with a light bulb over each box with a hole in it and label each box. Place a potted plant inside each of the four boxes. GALE GROUP.

Summary of Results After the experiment is completed, collect your data and display it for others to view. Make drawings of plants to demonstrate the effects of light intensity. Reflect on your hypothesis and draw some conclusions. What was the

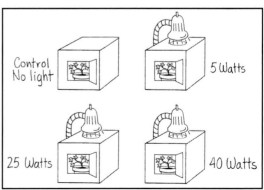

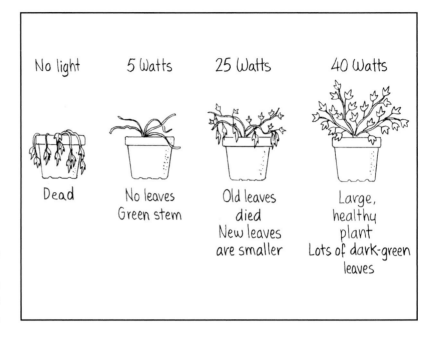

No light   5 Watts   25 Watts   40 Watts

Dead   No leaves Green stem   Old leaves died New leaves are smaller   Large, healthy plant Lots of dark-green leaves

Step 9: Each week record the changes in each plant. Illustration shows the likely outcome after four weeks. GALE GROUP.

best wattage or light intensity for the plants? If your hypothesis was that the 25-watt light would be best, and it turned out that the 40-watt light was actually the best, you weren't wrong—you just got a different result than predicted. You still learned something from the experiment.

Change the Variables Just as in Experiment #1, one way to change the variables is to change the plants being tested. Go to a plant nursery and find a type of plant that likes a low intensity light. Repeat the experiment to see which wattage bulb produces the best growth with the new plant.

Design Your Own Experiment

How to Select a Topic Relating to this Concept Photosynthesis is essential for a plant's survival and growth. Air, water, light, nutrients, and temperature are crucial elements that play a part in photosynthesis. You can select from the elements needed for photosynthesis to conduct an experiment. For example: temperature affects the function of the pigments responsible for photosynthesis. You can experiment to determine at what temperature photosynthesis stops in trees, that is, when they go into dormancy.

Check the Further Readings section and talk with your science teacher or school or community media specialist to start gathering information on photosynthesis questions that interest you. As you consider possible experiments, be sure to discuss them with your science teacher or another knowledgeable adult before trying them. Some of them might be dangerous.

Steps in the Scientific Method Here is your chance to answer questions or discover new facts. Design an experiment about a topic that interests you. To do this, you must follow some guidelines to help you stick to your goal and get useful information.

Here are the steps in designing an experiment:

- State the purpose of—and the underlying question behind—the experiment you propose to do.
- Recognize the variables involved, and select one that will help you answer the question at hand.
- State a testable hypothesis, an educated guess about the answer to your question.
- Decide how to change the variable you selected.
- Decide how to measure your results.

Recording Data and Summarizing the Results Experimenting is a means by which we discover the answers to our questions. It is important to record all the changes in the experiment as well as conclusions drawn from it. Others may use your experiment to answer questions or solve related problems regarding your topic.

Related Projects If you decide to test temperature and its effects, you may want to choose a plant that drops its leaves, known as deciduous, and monitor the temperature outside. In this sample experiment, all you have to do is choose a plant species, such as white oak, and monitor the average temperature when it drops its leaves.

Troubleshooter's Guide

Here is a problem you may encounter, a possible cause, and a way to solve the problem.

Problem: All the plants lost their leaves.

Possible cause: The plants are in shock. Grow them outside the box inside the house for a week or two before starting the experiment.

For More Information

Bonnet, Robert L., and G. Daniel Keen. *Botany: 49 Science Fair Projects.* Blue Ridge Summit, PA: Tab Books, 1989. Features seven projects on photosynthesis in Chapter 3.

Groleau, Rick. "Illuminating Photosynthesis." *Nova Online.* http://www.pbs. org/wgbh/nova/methuselah/photosynthesis.html# (accessed on March 1, 2008). Interactive animations on photosynthesis.

Lammert, John M. *Plants: How to Do A Successful Project.* Vero Beach, FL: Rourke Publications, Inc., 1992. Includes a chapter on photosynthesis.

"Photosynthesis: How Life Keeps Going." *FT Exploring.* http://www.ftexploring. com/photosyn/photosynth.html (accessed on March 2, 2008). Comprehensive information on photosynthesis and energy.

Budget Index

Chapter name in brackets, followed by experiment name. The numeral before the colon indicates volume; numbers after the colon indicate page number.

Level of Difficulty Index

Chapter name in brackets, followed by experiment name. The numeral before the colon indicates volume; numbers after the colon indicate page number.

EASY

Easy means that the average student should easily be able to complete the tasks outlined in the project/experiment, and that the time spent on the project is not overly restrictive.

EASY/MODERATE

Easy/Moderate means that the average student should have little trouble completing the tasks outlined in the project/experiment, and that the time spent on the project is not overly restrictive.

MODERATE

Moderate means that the average student should find tasks outlined in the project/experiment challenging but not difficult, and that the time spent on the project/experiment may be more extensive.

Experiment Central, 2nd edition

MODERATE/DIFFICULT

Moderate/Difficult means that the average student should find tasks outlined in the project/experiment challenging, and that the time spent on the project/experiment may be more extensive.

DIFFICULT

Difficult means that the average student wil probably find the tasks outlined in the project/experiment mentally and/or physically challenging, and that the time spent on the project/experiment may be more extensive.

Timetable Index

Chapter name in brackets, followed by experiment name. The numeral before the colon indicates volume; numbers after the colon indicate page number.

30 TO 45 MINUTES

2 HOURS

3 HOURS

2 DAYS

[Bacteria] Bacterial Growth: How do certain substances inhibit or promote bacterial growth? **1:90**

[Flowers] Sweet Sight: Can changing a flower's nectar and color affect the pollinators lured to the flower? **3:431**

[Genetics] Genetic Traits: Will you share certain genetic traits more with family members than non-family members? **3:556**

[Memory] Memory Mnemonics: What techniques help in memory retention? **4:701**

[Osmosis and Diffusion] Measuring Membranes: Is a plastic bag a semipermeable membrane? **4:798**

[Soil] Soil Profile: What are the different properties of the soil horizons? **5:1067**

3 DAYS

[Animal Defenses] Camouflage: Does an animal's living environment relate to the color of the animal life? **1:63**

[Chemical Properties] Chemical Patination: Producing chemical reactions on metal **1:173**

[Chemical Properties] Chemical Reactions: What happens when mineral oil, water, and iodine mix? **1:170**

[DNA (Deoxyribonucleic Acid)] Comparing DNA: Does the DNA from different species have the same appearance? **2:291**

[Dyes] Applying Dyes: How does the fiber affect the dye color? **2:301**

[Dyes] Holding the Dye: How do dye fixatives affect the colorfastness of the dye? **2:304**

[Ethnobotany] Plants and Health: Which plants have antibacterial properties? **2:392**

[Genetics] Building a Pedigree for Taste **3:559**

[Insects] Lightning Bugs: How does the environment affect a firefly's flash? **3:638**

[Oxidation-Reduction] Oxidation and Rust: How is rust produced? **4:817**

5 DAYS

[Food Spoilage] Spoiled Milk: How do different temperatures of liquid affect its rate of spoilage? **3:485**

[Nutrition] Daily Nutrition: How nutritious is my diet? **4:766**

General Subject Index

The numeral before the colon indicates volume; numbers after the colon indicate page number. **Bold** page numbers indicate main essays. The notation (ill.) after a page number indicates a figure.

A

A groups (periodic table), *4:* 829
A layer (soil), *5:* 1066–67, 1067 (ill.)
Abscission, *1:* 192
Absolute dating, *3:* 525
Acceleration
    bottle rocket experiment, *3:* 493–501, 495 (ill.), 498 (ill.), 499 (ill.)
    build a roller coaster experiment, *5:* 934–38, 935 (ill.), 936 (ill.), 937 (ill.)
    centripetal force experiment, *3:* 501–5, 503 (ill.)
    centripetal force in, *3:* 493, 493 (ill.)
    Newtonian laws of motion on, *3:* 492, 492 (ill.)
    of planetary orbits, *3:* 579–80
Acetate, *3:* 509, 511–14, 511 (ill.), 512 (ill.), 513 (ill.)
Acetic acid, *1:* 165, *4:* 820–23, 820 (ill.), 821 (ill.), 822 (ill.)
Acetone, *3:* 511–14, 511 (ill.), 512 (ill.), 513 (ill.)
Acid/base indicators, *4:* 860
    cave formation experiment, *1:* 134, 134 (ill.)
    pH of household chemicals experiment, *4:* 861–65, 861 (ill.), 863 (ill.)
Acid rain, *1:* **1–17,** 17 (ill.)
    brine shrimp experiment, *1:* 5–8, 7 (ill.)
    damage from, *1:* 1–3, *4:* 860–61
    design an experiment for, *1:* 15–16
    formation of, *1:* 1, 164
    pH of, *1:* 1, 2 (ill.), 3 (ill.), *4:* 860–61, 861 (ill.)

plant growth experiment, *1:* 9–12, 11 (ill.)
    structure damage experiment, *1:* 12–15, 14 (ill.), 15 (ill.), 16
Acidity
    in food preservation, *3:* 452
    in food spoilage, *3:* 478
    measurement of, *1:* 1
    neutralization of, *1:* 4
    for separation and identification, *5:* 1033, 1034 (ill.)
    of soil, *5:* 1064
    soil pH and plant growth experiment, *5:* 1074–77, 1074 (ill.), 1076 (ill.), 1079 (ill.)
    See also pH
Acids
    acid-copper reduction experiment, *4:* 813–17, 814 (ill.), 815 (ill.)
    cave formation experiment, *1:* 132–35, 134 (ill.)
    chemical properties of, *1:* 164
    chemical titration experiment, *4:* 865–68, 865 (ill.), 866 (ill.), 867 (ill.)
    copper color change experiment, *4:* 820–23, 820 (ill.), 821 (ill.), 822 (ill.)
    electricity conduction by, *2:* 334
    pH of, *4:* 859–61
    uses for, *4:* 859, 860
    See also Lemon juice; Vinegar
Acoustics, *5:* 1096
Acronyms, *4:* 700
Actions, reactions to every, *3:* 492, 494

C

C layer (soil), *5:* 1067, 1067 (ill.)
Cabbage, purple, *2:* 304–7, 306 (ill.), 307 (ill.)
Cactus, *5:* 899–900, 908, 908 (ill.)
　desert biome experiment, *1:* 108–11, 109 (ill.), 110 (ill.), 111 (ill.)
　saguaro, *1:* 105, *5:* 900
　water storage by, *5:* 884, 884 (ill.), 885
Calcite, *1:* 129–30, *4:* 862
Calcium
　bone loss experiment, *1:* 115–20, 119 (ill.)
　in bones, *1:* 114
　hard water sources experiment, *6:* 1231–34, 1232 (ill.)
　for nutrition, *4:* 761, *6:* 1226
　periodic table location for, *4:* 829
　in soil, *5:* 1064
　in water, *6:* 1225–26
Calcium carbonate
　bone loss experiment, *1:* 116–20, 119 (ill.)
　seashells of, *5:* 1020, 1022
　soil pH and plant growth experiment, *5:* 1074–77, 1074 (ill.), 1076 (ill.), 1079 (ill.)
　solubility of elements experiment, *4:* 835–38, 835 (ill.), 837 (ill.)
　stalagmites and stalactite experiment, *1:* 135–39, 137 (ill.)
Calcium chloride, *1:* 157–59, 157 (ill.), 158 (ill.), 159 (ill.)
Calories, *4:* 766–69, 768 (ill.), 769 (ill.)
Cambium, *6:* 1296, 1297 (ill.)
Camera lenses, *4:* 795 (ill.)
Cameras, *6:* 1125–28, 1126 (ill.), 1127 (ill.)
Camouflage, *1:* 61–62, 63–65, 64 (ill.), *5:* 1021
Canals, *2:* 375
Cancellous bone, *1:* 114
Canned food, *3:* 452–53, 479, 479 (ill.)
Capillary action, *6:* 1260
Carbohydrates
　dietary carbohydrate sources experiment, *4:* 761–64, 763 (ill.), 764 (ill.)
　muscle strength and fatigue experiment, *1:* 123
　for nutrition, *4:* 760, 761 (ill.)

Carbon, *2:* 230, 246 (ill.), *4:* 749, 829, *5:* 912
Carbon-carbon bonds, *5:* 912
Carbon dating, *3:* 525
Carbon dioxide
　in air, *1:* 33
　in bread making, *2:* 359
　burning fossil fuels experiment, *3:* 596–98, 596 (ill.), 597 (ill.)
　in cave formation, *1:* 127–29, 128 (ill.)
　comet composition experiment, *2:* 218–21, 220 (ill.)
　in dry ice, *2:* 220
　from fish, *3:* 402
　greenhouse effect, *1:* 46, 47 (ill.), *3:* 589–90, *5:* 941
　from leavening agents, *3:* 464
　leavening agents and carbon dioxide experiment, *3:* 470–73, 472 (ill.), 473 (ill.), 474
　nanosize and reaction rate experiment, *4:* 753–55, 754 (ill.), 755 (ill.)
　in plant respiration, *4:* 871, 872
　from power plants, *1:* 46
　temperature for yeast growth experiment, *3:* 544–49, 547 (ill.), 548 (ill.)
　from yeast, *2:* 359, *3:* 540–41
Carbon monoxide, *1:* 45, *2:* 231
Carbon nanotubes, *4:* 749
Carbonic acid, *1:* 127–29, 128 (ill.), 132–35, 134 (ill.), *3:* 544
Cardboard soundproofing, *5:* 1102–5, 1104 (ill.)
Cardiac muscles, *1:* 115, 115 (ill.)
Carlsbad Caverns, *1:* 129
Carotene, *1:* 192, 201 (ill.), *4:* 872
Cars, *1:* 3–4, 46, *3:* 590
Carson, Rachel, *4:* 846
Carson River, *5:* 955
Cartier, Jacques, *4:* 759
Cartilage, *1:* 114
Cartilaginous fish, *3:* 401
Casts, fossil, *3:* 523, 526–29, 528 (ill.)
Catalase, *2:* 361 (ill.), 362–65, 363 (ill.), 364 (ill.)
Catalysts, *2:* 359–60, 360 (ill.)
Catalytic converters, *1:* 3–4
Caterpillars, *3:* 633–34, *4:* 645
Caventou, Joseph Biernaime, *1:* 191
Caverns. *See* Caves

I

orbit of, *5:* 982, 986 (ill.)

phases of, *2:* 329–30, 330 (ill.), 331 (ill.)

tides and, *4:* 774, 775 (ill.), *5:* 983–84

in timekeeping, *6:* 1175

Mordants, *2:* 300–301, 300 (ill.), 304–7, 306 (ill.), 307 (ill.)

Mosses, *1:* 131

Motion

circular, *3:* 492–93, 493 (ill.), 501–5, 503 (ill.)

three laws of, *3:* 491–93, 492 (ill.), 493 (ill.)

Motors, electric, *2:* 358 (ill.), *5:* 1087–89, 1088 (ill.), 1089 (ill.)

Mount Everest, *4:* 735, 736 (ill.)

Mount Vesuvius, *6:* 1237, 1237 (ill.), 1239

Mountain range, *4:* 735

Mountains, *4:* **735–45,** 736 (ill.)

air density and, *1:* 36, 36 (ill.)

desert formation experiment, *4:* 741–44, 742 (ill.), 743 (ill.)

design an experiment for, *4:* 744–45

ecosystem of, *4:* 737–38

formation of, *4:* 735–37, 736 (ill.), 737 (ill.)

on the moon, *6:* 1109

mountain formation experiment, *4:* 738–41, 739 (ill.), 740 (ill.)

Mouths (insect), *3:* 632

Movement

by fish, *3:* 402–3, 403 (ill.), 407–9, 409 (ill.), 410

of heat, *3:* 615–17, 616 (ill.), 617 (ill.)

water bottle rocket experiment, *3:* 493–501, 495 (ill.), 498 (ill.), 499 (ill.), 500 (ill.)

See also Motion

MSG (Monosodium glutamate), *1:* 177

Mucus, *1:* 179

Multicellular organisms, *1:* 141, 144 (ill.)

Municipal water supply, *3:* 609–12, 610 (ill.)

Murray, John, *5:* 995

Muscle contractions, *1:* 115–16, 116 (ill.), 120–23, 122 (ill.)

Muscle fibers, *1:* 115, 115 (ill.), 124

Muscle strength, *1:* 115–16, 115 (ill.), 120–23, 122 (ill.)

Muscles, *1:* **113–25**

design an experiment for, *1:* 123–25

muscle strength and fatigue experiment, *1:* 120–23, 122 (ill.)

strength of, *1:* 115–16, 115 (ill.)

Mushrooms, *1:* 81, 108, *3:* 540, 550 (ill.)

Music, *4:* 700, 701–4, 701 (ill.), 702 (ill.), 703 (ill.)

Mutations, DNA, *3:* 555

Mycelium, *3:* 538, 539 (ill.)

Mystery powders experiment, *5:* 1009–13, 1011 (ill.), 1012 (ill.), 1013 (ill.)

N

Nails, magnetized, *4:* 674–78, 674 (ill.), 676 (ill.)

Nanometers, *4:* 787

Nanorobots (nanobots), *4:* 749, 750

Nanotechnology, *4:* **747–57,** 748 (ill.), 749 (ill.)

building blocks of, *4:* 747–48, 748 (ill.), 750 (ill.)

design an experiment for, *4:* 756–57

nanosize and properties of materials experiment, *4:* 750–53, 752 (ill.)

nanosize and reaction rate experiment, *4:* 753–55, 754 (ill.), 755 (ill.)

uses for, *4:* 749–50

Nansen bottles, *5:* 997

Napoleon Bonaparte, *3:* 452, 479

Nares, *3:* 403–4

National Weather Service, *6:* 1273, 1275 (ill.)

Native American baskets, *2:* 390–91, 396

Natural dyes, *2:* 299, 301–4, 302 (ill.), 303 (ill.), 304–7, 306 (ill.), 307 (ill.), 391

Natural fibers, *2:* 301–4, 302 (ill.), 303 (ill.)

Natural pesticides, *4:* 843, 844–46, 847–52, 851 (ill.)

Natural pollutants, *1:* 48

Nebula, *6:* 1124, 1124 (ill.)

Nectar, *3:* 425–26, 431–35, 433 (ill.)

Needles (tree), *1:* 103

Nervous system, *4:* 843–44, 844 (ill.)

Neutralization, *1:* 4, *4:* 860

Neutrons, *4:* 828

Newton, Isaac

energy, *5:* 930–31

gravity, *5:* 982

laws of motion, *3:* 491, 579, 580 (ill.), *6:* 1165

light, *2:* 203–5, 203 (ill.), 205 (ill.), *4:* 659–60, 659 (ill.)

tides, *4:* 774

Experiment Central, 2nd edition

W